THE COMPLETE IDIOT'S GUIDE® TO

Creative Writing

Second Edition

by Laurie E. Rozakis, Ph.D.

ALPHA

A member of Penguin Group (USA) Inc.

To Samara Kravitz and Shelby Kravitz, with much love. You make us all so proud and I expect to see your books in print very soon!

ALPHA BOOKS

Published by the Penguin Group

Penguin Group (USA) Inc., 375 Hudson Street, New York, New York 10014, U.S.A.

Penguin Group (Canada), 10 Alcorn Avenue, Toronto, Ontario, Canada M4V 3B2 (a division of Pearson Penguin Canada Inc.)

Penguin Books Ltd, 80 Strand, London WC2R 0RL, England

Penguin Ireland, 25 St Stephen's Green, Dublin 2, Ireland (a division of Penguin Books Ltd)

Penguin Group (Australia), 250 Camberwell Road, Camberwell, Victoria 3124, Australia (a division of Pearson Australia Group Pty Ltd)

Penguin Books India Pvt Ltd, 11 Community Centre, Panchsheel Park, New Delhi—110 017, India

Penguin Group (NZ), cnr Airborne and Rosedale Roads, Albany, Auckland 1310, New Zealand (a division of Pearson New Zealand Ltd)

Penguin Books (South Africa) (Pty) Ltd, 24 Sturdee Avenue, Rosebank, Johannesburg 2196, South Africa

Penguin Books Ltd, Registered Offices: 80 Strand, London WC2R 0RL, England

Publisher: *Marie Butler-Knight*
Product Manager: *Phil Kitchel*
Senior Managing Editor: *Jennifer Chisholm*
Senior Acquisitions Editor: *Randy Ladenheim-Gil*
Development Editor: *Michael Thomas*
Senior Production Editor: *Billy Fields*
Copy Editor: *Amy Borrelli*
Illustrator: *Chris Eliopoulos*
Cover/Book Designer: *Trina Wurst*
Indexer: *Heather McNeil*
Layout/Proofreading: *Angela Calvert, Mary Hunt*

Contents at a Glance

Contents

Part 2:   **Once Upon a Time: Writing Short Stories**   **63**

Foreword

In 1939, an ambitious young man in California who aspired to be a writer borrowed $75—an enormous sum in those Depression days—so that he could travel to New York City for the First World Science Fiction Convention. His goal in making the days-long bus trip was to meet an agent who would represent him and his work to the various science fiction pulp magazines of the day. He made his contact, and for the next two years manuscripts traveled back and forth across the country, until one day in 1941 when the young man received a check for the sale of "The Pendulum" to one of the magazines.

Over the next few years, the young writer successfully sold 70 stories—all handled by that same agent—and established his credentials as a premier author.

His name? Ray Bradbury.

In 1946, that same agent, now working as an editor for All-American Comics, received a very precisely written, spelled, and punctuated letter from a young fan. The purpose of the letter was to inquire whether or not the editor felt its sender showed any promise as a writer. The editor replied that he thought the young fan did indeed show promise. If he continued to work at his writing, the agent told him, he would one day surely become a well-known author.

His name? Harlan Ellison.

In my career as a literary agent and as an editor at DC Comics, I have worked with countless writers. Regardless of their level of skill and ability when I first met them, they had one thing in common with Bradbury and Ellison: the desire to write and be published. Since you are reading this book, I trust that you, too, share that goal.

At the risk of stealing some thunder from the text that follows this foreword, let me share some of the "hints" I've been passing along to writers for 60 years:

1. Be original! Many of my writers referred to me as "B.O. Schwartz" because I constantly demanded that they come up with something new and different. Surprise your reader; throw out the most obvious solutions to a problem— the ones your readers will think of themselves—and come up with something innovative and interesting instead.

2. Carry a notebook and pen at all times. Science fiction award-winning writer Alfred Bester always carried something to write on, and so should you. Something you read or something you hear can be the spark that inspires a story. Make sure to jot your ideas down.

Keep a notepad next your bed, too. Many of my writers will attest to the plotting sessions we've had that began with the words "I woke up at 3 this morning with this great idea …!"

3. Use a "narrative hook." Start your story with a sentence or idea that immediately grabs the reader's attention and lures him or her to read on. I became a science fiction fan for life after reading this opening: "It all started when the clock on Metropolitan Tower began to run backwards." The author hooked me and made me want to know what was going on. Do the same with your own manuscripts.

4. When you finish your manuscript, put it away for at least 24 hours before looking at it again. Take time to do something else before rereading your work. You'll be amazed at how flaws and errors jump out at you when you look at it with a fresh eye.

5. Keep writing. The only way to become a better writer is to practice. That means to keep working. As I recounted above, it took Ray Bradbury two years of writing before I sold his first story. He did not sit back and wait for the story to sell before writing a second; he continued to work until his efforts paid off.

Laurie Rozakis has put together a monumental volume here, covering an astonishingly wide variety of writing topics. I wish this book had existed years ago; I would have handed a copy to every writer who wanted to work with me. She answers virtually every question an up-and-coming writer could have.

There's plenty for experienced writers as well. Regardless of how much or how little writing you have done, you'll find invaluable tips throughout the book.

Skim the book for the areas that fit your interest, or read every word. Either way, any writer who follows the paths Dr. Rozakis sets out would be a client an agent would be proud to represent and an author any editor would find it a joy to work with!

That said, start reading … and then, start writing!

—Julius Schwartz

Julius Schwartz began his career as a literary agent in 1934 and continued representing a stable of prominent authors, including Ray Bradbury, Alfred Bester, Robert Bloch, and H. P. Lovecraft, until he joined DC Comics in 1944. At DC, he guided the destinies of virtually every prominent superhero, most especially Batman and Superman, until 1986. Since then, he has served as DC's goodwill ambassador to numerous comic book and science fiction conventions throughout the year. Mr. Schwartz passed away in February 2004.

Introduction

Has your creative urge been crushed by too many know-it-alls: teachers, critics, parents, spouses, and children who offer their bone-chilling suggestions too freely? "You're not smart enough to write a book," they may have said. "Don't give up your day job," they offered not-so-kindly. Posh.

Everyone is talented, original, and has something to say. You are interesting, funny, and important. Tell it all. Let it come out on paper.

If you want to write, you can. It's as simple as that. You have my promise.

As a matter of fact, you're probably writing far more than you realize, right now. How many of these kinds of writing do you do?

- Advertising copy
- Business letters
- E-mail
- Essays
- Fill-in-the-blank forms
- Journals and diaries
- Legal briefs
- Love letters
- Newspaper articles
- Photo captions
- Poems
- Reports
- Scientific papers
- School assignments
- Sermons
- Stories
- Technical manuals
- Thank-you notes

"But I'm not being creative," you claim. On the contrary, I say, the minute you put pen to paper or finger to keyboard, you're being creative. This book will help you learn to write more easily. Writing is work, but learning to write doesn't have to be.

What You'll Learn in This Book

This book is divided into five sections that take you through the process of developing your creative writing potential. You'll learn that before the actual writing comes detailed planning, analysis, and research. You'll find out that creative writing can take many different forms. Here's what the six parts of this book cover:

Part 1, "Unlock Your Creativity!," first explores creative writing by surveying the different forms it takes. Then I'll help you tap *your* creative potential through a series of fun and easy writing activities. Along the way, I'll teach you some of the most important secrets of creative writing!

Part 2, "Once Upon a Time: Writing Short Stories," gets into the nitty-gritty of writing narratives. Here's where you'll learn how to develop a compelling plot, realistic characters, vivid settings, authentic dialogue, and strong structure. You'll also learn how to develop your voice, your unique style.

Part 3, "Nonfiction," covers creative nonfiction, essays, memoirs, magazine articles, and poetry. I'll show you how to find a niche for your unique writing talents. In addition, there's an in-depth focus on hints you can really use to develop your skills. You'll also get an overview of the conventions of poetry: rhythm, rhyme, figurative language, and poetic technique.

Part 4, "Drama, Scripts, and Screenplays," opens with a discussion of writing plays. Then I survey the different types of screenplays you can write, including comedy, action/adventure, thrillers, and horror. You'll "toon" into the skills you need to write cartoons and the requirements for writing soap operas. Then I'll teach you all about story, structure, character, and how to write a *premise* and a *treatment*.

Part 5, "Living the Writer's Life," shows you how to tap additional resources as you develop your writing talents. These resources include creative writing classes, contests and grants, and editors (including self-editing and peer editing). You'll explore contemporary paths to publication, including self-publication and Internet publication. I describe writer's block and show you what to do if it strikes you. I'll teach you a series of easy methods for dispelling this affliction. Finally, I devote an entire chapter to how publishing works, so you can decide if going that route is right for you.

More for Your Money!

In addition to all the explanation and teaching, this book contains other types of information to make it even easier for you to unlock your creative abilities and learn how to write. Here's how you can recognize these features:

All the Write Stuff

Use these hints to make creative writing easier—and more enjoyable.

Wrong Turn

These warnings help you stay on track. They can help you avoid the little goofs … and the major pitfalls.

Words to the Wise

Like every other skill worth knowing, writing has its own jargon. Here's where I explain those useful terms so you can talk the talk and walk the walk!

Write Angles

This is interesting, useful background information that gives you even more of an "inside edge" to the writing biz. These are the facts that you can skim, but they're so nifty that you won't want to!

Acknowledgments

Much thanks to Randy Ladenheim-Gil, my brilliant editor, for her continuing wisdom, compassion, and support. Randy, it is always a pleasure dealing with you. Special thanks are also due to all the wonderful people who make me look so good: development editor Michael Thomas; senior production editor Billy Fields; and copy editor Amy Borrelli.

Trademarks

All terms mentioned in this book that are known to be or are suspected of being trademarks or service marks have been appropriately capitalized. Alpha Books and Penguin Group (USA) Inc. cannot attest to the accuracy of this information. Use of a term in this book should not be regarded as affecting the validity of any trademark or service mark.

Part 1

Unlock Your Creativity!

"People … automatically believe in books. This is strange but it is so. Messages come from behind the controlled and censored areas of the world and they do not ask for radios, for papers and pamphlets. They invariably ask for books. They believe in books when they believe nothing else."

—John Steinbeck

John Steinbeck, winner of the 1963 Nobel Prize for literature, recognized that books convey an authority that no other media can command. Plumbers may make more money, car mechanics may keep us tooling along, and fine chefs definitely make life more delicious. But writers fulfill a need that no one else can: They nurture our souls. This part of the book shows you why creative writing is so worthwhile—and how you can start unlocking your creativity!

Chapter 1

Write Away

In This Chapter

- Define *writing*
- Explore the four kinds of writing: narration, description, exposition, persuasion
- Define *creative writing*
- Distinguish between fiction and nonfiction
- Survey the top 10 types of creative writing

It is a delicious thing to write, to be no longer yourself but to move in an entire universe of your own creation. Writer John Updike compares being a creative writer to a sailor who sets a course out to sea. A creative writer is an explorer, a ground-breaker. Creative writing allows you to chart your own course and boldly go where no one has gone before.

In this chapter, you'll discover what creative writing is and why people feel so compelled to do it. You'll learn that the urge to write one's innermost thoughts is as old as time itself—and as powerful. This chapter will help you discover that you're not alone in your desire to produce the Great American short story, novel, memoir, article, essay, or screenplay.

What Is *Writing*?

We all know *writing* when we see it. Writing involves putting little marks on paper via a computer, pen, pencil, or crayon. But writing is more than mere scribbling.

When you write, you communicate a message to the reader. Communicating in writing means sending a message that has a destination. It takes two to tango, change a light bulb, and complete the function of the written word.

Words to the Wise

Writing is a way of communicating a message to a reader for a purpose.

The *message* of writing is its content. You can present your message in a variety of ways. Traditionally, the forms of writing are divided into *narration*, *description*, *exposition*, and *persuasion*. Let's look at each writing form in more detail.

Narration

Narration is writing that tells a story. The following chart shows different forms that narration can take:

Real-Life Narratives	Fictional Narratives
Memoirs	Short stories
Biographies	Novels
Autobiographies	Myths
Journals	Legends
Diaries	Narrative poems
TV and movie scripts	TV and movie scripts

Drama can be considered a type of narration because it tells a story, but drama is usually classified as its own *genre* or type of writing.

Words to the Wise

A **genre** is a major literary category. The three genres are prose, drama and poetry.

Description

Description is a kind of writing that creates a word picture of what something or someone is like. Description is made up of sensory details that help readers form pictures in their minds. Poetry is the most purely descriptive writing.

Description also uses *images*, words that appeal to one or more of our five senses: sight, hearing, taste, touch, or smell. Imagery can be found in all sorts of writing (and *should* be), but it is most common in poetry.

Exposition

Exposition is writing that explains, shows, or tells about a subject. As a result, it is the most common type of everyday writing. Exposition includes the following forms:

- News articles
- Memos
- Letters
- Manuals
- Recipes
- Business reports
- Term papers and research reports
- Notes to the butcher, baker, and candlestick maker

Words to the Wise

The term **exposition** can also be used to mean the opening parts of a play or story. During the exposition, the characters, action, and setting are introduced.

You can remember that exposition is writing that explains because both *exp*osition and *exp*lain start with *exp*.

Persuasion

Persuasion is a type of writing that tries to move an audience to thought or action. Newspaper editorials, advertisements, and letters to the editor are all examples of persuasive writing. So are resumés and cover letters, because they are designed to convince someone to give you an interview so you get hired. Persuasive writing that appeals to reason is often classified as *argumentation*.

Combo Platters

Even though I've separated the four types of writing so you can read about them on their own, it's rare that they're not combined. For example, you can't tell a story (a narrative) without adding adjectives and adverbs (description) or explaining what's happening (exposition). And how can you write a letter to the editor (a form of persuasion), without explaining the situation (exposition) and adding sensory words and details (description)? You can't!

What's the point of telling a story or describing something if there's no one to read it? Ditto with explaining and persuading. All four forms of writing share one crucial element—the *reader*, or *audience*.

What Is *Creative* Writing?

But what's *creative* writing? How is it different from garden-variety white-bread writing? How is it the same? I could argue that all writing is creative. I could also argue that baseball needs the designated hitter, all colas are the same, and pizza tastes best cold. But I won't make this argument because creative writing *is* different from everyday-ordinary-commonplace writing.

Take a look at the following definitions of creative writing. Which ones do you agree with? Circle the best definition of creative writing.

Creative writing is …

> A floor wax.

> A breath mint.

> A high-impact polymer used in food storage containers.

> The naughty bits.

> Nothing that a little Prozac wouldn't cure.

> Writing that uses language imaginatively.

Go for the last one: *Creative writing* is a kind of writing that uses language in imaginative and bold ways. So you're sure you'll know creative writing when you see it, I've charted some examples of creative and noncreative writing:

Creative Writing	Usually Not Creative Writing
Novel	Your tax return (unless you claim the lawn as a deduction because it would die without you)
Short story	A grocery list
Play	The check for a decaf mocha latte and a low-fat bran muffin
TV script	An excuse note (with the possible exception of "I didn't make it to work because I spent the night on a spaceship with Elvis")

Creative Writing	Usually Not Creative Writing
Poem	A losing lottery ticket
Autobiography	A report card (but we have some leeway here)
Memoir	A toe tag
Article	Your boss's memos
Love letter	Your online profile (well, it shouldn't be)

Creative writing falls into different categories. This means that there's something for everyone to read—and to write. No matter where your artistry lies, you can find a type of creative writing to suit your interests and taste.

We can divide creative writing into two main categories: *fiction* and *nonfiction*.

Fiction

Fiction is writing that tells about made-up events and characters. Fiction is obviously a very broad category, so we divide it into the following types:

- Short stories
- Novels
- Movie and TV scripts
- Drama (although it is usually classified separately)

Fiction that contains imaginary situations and characters that are very similar to real life is called *realistic fiction*.

Nonfiction

Nonfiction is a type of writing about real people and events. The main types of nonfiction are ...

- Memoirs.
- Essays.
- Biographies.
- Autobiographies.
- Articles.

But even these traditional categories aren't carved in granite, as writer Truman Capote (1924–1984) demonstrated in 1965 with the publication of his nonfiction novel *In Cold Blood*. A gripping account of the mass murder of a Kansas farm family, the Clutters, the book follows two young killers from the murder scene to their eventual execution five-and-a-half years later. Capote's meticulous research—he had even befriended the murderers—resulted in a literary landmark. Capote's "nonfiction novel" received extraordinary acclaim: *The New York Times* declared the novel a masterpiece. And Capote opened up an entire new genre for creative writers. Soon, other writers followed in his footsteps by merging fiction and nonfiction in short stories, novels, memoirs, and TV and movie scripts. Maybe you will, too!

Creative Writing Superstars

Below are the top 10 types of creative writing, the heavy hitters.

1. Article

An *article* is a short work of nonfiction. By "short," I mean that an article usually runs 750 to about 2,000 words and can easily be read in one sitting.

Creative writers of articles explore a variety of different topics, including medicine and health issues, sports and hobbies, pets, family life, culture, travel, leisure activities, humor, and social issues. You can find articles in magazines, newspapers, books, and online in *ezines* and web pages. Articles can be serious or humorous, depending on the topic and audience.

Words to the Wise

An **ezine** is an electronic magazine published only or primarily on the Internet. They are also called **zines**. Ezines are becoming more popular as printing costs rise and people increasingly turn to the Internet as a source for creative writing.

2. Biography

A *biography* is a true story about a person's life written by another person. Biographies are often written about celebrities, such as JLo, Michael Jackson, and Puff Daddy, and historical figures, such as Thurgood Marshall, Jonas Salk, and Eleanor Roosevelt.

3. Drama

Drama is a piece of literature written to be performed in front of an audience. The writer supplies dialogue for the characters to speak and stage directions that give information about lighting, scenery, props, costumes, and the actors' movements and ways of speaking. As a result, actors tell the story through their actions and the dialogue.

The audience accepts as believable many of the dramatic conventions that are used to tell the story, such as soliloquies (a long speech, made by a character who is alone on the stage, that reveals his or her private thoughts to the audience), asides (a speech delivered by an actor in such a way that other characters on the stage are presumed not to hear it), poetic language, and the passage of time between acts and scenes.

Dramas usually have three or five acts (major divisions). The acts are further divided into scenes (minor divisions). Dramas can be read as well as acted.

Write Angles

Although the term *drama* is often used to describe serious plays, *comedy* is actually a subcategory of this genre. (I would lie to you?) A subcategory of comedy is *farce*, a humorous play that is based on a silly plot, ridiculous situations, and comic dialogue. The characters are usually one-dimensional stereotypical figures. They often find themselves in situations that start out normally but soon turn absurd. Often, humor is created through an identity switch and the other characters' reaction to it.

---

4. Essay

An *essay* is a brief, nonfiction work on a particular subject or idea. The word comes from the French *essai* (an attempt or trial), first used in 1580 by the writer Montaigne to describe his short writings. As the history of the word suggests, an essay is meant to be exploratory. It is not meant to be a comprehensive treatment of a subject. An essay can be any length, from short (500–1,000 words) to long (book length).

Essays can be classified according to their topic and tone: formal or informal, personal or impersonal. They can also be classified according to their purpose—expository, persuasive, descriptive, or narrative. Essays are organized in a number of different ways, including comparison and contrast, cause and effect, and advantages and disadvantages.

5. Fantasy

Fantasy is a kind of writing that describes events that could not take place in real life. Fantasy contains unrealistic characters, settings, and events. *Science fiction* is fantasy writing that tells about make-believe events that include science or technology. Often, science fiction is set in the future, on distant planets, or among alien races.

6. Memoir

A *memoir* is a person's story of his or her own life. A type of nonfiction, a memoir may describe one or more key events from the person's life or encompass the person's entire life. A memoir may be written by a well-known person or an everyday individual.

Today, there's a keen interest in memoirs, and they have emerged as a front-runner in creative writing classes and book sales.

7. Novel

A *novel* is a long work of fiction. The elements of a novel—plot, characterization, setting, and theme—are developed in detail. Novels usually have one main plot and several less important subplots. Novels such as Victor Hugo's *Les Miserables* feature several main characters and a large cast of minor characters, while F. Scott Fitzgerald's *The Great Gatsby* has several main characters and only a few minor ones.

Novels can be classified in many ways, based on the historical periods in which they are written, such as Seventeenth-century novels, Eighteenth-century novels, and Nineteenth-century novels. They can also be classified according to their subjects and themes, such as Romance novels, African American novels, War novels, and Gothic (Horror) novels. Finally, novels can also be classified according to the literary movements that inspired them, such as Realistic novels, Naturalistic novels, and Local Color novels.

A work of fiction shorter than a novel but longer than a short story is often classified as a novella.

8. Poetry

Poetry is a type of writing in which words are selected for their beauty, sound, and power to express feelings. Most poems make use of highly concise, musical, and emotionally charged language. Many poems also contain imagery, figurative language, and follow a specific form.

Traditionally, poems had a specific rhythm and rhyme, but such modern poetry as *free verse* does not have a regular beat, rhyme, or line length. Most poems are written in lines, which are arranged together in groups called *stanzas*.

Song lyrics are poems set to music. All songs have a strong beat, created largely through the three R's: rhythm, rhyme, and repetition.

9. Script and Screenplay

Scripts and screenplays are pieces of literature written to be filmed and shown to an audience. They follow a specific format and since they are intended to be performed, tell the story through dialogue, action, and stage directions. Scripts are usually classified according to their genre, such as comedy, action/adventure, and thriller.

10. Short Story

A *short story* is brief work of fiction. Like its pumped-on-steroids cousin the novel, the short story has a plot, conflict, characters, setting, and dialogue. However, unlike the novel, the short story usually focuses on no more than two characters and a single event. Further, the short story tends to reveal character at a crucial moment rather than develop it through many incidents.

Most short stories can be read in one sitting and convey a single overall impression.

No matter what form it takes, creative writing is as crucial today as it was to the Egyptians sweating over their papyrus and the medieval monks hunched over their illuminated manuscripts. Perhaps the very qualities that would seem to make writing passé are the reasons it is more important than ever. As we litter the Information Superhighway with embarrassing, poorly written spam and communicate in itty-bitty sound bites, we need a medium that allows us to communicate, think, discover, and learn—creatively.

The Least You Need to Know

- ◆ *Writing* is a way of communicating a message to a reader for a purpose.

- ◆ Traditionally, the forms of writing are divided into *narration, description, exposition,* and *persuasion.*

- ◆ *Creative writing* is a kind of writing that uses language in imaginative and bold ways.

- ◆ You can be a creative writer. I promise.

Chapter 2

Music from the Heart

In This Chapter

◆ Learn about a creative writer who was ahead of her time

◆ Discover why people become creative writers

◆ Explore what creative writing can offer *you*

> This is my letter to the world,
> That never wrote to me—
> The simple news that Nature told,
> With tender majesty.
>
> Her message is committed
> To hands I cannot see;
> For love of her, sweet countrymen,
> Judge tenderly, of me!
>
> —Emily Dickinson

Every time we write for others, we send our "letter to the world." It is often terrifying to expose our innermost thoughts and private ideas to the judgment of others. "What will they think of my writing?" we worry. "What will they think of *me*?" It's no wonder that the poet Emily Dickinson begged her readers to judge her "tenderly."

There are many different *ways* that people write, just as there are many different reasons *why* they write. In this chapter, we'll explore these reasons in depth.

Being Ahead of the Curve

Today we regard Emily Dickinson as one of the foremost modern poets in America, if not the world. Yet during Dickinson's lifetime (1830–1886), few people outside her native Amherst, Massachusetts, had ever heard of her. And if they had, they considered her to be somewhat odd: a recluse who never married and dressed only in white. She never held a job; she never traveled.

During her lifetime, Dickinson wrote 1,775 poems—yet she published only seven, and all anonymously. The complete collection of her poetry wasn't published until 1955, long after her death.

There were many reasons why Emily Dickinson didn't share her creative writing with others. In part, her hesitancy was based on the unusual form of her poems. Her writing was so creative that it was unlike anything ever seen before.

In her day, poems rhymed and concerned "acceptable" topics such as nature, love, and famous people. Dickinson wrote about radical topics in radical ways. Her topics include death, sex, and individuality—all shocking subjects for genteel writers at that time. In fact, the poem you read in the beginning of this chapter didn't look that way at all originally. Dickinson's first editor "cleaned up" the poem to pass muster with readers. Here's the original version:

> This is my letter to the World
> That never wrote to Me—
> The simple News that Nature told—
> With tender Majesty
>
> Her Message is committed
> To Hands I cannot see—
> For love of Her—Sweet—countrymen—
> Judge tenderly—of Me

As you can see, Dickinson didn't use conventional punctuation. Instead, she used dashes in place of commas, semicolons, periods, and colons. She also shunned the everyday rules of capitalization. Her poems just didn't look and sound like poems were supposed to look and sound, and so she could not get them published. So why did she persist writing in the face of such disappointment?

Why Write?

Several years ago, my local school district held a "Celebrate the Arts" day. I was invited to be a guest speaker on the "writing process." Because it had been awhile since I had shaved both legs on the same day, I decided to spiff up a bit and get a free lunch.

The first speaker on the panel, a local novelist with two published books to his credit, stood straight and tall. "Writing is a tremendous amount of fun," he proclaimed. "The words flow like honey," he said. Writing was as easy as falling off a log, shooting fish in a barrel, or stealing candy from a baby, he asserted.

"Liar, liar, pants on fire," I thought. The previous week I had fallen off a ladder trying to get some leaves out of the gutter, and that was not fun. And many days, neither is creative writing. It is often lonely, hard, and as mucky as leaf removal. The words seldom flowed like honey. I eat too much candy and clean too many cabinets to avoid writing. But still I keep at it. Why?

Emily Dickinson wrote because she wanted to; she wrote because she *had* to. Creative writing filled her soul with joy, as it does yours and mine. She wrote because it fulfilled a need, because she had something to say. She wrote because creative writing nourishes the soul as few other artistic endeavors can. Writer Kate Braverman put it this way: "Writing is like hunting. There are brutally cold afternoons with nothing in sight, only the wind and your breaking heart. Then the moment when you bag something big. The entire process is beyond intoxicating."

There are many different *ways* that people write, just as there are many different reasons *why* they write. Read on as we explore some more of those reasons in depth.

What, Me Write?

As any good ballplayer will tell you, you can't steal second base and keep one foot on first. So what stops most people from writing?

- It's not lack of talent, whatever "talent" is. Everyone has talent to spare, if they only tap it.

- It's not lack of time, because we always manage to make time for the things we want to do.

- It's not lack of supplies, because all you need is a pencil or pen and some paper. Centuries of creative writers did just fine without computers or even typewriters.

Write Angles

The first novel ever written on a typewriter was Mark Twain's *The Adventures of Tom Sawyer*, in 1876. Mark Twain (the pen name of Samuel Langhorne Clemens) is ranked as the greatest humorist of nineteenth-century American literature. But he's more than a funnyman. Twain established himself as one of the best writers in the history of American literature by transmuting his childhood experiences into the classic American novels *Tom Sawyer* and *The Adventures of Huckleberry Finn* (1885). The influence of *Huck Finn* was so great that Ernest Hemingway, not noted for his generosity toward other writers, gave it his stamp of approval, saying, "All modern literature comes from one book by Mark Twain called *Huckleberry Finn.*"

So why don't people fulfill their dreams by starting to write creatively? It's fear. "Who am I?" most beginning writers think. "What right do I have to think I can be a writer? Besides, no one will listen to me."

Nonsense. You are a person with a unique story to tell. I've been teaching creative writing for more than (gulp) 25 years. I've been publishing my work for nearly 20 years. And I tell you that everyone has a story that should be told.

Why Do You Want to Be a Creative Writer?

Take this quick quiz to learn why you should be writing creatively.

I want to write creatively because …

____ 1. I want to learn more about myself.

____ 2. I want to learn more about the world.

____ 3. I need to heal old wounds.

____ 4. I have a story I want to hand down through the ages.

____ 5. I have information to share.

____ 6. I want to entertain people with the power of my pen.

____ 7. I want to make the world a better place.

____ 8. I want to fulfill a dream.

Let's take a look at each reason in greater depth.

I Want to Learn More About Myself

How can you know what you mean until you write it? The act of writing allows you to make unexpected connections among ideas and language. Creative writing helps you get your ideas across in fresh, new ways.

Below is part of a journal written in the last century. As you read, decide why the author wrote the entry.

> May 31, 1889
>
> I think that if I get into the habit of writing a bit about what happens, or rather doesn't happen, I may lose a little of the sense of loneliness and desolation which abides with me. My circumstances allowing of nothing but the ejaculations of one-syllabled reflections, a written monologue by that most interesting being, myself, may have its yet to be discovered consolations. I shall at least have it all my own way and it may bring relief as an outlet to that geyser of emotions, sensations, speculations and reflections which ferments perpetually within my poor old carcass for its sins; so here goes!
>
> Alice James (1848–1892)

Self-discovery is one of the most beneficial ways to spend our time, because understanding who we are can help us get where we want to be. Alice James knew how to use writing to look inward. The sister of a world-famous writer (Henry James) and a world-famous writer-psychologist (William James), Alice had an especially hard time carving out a niche out for herself in the world.

You may have been using writing as a voyage of creative self-discovery for quite some time—or you may have decided that an unexplored life *is* indeed worth living. It's natural for us to swing from one extreme to the other as we mature.

I Want to Learn More About the World

The act of writing can also help us peel back layers of meaning, as well as create meaning. The following passage by my son, written when he was a senior at Princeton University, explores the topic of language acquisition.

> Is language innate in humans? I say, at least in part, that it is. We can say that if a major component of language—grammar—is innate, then language itself should be as well. "Complex language is universal because children actually reinvent it, generation after generation," says Pinker. Based on this, I will examine several cases of spontaneous grammar formation by children. If children are

capable of creating grammar without any instruction, then such grammar might preexist in their brains.

—Charles Rozakis

"How can I know what I think before I write it?" a student once asked me. Good question! Fortunately, creative writing is a great way to probe ideas before you commit yourself to one position. As the paragraph above shows, you can write to discover something rather than assert it. Your ideas develop as you write.

Although the writer is making a case for language being inborn rather than acquired, he has not committed himself to making a sustained argument. Instead, we get the sense that the writer is thinking aloud. You can tell from the phrases *at least in part*, the preposition *if*, and the word *might* that the writer is testing a hypothesis.

Writing for knowledge is like free association. That's because you're exploring ideas as you write. The example here is tightly woven, but it is perfectly okay to let your mind wander on different tangents to see what emerges. Actually, in some instances it might be preferable to explore rather than lock yourself into a position. Don't be afraid to pick up one thread and let another dangle—or go back and pick up that loose one as you write in this mode.

As you write, you are trying to find new avenues to explore, new things to discover. By providing an opportunity to try and test new ideas instead of proving concepts that are already accepted, writing for knowledge opens up vast new creative vistas.

Writing is a way of thinking and learning. Creative writers have a unique opportunity to explore ideas and acquire information. Writing allows you to …

- Know subjects well.
- Own the information.
- Recall details years later.
- Gain authority and credibility.
- Organize and present ideas logically and creatively.

I Need to Heal Old Wounds

How do you think writing the following diary entry might help the author resolve some key issues in his or her life?

I finally put two and two together. I had buried myself under so many protective layers that it took three months to even cry about it. Crying comes more easily now, though. I have had to stop three or four times while writing this. My emotions are raw, but I think that is for the best. Feeling bad now is better than twenty years of feeling nothing.

—Anonymous

Writing can help you work through a crisis. Julia Cameron, a writer who is also the former wife of movie director Martin Scorsese, started using writing as a healing tool after she suffered some great disappointments. "I very rapidly saw that [the pages] washed away my bitterness, introduced new characters, and seemed to give me a healthier set of priorities," she noted in her book *The Artist's Way.*

Venting your emotions through writing carries a great bonus, too: As you heal, you often tap your hidden creativity. Later, we'll look more deeply into this use of creative writing. I'll teach you some ways to make this method work for you.

I Have a Story I Want to Hand Down

What events have had a strong impact on you? The following passage describes a terrifying event that the writer witnessed. What purpose do you think his account serves for contemporary readers?

> This was a mournful scene indeed, and affected me almost as much as the rest; but the other was awful and full of terror. The cart had upon it sixteen or seventeen bodies; some were wrapped up in linen sheets, some in rags, some little other than naked, or so loose that what covering they had fell from them in the shooting out of the cart, and they fell quite naked among the rest; but the matter was not much to them, or the indecency much to anyone else, seeing they were all dead, and were to be huddled together into the common grave of mankind, as we may call it, for here was no difference made, but poor and rich went together; there was no other way of burials, neither was it possible there should, for coffins were not to be had for the prodigious numbers that fell in such a calamity as this.
>
> —from *A Journal of the Plague Year* by Daniel Defoe (1660–1731)

Have you witnessed an event that you know will become a part of history? The event might touch many lives, such as President Kennedy's assassination, Martin Luther King's assassination, or 9/11. Such was the case with the terrible outbreak of plague that Defoe recorded in his *Journal.* All told, more than a thousand people died in just his small town. Defoe knew that he was *seeing* history and his writing ended up *preserving* history.

Create Living History

But the event that touches your heart might be private rather than public. Perhaps you want to record your child's first steps, your arrival in this country, or your recovery from an illness. These seemingly small events become part of the larger fabric of history as much as the bigger events. For example, the journals, letters, and diaries of the pioneers help modern readers understand the triumphs and tragedies of trailblazer life a century ago. These primary documents are invaluable for our descendants as they seek to understand our time and place.

Leave a Legacy

The wish to record a memory is one of the most common ways people express their creativity in writing. This is no accident: Writers have memories and writing helps save these memories from loss. By passing on our memories in writing, we are actively preserving and creating as we bring order to our lives.

Writing for the future can take many forms. Here are some of the most common ones:

- ◆ Articles
- ◆ Autobiographies
- ◆ Diaries
- ◆ Memoirs
- ◆ Eyewitness accounts
- ◆ Interviews
- ◆ Journals
- ◆ Letters
- ◆ Oral histories
- ◆ Postcards

Wrong Turn

Increasingly, "letters" are taking the form of e-mail. Since electronic mail is an ephemeral form because is not permanent, be sure to print out any e-mail letters that you wish to save for posterity.

Later in this book, you'll learn how to write memoirs, a great way to record your impressions for future generations.

I Have Information to Share

Writing is a powerful means of communication because it forms and shapes human thought. In an open society, everyone is free to write and thereby share information with others. And beyond sharing information, writing helps change ideas and attitudes through persuasion.

Want to spread the news? The written word has been used for centuries to keep people informed. What information does the following passage report?

Butterflies in My Stomach

In Japan, gourmets relish aquatic fly larvae sautéed in sugar and soy sauce. Venezuelans feast on fresh fire-roasted tarantulas. Many South Africans adore fried termites with cornmeal porridge. Merchants in Cambodia sell cooked cicadas by the bagful. Diners cut off the wings and legs before eating them. People in Bali remove the wings from dragonflies and boil the bodies in coconut milk and garlic.

Insect cuisine may not be standard food in the U.S., but Miguel Vilar notes in Science World that eighty percent of the world's population savors bugs, either as staples of their everyday diet or as rare delicacies. Entomophany (consuming insects intentionally) has yet to catch on in America and Europe.

—Laurie Rozakis

Sometimes we think that all creative writing is soft, such as love poetry and self-revelatory essays. In fact, creative writing can be very specific, as this example shows. It's part of an essay I wrote to report the popularity of eating insects.

Much of the writing you do every day involves stating facts. This type of writing is every bit as creative as diaries, journals, letters, and poems. When you write to report information, you are sorting data—details—and selecting the ones that express your ideas in the order you have decided is important.

I Want to Entertain People

Imagine that it's a cold winter night and you're curled up in bed with a cup of hot cocoa and the following two poems. They're both by the famous poet "Anonymous." Get comfy and read the poems. Then decide what made them entertaining.

Example #1: Judged by the Company One Keeps

One night in late October,
When I was far from sober,
Returning with my load with manly pride,
My feet began to stutter,
So I lay down in the gutter,
And a pig came near and lay down by my side;
A lady passing by was heard to say:
"You can tell a man who boozes,
By the company he chooses,"
And the pig got up and slowly walked away.

Example #2: Where Are You Going, My Pretty Maid

"Where are you going, my pretty maid?"
"I'm going a-milking, sir," she said.
"May I go with you, my pretty maid?"
"You're kindly welcome, sir," she said.
"What is your father, my pretty maid?"
"My father's a farmer, sir," she said.
"What is your fortune, my pretty maid?"
"My face is my fortune, sir," she said.
"Then I can't marry you, my pretty maid."
"Nobody asked you, sir," she said.

"Laughter is the best medicine," a wise person once said. Writing that entertains is fun to write as well as fun to read. If you find joy in writing to entertain others, it will come from knowing that you brought them pleasure. It is a rare and wonderful piece of writing that can make us laugh out loud, but even sparking a smile can make you say, "I did a good job with that piece!" Using words to bring a twinkle of recognition shows you have a good-humored, sympathetic nature.

In a larger sense, when you help readers laugh about their tragedies as well as their triumphs, you help them deal with difficult situations. By reminding people that we all have tough times, you help them feel part of a larger community. Humor thus helps people deal with human imperfection.

I Want to Make the World a Better Place

With his writing, Dr. Martin Luther King Jr. changed the world. Do you remember these historic words?

I have a dream that one day this nation will rise up and live out the true meaning of its creed: "We hold these truths to be self-evident, that all men are created equal." ... I have a dream that one day my four little children will live in a nation where they will not be judged by the color of their skin, but by the content of their character.

—Dr. Martin Luther King Jr., 1963

Dr. King delivered his famous "I Have a Dream" speech on the steps of the Lincoln Memorial in Washington, D.C., on the hundredth anniversary of Lincoln's Emancipation Proclamation.

Since ancient times, people have written speeches, letters, books, and articles in an effort to change the world. When you write to make a difference, you use language to move people to action or belief. You appeal to their reason, emotion, or ethics, or any combination of these three factors.

I Want to Fulfill a Dream

Writing creates a permanent, visible record of your ideas for others to consider and ponder. Writing gives you a taste of immortality.

Writing can change the world—and it can change your life. That's because words themselves are power. More than 2,000 years ago the ancient Greek mathematician Archimedes wrote, "Give me a lever long enough and a prop strong enough, and I can single-handedly move the world." But the celebrated novelist Joseph Conrad realized that true power lies with language. "Do not talk to me of Archimedes' lever," Conrad said. "He was an absent-minded person with a mathematical imagination. Give me the right word and the right accent, and I will move the world."

You have the power to use your words to move the world.

The Least You Need to Know

- Creative writing is self-expression, liberation from the constraints of everyday life.

- People write creatively for self-discovery, to gain knowledge, and to heal hurts.

- They also write to leave a legacy for future generations and to share information.

- Some writers use their creativity to entertain their readers, while others seek to improve the world through the power of their prose.

- No matter why you want to become a writer, unlocking your creativity can unlock your power to make the world a better place.

Chapter 3

The Power of the Pen

In This Chapter

- ◆ Explore some excuses people give for not writing
- ◆ See why these excuses are silly
- ◆ Start releasing your talent

A well-known writer once claimed that writing is the most difficult work that doesn't involve heavy lifting. He was right on the money. So why should you put all your blood, sweat, and yes, even tears into writing creatively? Here's how Emily Dickinson put it:

> In this short Life
> That only lasts an hour
> How much—how little—is
> Within our power.

I know what you're thinking: "That's all well and good, Rozakis, but I'm not a writer. Writers are born, not made. I could never be a *real* writer."

Yes, you can.

In this chapter, you'll first explore some reasons why people claim they can't write. Then we'll explode those excuses, one by one. Along the way, you'll have fun with a creative writing exercise. This activity will help you tap your talent and get started writing.

Excuses People Use to Avoid Becoming Creative Writers ...

Despite the tremendous advantages that creative writing can bring both personally and professionally, many people convince themselves that they can never learn to write what they want, be it a short story, memoir, script, or any other form. Have you ever heard (or used!) these excuses?

1. "Writing is a talent I was denied at birth."

2. "I'm too old to write."

3. "I'm just not smart enough to write."

4. "I'm not well educated enough to write."

5. "I don't have any original ideas. What could I possibly write about?"

6. "I was never taught to write and so I've missed the chance."

7. "I don't have the time to write. After all, I work full-time and have a family, too."

8. "I don't have the right equipment in my house and I can't afford it."

9. "I'm not good at all that grammar stuff."

10. "I can't write what I really want because it might embarrass people."

Bonus Excuse: "Why bother? Who's going to read my stuff after all?"

No Excuses, Part 1

Let's take a look at the first five excuses that people give for not becoming creative writers. Then we'll see why they don't hold water.

1. "Writing is a talent I was denied at birth."

Unfortunately, this line of thinking often becomes a self-fulfilling prophecy. People who use this excuse rarely do learn to write imaginatively, because they have convinced themselves that they can't. Convince yourself that you will fail, and you most likely will.

Now, I would be lying to you if I claimed that life is a level playing field. Some people are born with a certain aptitude for creative writing, just as some people are born with a better pitching arm or a good sense of direction. But to a very large extent, just as anyone can learn to throw a ball or follow a map, so anyone can learn to write well.

Convince yourself that you can succeed as a creative writer, and you will. As with any skill worth mastering, original writing involves hard work. It will take time, effort, and a certain amount of looking inward to write with imagination and a fresh eye, but the investment will pay off manifold.

2. "I'm too old to write."

The following passage was first published in 1791:

> Of all the pleasures derivable from the cultivation of the arts, sciences, and liter-ature, time will not abate the growing passion; for old men still cherish an affec-tion and feel a youthful enthusiasm for those pursuits, when all others have ceased to interest.... In advanced life we may resume our former studies with a new pleasure, and in old age we may enjoy them with the same relish with which more youthful students commence.
>
> —Anonymous

Did you know …

♦ Laura Ingalls Wilder wrote her marvelous *Little House* series when she was in her 60s. These nine young adult novels were her first books.

♦ Geoffrey Chaucer began writing his *Canterbury Tales* when he was 54 years old; he finished when he was 61.

♦ Sophocles' sons are said to have summoned him to court in his old age (he lived to be 90) so a jury could find him incompetent to manage his affairs. After Sophocles read the jury the play he had just finished, *Oedipus at Colonus*, the jury sided with him, reasoning that no man in his dotage could write such a masterpiece. They even escorted him home as an honor.

♦ When he was an old man, the American poet Henry Wadsworth Longfellow was asked how he could write so many happy, childlike poems, full of wonder and joy. He

---

Write Angles

The first woman to earn her living as an author seems to have been Aphra Behn (1640–1689). She wrote several plays, poems, and novels, including such tales of adventure and romance as *The Fair Jilt*, *The Rover*, and *Sylvia*.

replied that Governor Endicott's pear tree, 200 years old, "still bears fruit not to be distinguished from a young tree in flavor."

♦ When he was a senior citizen, Michelangelo created a statue of an old man holding an hourglass. The inscription read: "Yet I am learning." And so are you. Age is no barrier to self-expression, especially when it comes to creative writing.

3. "I'm just not smart enough to write."

Psychologist Catherine Morris Cox studied the lives of over 300 famous creative writers and ranked them according to their IQs on a standard intelligence test. The "average" person has an IQ of about 100. The famous creative writers John Stuart Mill and Johann Wolfgang von Goethe came in with IQs in the whopping 200 range. Voltaire, author of the classic French novel *Candide*, came in around 170; George Sand (a woman) wasn't far behind at 150.

Charles Darwin, whose book *The Origin of Species* revolutionized the way we look at evolution, had an above-average IQ. Miguel Cervantes, author of the Spanish classic *Don Quixote*, had an average IQ, around 105. Many other famous writers were equally "average."

Assuming we accept tests of intelligence as real measures of a person's intelligence (and I'm not sure that I do), I've just shown that people who wouldn't be considered "smart" according to the IQ tests have written masterpieces. And so can you.

4. "I'm not well educated enough to write."

It's not surprising that many celebrated creative writers earned advanced college degrees from the top universities. The Romantic British poet William Wordsworth was educated at England's elite Cambridge University, as were Lord Byron; Alfred, Lord Tennyson; and Margaret Drabble. Percy Bysshe Shelley, Matthew Arnold, Gerard Manley Hopkins, A. E. Housman, and V.S. Naipaul all earned degrees from England's Oxford University.

On our own side of the pond, the wildly creative poet e. e. cummings graduated from Harvard University. (He's the poet who wrote without capital letters and included some very odd arrangements of letters.) Contemporary short story writer and novelist John Updike also graduated from Harvard's ivy halls. The Native American writer M. Scott Momaday earned a Ph.D. in literature from Stanford University. But hold on a minute!

An astonishing number of famous creative writers were school dropouts. Masters of imaginative writing who never finished grade school include:

- ◆ Celebrated British novelist Charles Dickens

- ◆ American idol Mark Twain

- ◆ Russian novelist Maxim Gorky

- ◆ Irish writer Sean O'Casey

- ◆ Italian novelist Alberto Moravia

Adventure writer Jack London, humorist Will Rogers, and short story writer William Saroyan are among the famous creative writers who never finished high school. American poet Carl Sandburg had little formal schooling. The great English novelist and poet Thomas Hardy dropped out of school at age 15.

Nobel laureate playwright George Bernard Shaw never went to college. Neither did Virginia Woolf. Nobel laureates in literature William Faulkner and John Steinbeck started college, but never made it to the finish line. They weren't alone. African American poet Langston Hughes dropped out of Columbia University; experimental poet H. D. (Hilda Doolittle) dropped out of Bryn Mawr College.

And many superb writers who went to school failed their writing classes! The celebrated French novelist Émile Zola, for instance, is said to have gotten a zero in a writing class while attending the Lycée St. Louis.

This is not to say that you should avoid school if you want to be a writer—quite the contrary! I devote an entire chapter to the advantages of attending creative writing classes, seminars, and programs. It *is* to say that you can be a happy and successful writer if you haven't been able to get as much formal education as you want.

5. "I don't have any original ideas. What could I possibly write about?"

Leonard Bernstein/Stephen Sondheim/Jerome Robbins's brilliant musical play *West Side Story* is a revision of Shakespeare's *Romeo and Juliet* … which is itself a retelling of a 1530 Italian story by Luigi da Porto, which is itself a retelling of Masuccio of Salerno's 1476 tale of star-crossed lovers, which is a retelling of *Ephesiaca*, written in the fourth century by the Greek historian Xenophon.

Cole Porter's delightful musical play *Kiss Me Kate* is a reworking of Shakespeare's *The Taming of Shrew*, which is itself a retelling of ….

You get my point: Many of our most "original" ideas are creative reworkings of very old, traditional stories. So why not take an old plot and make it your own by adding an individual twist? In the next section, let's do this by using some plots we all know: fairy tales.

Let's Do the Twist Like We Did Last Summer

Let your creativity emerge by changing one of the following elements commonly used in fairy tales. Here are some ideas to get you started:

◆ Character(s): Change their gender or personality; make a man into a woman, or make a fierce character mild-mannered.

Words to the Wise

The **protagonist** is the most important character in a work of literature. The protagonist is at the center of the conflict and the focus of our attention. The **antagonist** is the force or person in conflict with the protagonist. An antagonist can be another character, a force of nature, society, or something within the character.

◆ Setting: Update the time and place. For instance, reset "Cinderella" in the White House or "The Three Little Pigs" in a major-league ballpark.

◆ Conflict: Switch the *protagonist* and *antagonist*; consider making the good guy into the villain.

◆ Point of view: Switch from the third-person omniscient (all-knowing) point of view to the first person (*I*) or vice versa.

◆ Plot: Change the ending. For instance, instead of having the woodchopper kill the Big Bad Wolf, why not have Little Red do it?

◆ Mood: Turn a calm mood into a frightening one.

Story	Twist
"Little Red Riding Hood"	_____
"Cinderella"	_____
"The Three Little Pigs"	_____
"The Three Bears"	_____
"Hansel and Gretel"	_____

Now, choose the twist you like the best and write the story. Aim for 350–500 words, about two typed pages.

No Excuses, Part 2

What about the rest of those excuses? Here are my rebuttals.

6. "I was never taught to write and so I've missed the chance."

It's only too late when you've shuffled off this mortal coil. As long as you're still with us, you can always learn to write with originality. This is one train you can't miss! You can learn to write creatively on the job, through community service, and at home through online classes and groups. You can join a writer's group and take classes, too.

7. "I don't have the time to write. After all, I work full-time and have a family, too."

Nobel Laureate in literature T. S. Eliot worked full-time in a publishing house; poet William Carlos Williams worked as a pediatrician in Paterson, New Jersey. Poet Wallace Stevens worked his way up the ladder of an insurance company in Hartford, Connecticut, eventually becoming the vice president. Four-time Pulitzer prize–winning poet Robert Frost was a farmer, mill hand, newspaper writer, and school teacher.

Nearly all creative writers have families; like many people in the world, wordsmiths sometimes have more than one set of spouses and children, too. Charles Dickens had 10 children by his wife, and somehow found time to write 14 novels. (He died before completing his fifteenth novel, *The Mystery of Edwin Drood*.) Dickens also had numerous lovers, including the famous actress Ellen Ternan.

Wrong Turn

When you write, don't worry about competing with anyone. Creative writing isn't a sport like pole vaulting.

It *can* be difficult to find the time to write with originality and style. Some days, finding the time to think—much less write!—can seem downright impossible. That's because we're pulled in an extraordinary number of directions today: work, family, community. But imaginative writers are a hardy and inventive bunch. What happens if you don't have the time to write? Make some time by carving a little here and a little there from your day. Try these methods:

◆ Write before you shower, eat, or get dressed. Karen Hesse, winner of the Newbery Award (the top award for young adult writing), is up at 5 every morning and at her desk soon after.

- ◆ Write at breakfast.

- ◆ Write on the bus or train on the way to work and on the way home. That's how lawyer Scott Turow created his first best-seller, from stolen minutes while he commuted by public transportation. An hour here, an hour there: It all adds up to writing time.

- ◆ Write during your coffee break.

- ◆ Write at lunch while chowing down on your tuna wrap. Pediatrician William Carlos Williams wrote landmark poems at his desk during lunch hour. (He even managed to get a few lines down on paper between seeing patients.)

- ◆ Write between meetings.

- ◆ Write on the way home from work, on the bus, subway, or train (but not while driving the car, please!).

- ◆ Write before you go to sleep, or in place of watching TV or surfing the Net.

All the Write Stuff

If you write just one page a day, in a year you will have 365 pages—enough to be a collection of essays, a book of short stories, or a memoir!

Write all alone, with no one looking over your shoulder, tugging at your leg, or calling for a ride to the mall. When the novelist Barbara Rogan is writing, she instructs her children not to disturb her unless the house is on fire. And so she has produced an impressive number of wonderful books—as well as two wonderful sons who respect and admire her work.

8. "I don't have the right equipment in my house and I can't afford it."

Don't get hung up on equipment. "Real writers have fancy computers and all that stuff," people tell me. "I can't write with old-fashioned paper and pencil." Why not? Most of the world's masterpieces were written longhand.

Now, I'm not claiming that it's easier for everyone to write with pen and paper; computers certainly make it easy for many people. But people were writing magnificent literature long before computers were invented. And so can you.

9. "I'm not good at all that grammar stuff."

"I'm terrible at spelling, punctuation, and grammar," you say. When you're creating a first copy, it's time to let your creative energy flow. No one has to see your writing now, if you don't want them to.

10. "I can't write what I really want because it might embarrass people."

And well it might. Families and friendships have been shattered by someone's writing. They have also been created or reconciled by words, but you may not want to take the risk of alienating people.

What happens when you want to write—or *need* to write—about a very sensitive family subject, such as abuse, betrayal, or theft? You have four choices here:

- Write what you want but don't publish it. This is a perfectly valid choice, but what do you do with the manuscript? Unless you destroy it, you don't have any guarantee that it won't fall into the wrong hands … the very hands you were trying to keep it from. So unless you intend to write the manuscript and immediately shred it, you might as well assume it's going to be read by others.

    Besides, you might really want to publish your work because you feel that your message is vitally important. By writing your story, poem, or memoir, you might be saving someone the tough times you experienced—or helping them get through their hardships and overcome their challenges.

- Write what you want, publish it, and let the chips fall where they may. Judging from the ever-increasing numbers of "tell-all" memoirs crowding the shelves, this is a popular choice. It can certainly be *your* choice, but the fallout can be toxic. It's your call.

- Censor your writing to spare people embarrassment. If you take this option, then you're not writing about the topic you chose. Rather, you're writing about an entirely different topic. The original topic will always be in your soul, unexpressed.

- Write what you want—but not under your own name. Many authors adopt a *pseudonym*, a pen name. There are several reasons they do this. For example, William Sidney Porter took the pen name O. Henry to spare his family embarrassment, since he was serving a jail sentence for bank fraud. Stephen King took the pen name Richard Bachman to publish more than he could under his own name, since he had saturated the market as Stephen King.

You can use any name you wish when you publish. This literary convention allows you the freedom to say what you want without fear of identification.

Bonus Excuse: "Why bother? Who's going to read my stuff after all?"

"No one will read my work, much less publish it," you claim. So what? No one says that you *have* to publish your work. No one says that anyone else has to read it, either. You can write creatively for the sheer pleasure of writing, for healing, for your self-esteem.

And if you do decide to publish your creative writing, today's writers have exciting new avenues never before open. For example, you can create your own web page and share your work on the Internet. You have the potential to attract millions and millions of readers, at virtually no cost.

The Least You Need to Know

- You can develop the talent to be a writer. You're never too old to get started.

- Start with your own ideas or adapt traditional plots.

- It's not as difficult as you may think to make the time you need to write creatively. You don't need any special equipment, either.

- Whether you publish or not, your original and imaginative writing will bring you pleasure.

- You have no excuse not to start writing. Start telling your story now!

4

Motivation, Muse, and Model

In This Chapter

- ◆ Discover how writing and speaking differ
- ◆ Learn surefire ways to get started writing creatively
- ◆ Find out which jump-start methods work best for you—and why

Creative writing is easy; you just jot down ideas as they occur to you. The jotting is simplicity itself—for most writers, it's the *occurring* that's difficult.

In this chapter, you will learn how to get started writing. I'll teach you different methods to make it easier for you to get your ideas down on paper. You'll learn proven techniques used by creative writers of all different types of writing, from fiction to nonfiction, poetry to prose. I'll show you how to select the routines that work best for you and your individual writing style. It's time to kick off the high board and dive right in. (Not to worry; the water's fine!)

Writing vs. Speaking

We all know how to talk. In fact, you probably can't remember a time when you didn't know how to talk. It's easy to talk to our friends … so why can it be difficult to write to them?

To answer that question, we must analyze how writing differs from speaking. Take a few minutes to write down all the differences you can think of between these two vital activities.

Use the spaces provided below to compare speaking and writing.

Speaking   **Writing**

_____   _____

_____   _____

_____   _____

_____   _____

_____   _____

As you can see from your chart, writing and speaking differ in several important ways. First of all, speech vanishes faster than yesterday's media darling. This is not necessarily a bad thing; for one, it means that any mistakes we make as we speak are likely to glide right by before they register in our listener's consciousness. In contrast, any mistakes we make when we write tend to stick around like an especially vile hangover. This gives people a chance to comment on our faux pas.

In addition, speech is immediate. There is a good point to this: The message gets across fast. But there is also a bad point to this: Sometimes we jump-start our mouths before our brains have had a chance to kick in. The immediacy of spoken communication gives people a chance to respond right then and there. If our message is garbled, our audience can say, "Huh?" and give us a chance to clarify our words. But when we write, our words may not be read for hours, days, months, or even years. As a result, a great deal of time may pass before we know if we have communicated successfully. Sometimes, we may not even remember what we intended to write and so cannot straighten out any miscommunication.

All the Write Stuff

Want to capture the cadences of speech in your written dialogue? Use a tape recorder to record an actual dialogue, then study the speech patterns.

Nonetheless, speech and writing are similar in one important way: Both methods of expression have patterns, such as accent, speed of delivery, and repetition. But writing has several unique conventions not shared by speech, such as spelling, punctuation, and capitalization. If we do not master these customs, our written communication will be flawed. People may judge us harshly as a result of our written errors.

Whether you realize it or not, you've worked to master the conventions of speech. You can do the same to master the conventions of writing.

Because of all these differences between writing and speech, you cannot simply write the way you speak. Instead, you have to learn to use those features of written communication that will enable you to communicate your ideas clearly and creatively. That's what you'll learn next in this chapter.

The Right Way to Write?

Certain processes have a right way and wrong way. We *all* know that to eat a chocolate Easter bunny properly, you start by biting the head off. Even a toddler knows that you put the cereal in the bowl first, *then* you pour in the milk. What car owner doesn't know that you take off the lug nuts *before* you change a tire? (Actually, changing a tire is an entirely different matter. That's why we have road service.) Need I get into lather, rinse, repeat?

But what about getting started writing imaginatively? Is there a right way and a wrong way with this all-important procedure? Take this true/false quiz to see how much you know about starting the process of creative writing.

Write *true* if you think the answer is true; write *false* if you think it is a bold-faced lie.

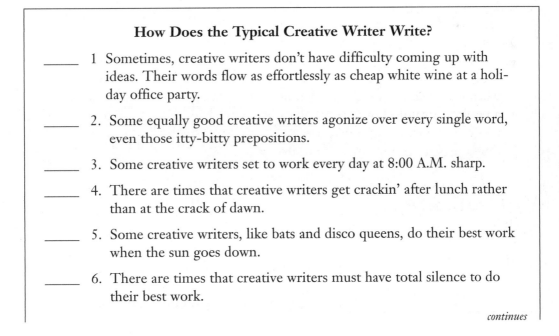

How Does the Typical Creative Writer Write?

_____ 1 Sometimes, creative writers don't have difficulty coming up with ideas. Their words flow as effortlessly as cheap white wine at a holiday office party.

_____ 2. Some equally good creative writers agonize over every single word, even those itty-bitty prepositions.

_____ 3. Some creative writers set to work every day at 8:00 A.M. sharp.

_____ 4. There are times that creative writers get crackin' after lunch rather than at the crack of dawn.

_____ 5. Some creative writers, like bats and disco queens, do their best work when the sun goes down.

_____ 6. There are times that creative writers must have total silence to do their best work.

continues

continued

_____ 7. Other creative writers can't write without the radio or stereo blaring, preferably with oldies, show tunes, or opera.

_____ 8. Many creative writers do their best work on a computer.

_____ 9. Some creative writers sprawl on their stomach and write parts of their first drafts in longhand.

_____ 10. All creative writers write the same way.

Answers

Items 1–9 are true; only item 10 is false.

What does this quiz prove? It shows that there isn't a "right" way to write. Creative writing is so intensely personal that there are all kinds of methods that accomplish the same aim. But imaginative writers are usually vulnerable and tense. Driven by a compulsion to put the best of themselves down on paper, they are terrified by their audacity.

CAUTION

Wrong Turn _____

Don't be taken in by those people who try to force you into using a specific writing method. Write the way that feels most comfortable to you. This will help you spark and maintain your creativity.

Even though anyone who's ever written knows that creative writing is a high-wire act performed without a net, many people assume that writers can just sit down and flip on their creative juices any old time. Some imaginative writers *can* sometimes start cold, but most creative writers can't pen glittering prose first thing in the morning. Experienced creative writers know that fresh and original writing is a series of activities, a process as much as a product. But like plants, all creative writers need the same things for their originality to germinate. Let's look at some of these tools now.

Space, the Final Frontier

Nearly all experienced creative writers find that they compose most easily in a quiet and calm place, free from distractions. To paraphrase the famous British writer Virginia Woolf, every creative writer needs a "room of their own" in which to compose. I agree, but nowadays this isn't always possible. Few worker bees today have the luxury of having their own personal offices, much less a home office dedicated to nothing but creative writing.

However, it usually isn't difficult to carve out a small space for yourself somewhere in your home. Your "office" can be a desk in the corner of the kitchen, bedroom, or hall. It can be an unused closet converted to a writing "room" or an attic finished off with a desk, light, and coffeemaker. I know aspiring creative writers who made over part of the garage or shed as their offices. A close friend created an office in her mother's house. With the kids grown and flown the coop, there's plenty of room in the old split-level homestead. Mom even makes lunch sometimes.

Try to avoid writing creatively in the kitchen, dining room, or family room. Aside from the natural distractions in these high-traffic areas, you'll have to sweep aside your papers every time someone walks in and wants to eat. And if your house is like mine, someone is *always* eating something. If you use a crowded place in your house, you also run the risk of having your manuscript used to wrap fish and your floppy disks becoming props for uneven table legs.

Smashing the Sound Barrier

Some creative writers require absolute pin-drop silence as they tap their heart and soul. Others like a little background noise while they write, such as radio music. The music matters, too. For example, I can't write to "lite" feel-good elevator music; it turns my prose to sludge. Hard rock makes me twitch; opera makes me doze off faster than Uncle Harry's war stories.

Experiment with different noise levels as you start off. Find your comfort zone. But don't delude yourself: Aside from Geraldo, no one writes his or her best in the middle of a war zone. It stands to reason: You cannot concentrate if people are distracting you with bullets, bongos, or burgers.

On Your Mark, Get Set ... Go!

Following are some tried-and-true methods that successful creative writers use to get started. These methods are not designed to produce final, polished drafts. Rather, they are intended to help you get your ideas down on paper. The key to all these suggestions is kindness: Be nice to yourself. Suspend your criticism until you have enough words on the page to do some serious revision. Evaluating too soon can stall even the most self-assured writer. So use these ideas as a springboard rather than as a truncheon.

Words to the Wise

Listing, a brainstorming technique, involves listing all the ideas that come to mind associated with a topic.

Listing

Listing is one of the easiest ways to get a lot of ideas. Start by thinking of a subject and then list all the ideas that come to mind about it. You can list the ideas as words, phrases, or even sentences. This technique is great because it helps you narrow down a broad subject into something original and manageable.

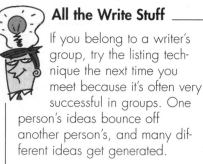

All the Write Stuff

If you belong to a writer's group, try the listing technique the next time you meet because it's often very successful in groups. One person's ideas bounce off another person's, and many different ideas get generated.

Listing works best when you let your mind free-associate, so try to work in one concentrated burst of energy. You can always add as many ideas as you like later on, but your mind will kick in faster if you try to write as fast as you can without analyzing your thoughts. Start by writing briefly, for about five minutes.

Try it now. If you're stuck for ideas, here are some subjects to consider:

- A person who has had a significant impact on your life, positive or negative

- Music, plays, TV shows, books, trends, fashions

- A problem that you now face or have overcome

- Places to visit, real or imaginary

- Controversial topics that you feel strongly about

Subject:_____

1. _____
2. _____
3. _____
4. _____
5. _____
6. _____
7. _____
8. _____
9. _____
10. _____

There are various ways to use your list. For example:

◆ Circle the ideas that strike your fancy because they are especially ingenious or original. Make another list with them or use them as the basis for the next activity we'll discuss, webbing.

◆ Group the ideas into categories. Develop these groups into memoirs, stories, or any other form they seem to fit.

Webbing

Also known as *clustering* and *mapping, webbing* is a more visual means to plan your creative writing. A web looks different from a list of words, and so it helps some writers branch off in exciting new directions.

To start a web, draw a circle in the middle of a sheet of paper. Then draw lines radiating out from the circle. If you want, you can label each line with a major subdivision of your topic, but this isn't necessary. At the end of each line, draw a circle and fill it in with a subtopic.

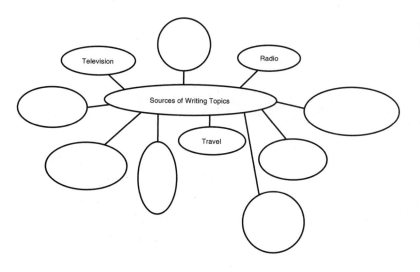

Complete this web to spark ideas about creative writing.

Web for a poem on identity.

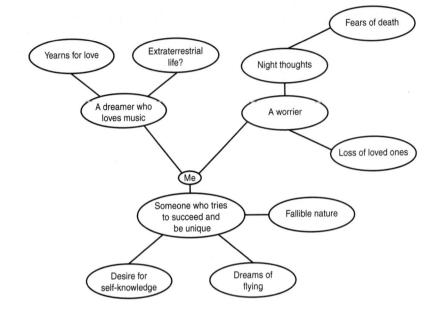

Here's how the same web looks as an outline:

A Poem About Me

    I. Stanza 1: A dreamer who loves music

        A. Extraterrestrial life?

        B. Yearn for love

   II. Stanza 2: A worrier

        A. Night thoughts

        B. Fears of death

        C. Loss of loved ones

 III. Stanza 3: Someone who tries to succeed and be unique

   A. Fallible nature

   B. Dreams of flying

   C. Desire for self-knowledge

Freewriting

Freewriting is just what its name suggests: writing freely without self-censure. To freewrite, think of a topic. Write nonstop for 10 to 15 minutes on your topic. If you're writing longhand, try not to lift your pen. If you're keyboarding, try not to stop typing. Don't worry about grammar, spelling, or punctuation. Instead, concentrate on getting your ideas down on paper in the most original way you can.

Try it now. If you're stuck for some topics, consider these general ideas:

◆ A handsome stranger, a deserted cottage on the English moors, and a passionate love affair.

◆ A significant childhood memory, such as the birth of a sibling, moving to a new place, or the death of a loved one.

◆ A traumatic event that you saw in person or on TV.

◆ Someone you admire very much. The person can be famous or not well known, real or fictional.

◆ A haunted house.

◆ A spaceship landing in your backyard.

_____

_____

_____

_____

_____

_____

_____

_____

_____

_____

_____

_____

Now, go back and read what you wrote. Pick out one or more sentences that look promising. You can always find at least one nice, juicy sentence, I promise. Then start writing again with these sentences. You'll have warmed up and gotten your writing pointed in a promising direction.

Here are some models. The following is an idea for a memoir:

> I will always remember my first view of Prince Edward Island where we lived when my family left the mainland. It was sunset when we arrived. The lighthouse looked down on us like a tall, black-capped giant.

Here's an idea for a short story:

> It's dress-down Friday at the brokerage house. Mr. Fitzpatrick, the big boss, is wearing an open-necked sports shirt. Brian, the new guy in accounts, comes walking down the hall—in a suit and tie.
>
> "It's Friday," Mr. Fitzpatrick said. "You're not supposed to wear a tie."
>
> Brian (crushed), "But it's not silk."

Picture a Scene

Some people are intensely visual. How can you tell if you're one of these lucky people? Try these simple tests. Are you able to tell how much furniture will fit in a room, how many people you can pack around a holiday table, and how much room is left in the freezer? Can you pack a suitcase with everything you need for a week's trip and close it without having to hire an elephant to jump on the lid? Do you have a reliable sense of direction?

If so, this brainstorming method will likely work well for you. Close your eyes. Now imagine a scene. Try to evoke all five senses by considering how things taste, smell, feel, sound, and look. Here's an example:

> You're at a circus. Listen to the happy crowds roaring, smell the rich odor of peanuts roasting, feel the sticky cotton candy on your fingers and taste it melting on your tongue. See the raggedy clowns packing into the tiny red car.

Choose a scene that's evocative for you. Describe it. Here are some ideas to consider if you're stumped:

- A wedding, funeral, or other important occasion
- A day at the ocean, a lake, a campground, the desert
- Repairing, building, or cooking something

- ◆ Leaving your homeland to come to America
- ◆ Being at an amusement park, roaring down a roller coaster or other thrill ride

_____

_____

_____

_____

_____

_____

_____

_____

_____

_____

Now go back over your writing and label the details that appeal to each sense. See what other details you could add to make your writing more descriptive and evocative.

Experiment with Format

Creative writing is a pressure situation because you're trying to squeeze out every drop of imagination. Fortunately, many people don't think of writing to a friend as tense at all. Even though it's still writing, people imagine it as an easy chat between friends, a pleasant tête-à-tête. Take advantage of this perception by starting to write as though you were addressing a friend. Use this creative writing event as an opportunity to chat with a friend. With luck, you'll relax and your ideas will flow. Try having a brief written "conversation" with a friend, living or dead, close or estranged.

_____

_____

_____

_____

_____

_____

_____

_____

_____

_____

Now transmute this letter into the form you want. For example, revise and expand the letter into the beginning of a short story, the first act of a play, or the introduction to a memoir.

Don't Start at the Beginning

Julie Andrews in _The Sound of Music_ aside, who says you have to start at the very beginning? You can just as easily (and often much more easily) start at the middle or even at the end. This method works especially well if you don't know how you want to start your creative writing. Compose your draft from the middle out or from the end to the beginning.

As a nice bonus, this method makes it unlikely that you'll end up with the hackneyed _Peanuts_ opening, "It was a dark and stormy night."

Try it now by recounting an event that happened to you. Start in the middle or even the end. Then go back and fill in the beginning.

_____

_____

_____

_____

_____

_____

_____

_____

_____

_____

_____

We've discussed a lot of different methods here. Which one should you use? Why not experiment with them all to discover which ones work best for you? If you're having trouble getting your ideas down on paper, try a new method of releasing your creativity. Often, just substituting a web for listing, or starting in the middle of a story rather than at the end, will free your mind to narrow your subject in exciting new ways.

The Least You Need to Know

- ◆ You cannot write the same way you speak because speech and writing are too dissimilar.

- ◆ There isn't a "right" way to write. Creative writing is so intensely personal that many methods can help you accomplish the same goal.

- ◆ Try to create a physical space for your writing in your home and consider how sound affects your ability to be creative.

- ◆ Use brainstorming techniques such as listing, webbing, freewriting, picturing a scene, experimenting with format, and starting in the middle of a story to jump-start your creativity.

Chapter 5

Release Your Imagination Through Journaling

In This Chapter

- ◆ Find out what a journal is … and what it is not
- ◆ Explore how a journal can help you become a more creative writer
- ◆ Learn how to set up your journal
- ◆ See how to make the most of your journal
- ◆ Read excerpts from famous journals

> My journal is the heart of my writing. There I record dreams, memories, funny happenings, and wild ideas. Free to play, I write in different directions and colors; I draw, I tape in leaves, notes from kids, boarding passes. From such compost, poems, stories, and even novels grow.
>
> —George Ella Lyons

"Where do you get your ideas?" people ask me all the time. Sometimes I think that people feel that creative writers have a special idea hot line: We just dial 1-800-IDEAS and Voilà! We get a slew of ideas.

A poem about doomed love. A novel about a child who keeps a pig named Charlotte as a pet. A short story about a jumping frog that a stranger fills with buckshot. A screenplay about the "unsinkable" ocean liner. So where do creative writers get all those ideas? They're not from an idea hot line. Here's the scoop: Great ideas are all around you. However, if you want to find them, you have to look carefully and listen closely. In Chapter 4, you learned many fun and easy ways to spark your artistry. Keeping a journal is such an important way to unlock your creativity that it deserves an entire chapter.

In this chapter, you'll first learn what a journal is … and what it is not. Then you'll discover how to use journals to improve your writing. We'll explore the advantages of keeping a journal, too. Then I'll help you start this superb "writing idea storehouse" of your own.

What Is a Journal?

Good question. Some people think a journal is a book in which you note the things you have to do every day. Okay, but if that's a journal, then what's a diary? For starters, you need to know the difference between a journal and a diary.

Both a journal and a diary are books that you write in. (More on that "book" part later.) However, since a diary usually has a space for each day of the year, there's a built-in expectation that you'll write something every day. Further, the amount you choose to write will be defined by the space you're allocated in the diary. If the diary allows you 1 inch, you'll be able to write 1 inch worth—and no more.

Journal writing is generally used to spark self-reflection, to get in touch with your deepest feelings, and to sort out your emotions (although you can, of course, record daily activities in your journal). This is what makes journal writing, when done often, such a powerful tool for creative writers.

In addition to your own words, journals can include pictures, photographs, articles clipped from newspapers and magazines, pressed flowers, and other artifacts that spark your imagination.

Think of your journal as …

- A giant safe deposit box that holds the most valuable stuff of all: your thoughts.
- A mailbox where you store letters to yourself.
- Your best friend, who listens and responds with encouragement.
- A sketchbook for drawings, paintings, cartoons, doodles.

- A place to make your deepest confessions.

- A safe place where you work out a problem.

- A photo album.

- A record of your life and the lives of those whom you love.

- A collection of quotations. These can be funny, inspirational, or life-affirming.

- An inspiration for days when your pen runs dry.

- A combination of all these things—and more than the sum of their parts.

It's clear that a journal is different from a diary. A *journal* is an idea book, a record of your thoughts, emotions, and reflections. A *diary*, in contrast, is used to record the day's events, like a Filofax or Day-Timer. Diaries are not used for reflection or experimentation. As such, they don't help you improve your writing skills while you grapple with life issues. A diary can help you make it to that 10 o'clock meeting on Tuesday, however.

The following chart summarizes the differences between a journal and a diary:

Journal	Diary
Book you write in	Book you write in
Place to write ideas	Record of social engagements
Way to spark self-reflection	Way to avoid social embarrassment

What Can a Journal Offer *Me?*

Journals fulfill many wonderful functions for writers. Journals can ...

- Help you come up with writing ideas. Those random scraps of memory you've stored in your journal can coalesce into a stunning new idea for a song, short story, or script, to name just a few.

- Be a place where you store ideas. You can draw on these ideas now, in a few weeks, in a few months, or even in a few years. But if you don't write the ideas down, they can be lost forever.

- Provide a risk-free venue for trying out creative new writing techniques and story ideas. Since no one has to see your journal but you, your journal provides a safe place to take bold risks as you write.

◆ Relieve stress. Describing upsetting experiences in a journal often helps relieve tension, so you can turn your thoughts to being truly creative in writing.

◆ Help you become a better writer through practice. When it comes to writing, that old saying is true: Practice *does* make perfect. Since keeping a journal encourages you to write, it provides invaluable practice. Whether you keep a journal to help you express your feelings or gather ideas for your creative writing, the very act of journaling will help you become a more skilled, confident, and imaginative writer.

◆ Increase your literary output. Writers who keep a journal tend to produce more complete projects than writers who don't have journals. In part, this is because keeping a journal demonstrates a commitment to the writer's craft.

◆ Make you a more successful writer. The more productive you are, the better you'll feel about your progress as a creative writer. Success engenders more success.

◆ Alleviate writer's block. Experimenting on paper when it doesn't count, as in a journal, takes a lot of the anxiety out of writing. This can often help get the creative juices flowing again for people who suffer from writer's block.

Setting Up Your Journal

So you've decided that keeping a journal is for you. Here's how to get started and get the maximum benefit as a creative writer.

Types of Journals

Keeping a journal is easy and inexpensive. You just need something to write *in* and something to write *with*. In my workshops on journaling, I share the following suggestions to get creative writers pointed in the right direction:

◆ Use a small notebook. You know the kind: They used to cost a quarter; now they cost a dollar. The notebook should be small enough to fit into your pocket or purse but big and thick enough to give you sufficient space to jot down ideas.

◆ Use a large notebook. There are many different possibilities if you want a large book for your journal. You may want a $9^1/_2$ x 11" sketchbook with rich pale cream-colored pages, for example, or a basic spiral notebook like you used in school. Some writers find a stenography pad works well for their journals; others like composition books, the ones with the black-and-white marbleized covers.

◆ Use a small tape recorder. A mini-tape recorder is another good way to keep a creative writing journal. It's difficult to walk and write creative ideas at the same time, but it's easy to walk and talk into a tape recorder at the same time.

◆ Use a computer. You can use a desktop, laptop, or PDA—whatever you prefer. Just be sure to back up the files on a disk or Zip drive. As an extra precaution, print out your journal entries weekly.

◆ Use paper scraps. Some writers keep their journals on scraps of paper. I don't recommend this method because it's too easy for the scraps to get lost. "I'll tape, glue, or staple every scrap into a notebook," you say. If you're compulsive enough to do that, you're compulsive enough to write in a notebook in the first place.

CAUTION

Wrong Turn

I don't recommend a loose-leaf notebook as a journal, because the pages can fall out easily and become scrambled.

Each journal method has its advantages and disadvantages. Study the following chart to help you decide which method is best for you.

Journal	Advantages	Disadvantages
Notebook	Inexpensive	Limited space in which to write
	Portable	Always need a pen or pencil
	Easy to use	May be hard to read your writing
	Always at hand	Large books are hard to carry
Tape Recorder	Portable	Need to buy tapes and batteries
	Easy to use	May break
	Inexpensive	May malfunction at a critical time
	Great if your hand-Writing is bad	Easy to steal
Computer	Easy to read	Time-consuming if you don't type fast
	Ideas easy to categorize	May crash
	Hard to lose	Expensive

Try different journals to find the ones that work best for you. If inspiration is slow to come, you can change journaling methods. This often sparks imaginative ideas.

Journal Tools

Now, let's turn to the tools you need to write *with* in your journal. Here you have three basic choices:

Write with a Pen

Many writers love the feel of a good pen. Some like the way the ink flows smoothly from their expensive fountain pens; others write best with a cheap ball-point pen. (You know the one: It has a gnawed end and missing cap. The writer stole it from the doctor's office or gas station.)

All the Write Stuff

If you decide to write in pencil or erasable pen, *never* erase any entry in your journal. After all, you don't know if you'll ever want to use that material down the road.

To some writers, the color of the ink also matters. One of my dearest friends, a truly gifted creative writer, writes in purple ink. It's been her special "signature" for more than 30 years.

Write with a Pencil

Colored pencils? Standard No. 2 pencils? Super-sharp long pencils? Pencils reduced to nubs? I'll let you in on a secret: If I have to write longhand, it's always in pencil. Pens are so, well, *final*, that they make my writing stilted and artificial. It loses all its sparkle.

Highlight with a Marker

Markers have a loyal group of followers, too. Many writers use neon markers to highlight key passages in their journals. The colors rank ideas: Yellow might mean "super idea"; pink, "keep on the back burner." Try variations on this technique. Here are two different ways to use this method:

- Read through your journal looking for a specific theme. Highlight each entry on this theme and see how the ideas fit together.

- Highlight ideas for a memoir in one color and ideas for a short story in a different color.

The tools you use as a creative writer matter a great deal, especially when it comes to your journal. This is because the most comfortable tools make your writing natural, almost automatic. The tools tell your brain, "Hey, it's time to write now," and your brain spins into action.

My house is filled with whiz-bang computers, but I write best on an ancient PC, a 386. My son souped it up so it has much more memory, but as far as my brain and hands are concerned, it's still the same sweet machine I'm been pounding on for close to a decade. And it works for me, so that's all that matters.

Writing in Your Journal

You've been planning to keep a journal—to jot down song ideas, reflect on watershed experiences, or sort through puzzling encounters. But where to begin? It's easier than you think. You may have already begun! If not, there's no time like the present.

Step #1: Ready → Consider whether you want to cover everything you experience or focus this journal on one aspect of your life.

Step #2: Set → Put the page number *1* on the top of the paper, or number a few pages in the notebook. It might sound silly to number your pages, but it gets you started writing. Suddenly, the page is no longer blank.

Step #3: Go! → Write for a predetermined time, for as long as you feel like it, or until you're interrupted. Try to write every day. If that's not possible, try to write at least three days a week. Keeping a journal is like any beneficial pastime; the more often you do it, the easier it is and the most you'll get from it.

If possible, try to write at the same time every day. This makes writing a priority in your life and shows your commitment to learning. For many people, writing in their journals is a good way to start the day, while others use it at night to decompress.

Write Freely

Remember that a journal is for you and you alone. Don't worry about spelling, punctuation, or grammar.

Don't censor your ideas, either. If you're using your journal to blow off steam or express ideas that you don't want anyone else to see *ever*, you can always destroy those pages right after you write them.

All the Write Stuff

Instant Journal: Print out and bind your recent outgoing e-mail. You've now got your most urgent concerns and projects, already written down. Add copies of any handwritten correspondence, a couple of unsent letters, and you've got an up-to-date slice of your life.

If you feel stuck, refer to things you've written lately: e-mail to friends, to-do or shopping lists, office memos. Consider these experiences to help spark ideas. You can also record your dreams, hopes, and desires.

Remember that a journal can become an extension of your thinking. By writing in a journal, you're taking the ideas out of your head and putting them down on paper.

A Note About Privacy

If you don't want people to read your journal, put it in a secure place, or write a note on the first page for people who might open your journal, accidentally or on purpose. For example: "This is my personal journal. Please respect my privacy and return the journal to me without reading it."

Under no circumstances keep your personal journal on your office computer; increasingly, courts are upholding the rights of employers to read any writing done on office time and even use it in court cases.

Making the Most of Your Journal

Fortunately, keeping a journal is easy and fun—and it's probably the single best way to spark your creative writing juices and gather ideas. The following suggestions will help you get the most from your journal and enjoy the experience as you write. Reread this list from time to time, especially if you find it hard to stick to a journal-writing schedule.

Be Nice to Yourself

Experienced or novice, many creative writers are tortured by self-doubt. Even the most imaginative writers may feel that what they've written just doesn't measure up. And like a sleepless night, one doubt leads to another and another, until you're wracked by fears that your work is flat, dull, and unimaginative. This can be an even worse problem if your writing has been raked over the coals before.

Ignore the doubts and the fear they raise. Your journal is for your eyes only so you're not serving any master at all. What you write in your journal doesn't have to be perfect. It only has to be honest.

Keep Track of Your Entries

Date every entry to help track ideas. When I kept a handwritten journal, I'd often write so fast and furiously that I'd turn two pages at a time. This left a blank page in the middle, which I'd often fill up at a later date. If I didn't date my entries, I'd never be able to track the parts of each story I'd written.

Write for Yourself

Remember: Your journal is for *you*. Of course, you're free to share entries with anyone you choose, but you're under no obligation to do so. When you know that someone else is going to read your journal, you may not be as open and honest as you would be if you were writing for yourself alone.

Don't Worry About Neatness

It's perfectly okay to be sloppy. If you're concerned about creating a perfect or beautiful journal, you'll never take any risks with your imagination. And it's only when you take a chance with your writing that you'll spread your wings.

Don't Erase or Throw Out

Save all your writing, even the stuff you're convinced is worthless. I can't stress this enough. For the sake of your art and future generations, don't be short-sighted and destroy your work.

The following drafts show how the poet William Blake worked out the different versions of his famous poem "The Tyger" in his journal. Notice how messy the first drafts are!

So far, journals sound like the best thing since sliced bread. After all, they can help you become a more creative writer as you're dealing with the stress of everyday life. But keeping a journal isn't for everyone.

Journal writing may *not* be for you if …

◆ You are obsessive, because the technique itself could become an obsession. In that case, you would get little benefit from the writing, since you're not doing it to explore technique or content but rather just for the sake of doing it.

◆ You are coping with a terrible loss. For some people in a tragic situation, writing in a journal becomes a substitute for taking action.

What differences and similarities do you see among these drafts?

WILLIAM BLAKE
The Tyger

[First Draft]

The Tyger

1   Tyger Tyger burning bright
     In the forests of the night
     What immortal hand or eye
     ~~Dare~~ ~~Could~~ frame thy fearful symmetry

                    Burnt in
2   ~~In what~~ distant deeps or skies
     ~~The cruel~~ ~~Burnt the~~ fire of thine eyes
     On what wings dare he aspire
     What the hand dare sieze the fire

3   And what shoulder & what art
     Could twist the sinews of thy heart
     And when thy heart began to beat
     What dread hand & what dread feet

     ~~Could fetch it from the furnace deep~~
     ~~And in thy horrid ribs dare steep~~
     ~~In the well of sanguine woe~~
     ~~In what clay & what mould~~
     ~~Were thy eyes of fury rolld~~

          ~~Where~~   ~~where~~
4   ~~What~~ the hammer ~~what~~ the chain
     In what furnace was thy brain

                               dread grasp
     What the anvil what ~~the arm~~ ~~arm~~ ~~grasp~~ ~~clasp~~
     ~~Dare~~ ~~Could~~ its deadly terrors ~~clasp~~ ~~grasp~~ clasp

6   Tyger Tyger burning bright
     In the forests of the night
     What immortal hand & eye
                  frame
     Dare ~~form~~ thy fearful symmetry

[*Trial Stanzas*]

Burnt in distant deeps or skies
The cruel fire of thine eye,
Could heart descend or wings aspire
What the hand dare sieze the fire

               dare he smile laugh
5   And did he laugh his work to see
          ankle
   What the shoulder what the knee
  Dare
4   Did he who made the lamb make thee
1   When the stars threw down their spears
2   And waterd heaven with their tears

[*Second Full Draft*]

Tyger Tyger burning/bright
In the forests of the night
What Immortal hand & eye
Dare frame thy fearful symmetry

And what shoulder & what art
Could twist the sinews of thy heart
And when thy heart began to beat
What dread hand & what dread feet

When the stars threw down their spears
And waterd heaven with their tears
Did he smile his work to see
Did he who made the lamb make thee

Tyger Tyger burning bright
In the forests of the night
What immortal hand & eye
Dare frame thy fearful symmetry

[*Final Version,* 1794]

The Tyger

Tyger Tyger, burning bright,
In the forests of the night;
What immortal hand or eye,
Could frame thy fearful symmetry?

In what distant deeps or skies
Burnt the fire of thine eyes!
On what wings dare he aspire?
What the hand, dare sieze the fire?

And what shoulder, & what art,
Could twist the sinews of thy heart?
And when thy heart began to beat,
What dread hand? & what dread feet?

What the hammer? what the chain,
In what furnace was thy brain?
What the anvil? what dread grasp,
Dare its deadly terrors clasp?

When the stars threw down their spears
And water'd heaven with their tears:
Did he smile his work to see?
Did he who made the Lamb make thee?

Tyger, Tyger burning bright,
In the forests of the night:
What immortal hand or eye,
Dare frame thy fearful symmetry?

Peak Inside Some Journals

As you learned in previous chapters, reading widely will help you become a more creative writer by giving you ideas, models, and templates. To that end, here are some sample journal entries to show you how other writers approach their journals. See which models most closely fit *your* journal ideas.

From Samuel Pepys's Journal

Samuel Pepys (1633–1703) is one of the most curious figures in English literature because his fame rests on only one work that he never intended for publication: his diary. Could that man dish the dirt! Pepys's diary (a journal, by our definition) is a vivid portrait of seventeenth-century life, filled with candid, private revelations and keenly observed public scenes. The following excerpt falls into the latter category, as it describes London's Great Fire of 1666.

> So near the fire we as could for smoke; and all over the Thames, with one's face in the wind, you were almost burned with a shower of firedrops. This is very true; so as houses were burned by these drops and flakes of fire, three or four, nay, five or six houses one from another.… As it grew darker, it appeared more and more, and in corners and upon steeples, and between churches and houses, as far as we could see up the hill of the city, in a most horrid malicious bloody flame, not like the fine flame of an ordinary fire. We saw the fire as only one entire arch of fire from this to the other side of the bridge, and in a bow up the hill for an arch of above a mile long; it made me weep to see it. The churches, houses, and all one fire and flaming at once: and a horrid noise the flames made, and the crackling of houses at their ruin.

From Virginia Woolf's Journal

Considered one of the most influential writers of the twentieth century, Virginia Woolf's novels include *Mrs. Dalloway* (1925) and *To the Lighthouse* (1927). The following journal entry reveals her despair at a critical moment in her life as a creative writer.

> Thursday 5 September 1941 Hot, hot, hot. Record heat wave, record summer if we kept records during this summer. At 2:30 a plane zooms; ten minutes later air raid sounds; twenty later, all clear. Hot, I repeat; and doubt if I'm a poet. An idea. All writers are unhappy. The picture of the world in books is thus too dark. The wordless are the happy; women in cottage gardens. Now, in my nightgown, to walk on the marshes.

From Susy Clemens's Journal

In 1885, when Susy Clemens was thirteen years old, she began to write a memoir of her celebrated father, Samuel Clemens (Mark Twain). "I shall have no trouble in not knowing what to say about him," she observed in its opening paragraph, "as he is a very striking character." For a year, she recorded her observations of her father, his writings, and his reputation in a journal that she kept safely tucked beneath her pillow. Here is an excerpt:

> Papa has the mind of an author exactly, some of the simplest things he cant understand. Our burglar-alarm is often out of order, and papa had been obliged to take the mahogany-room off from the alarm altogether for a time, because the burglar-alarm had been in the habit of ringing even when the mahogany-room was closed. At length he thought that perhaps the burglar-alarm might be in order, and he decided to try and see; accordingly he put it on and then went down and opened the window; consequently the alarm bell rang, it would even if the alarm had been in order. Papa went despairingly upstairs and said to Mamma, "Livy the mahogany-room won't go on. I have just opened the window to see."
>
> "Why, Youth," Mamma replied "if you've opened the window, why of coarse the alarm will ring!"
>
> "That's what I've opened it for, why I just went down to see if it would ring!"
>
> Mamma tried to explain to Papa that when he wanted to go and see whether the alarm would ring while the window was closed he mustn't go and open the window—but in vain, Papa couldn't understand, and got very impatient with mamma for trying to make him believe an impossible thing true.

Susy died from spinal meningitis in August, 1896. Ten years later, Twain discovered Susy's journal among the family's records and incorporated much of it into his autobiography, often using it as a prompt for his own memories.

From Governor Endicott's Journal

This is one of my favorite journal entries because of what it reveals about the attitude people had toward female creative writers in the seventeenth century. I know that you'll enjoy it as much as I do.

> April 13, 1645
>
> Mr. Hopkins, the governor of Hartford upon Connecticut, came to Boston, and brought his wife with him, (a godly young woman, and of special parts,) who was fallen into a sad infirmity, the loss of her understanding and reason, which had been growing on her diverse [many] years, by occasion of her giving herself wholly to reading and writing, and had written many books. Her husband, being very loving and tender of her, was loath to grieve her; but he saw his error, when

it was too late. For if she had attended her household affairs, and such things as belong to women, and not gone out of her way and calling to meddle in such things as are proper for men, whose minds are stronger, etc., she had kept her wits, and might have improved them usefully and honorably in the place God had set her. He brought her to Boston, and left her with her brother, one Mr. Yale, a merchant, to try what means might be had for her. But no help could be had.

The Least You Need to Know

◆ A *journal* is an idea book, a record of your thoughts, emotions, and reflections.

◆ Journals help you come up with writing ideas, take risks, relieve stress, practice your craft, and ease writer's block.

◆ Keeping a journal is easy and inexpensive. Your journal can be a book or electronic. Choose the method and tools that help you write most freely and creatively.

◆ Write openly in your journal, without censoring yourself.

Part  Once Upon a Time: Writing Short Stories

Once upon a time there was fiction and nonfiction and everybody knew which was which: Fiction told stories and nonfiction reported facts and opinions. But now, all that has changed—twentieth-century writing has fogged the distinction between the forms.

For more than 30 years now, nonfiction writers have been swiping tasty morsels from the fiction writer's table. Not to be outdone, fiction writers have been using some of the techniques traditionally associated with nonfiction. This is a good thing, for it allows much greater freedom in writing.

Building on that freedom, I'll help you learn how to write fiction in this part of the book. I'll take you step-by-step through the elements of a short story, including plot, voice, characterization, dialogue, conflict, and atmosphere.

Chapter 6

The Inside Scoop

In This Chapter

◆ Learn how to use words in fresh, new ways to spark your reader's imagination

◆ Discover the power of *parallelism*

◆ Use *repetition* to create emphasis and unity

◆ Explore the importance of *diction* in writing

◆ Find your *voice* and create an individual *style*

The late author Truman Capote once said, "Writing has laws of perspective, of light and shade, just as painting or music does. If you are born knowing them, fine. If not, learn them. Then rearrange the rules to suit yourself."

You say the dishes are done, the kids are in bed, and there's nothing on TV? Good. This is your chance to take a few minutes to discover the secrets of really creative writing—and I don't mean onomatopoeia and foreshadowing. *They're* for high school sophomores. We're into the big leagues here. It's time to meet the real keys to finding your original voice: *parallelism*, *repetition*, *diction*, *style*, *voice*, and *wit*.

I Know It When I See It

Can you recognize creative writing when you see it? There are a lot of myths and half-truths about creative writing. Take this snap quiz to see how much you know about the Real Thing.

Write T if you think the statement is true or F if you think it's false.

If It Walks Like a Duck and Quacks Like a Duck ...

_____ 1. We all know good writing when we see it.

_____ 2. Good creative writing is the novel you stay up all night to finish.

_____ 3. Great creative writing is the short story you insist on sharing with all your friends.

_____ 4. It's the play you want to see over and over.

_____ 5. Really imaginative writing is the movie that makes you laugh and cry at the same time.

_____ 6. You can find original writing in song lyrics that you can't get out of your head.

_____ 7. Great creative writing is the poem that comforts you when times are tough.

_____ 8. Good creative writing can be poetry or prose.

_____ 9. Superb creative writing can be fiction or nonfiction.

_____ 10. Only geniuses can create great creative writing.

Answers

Items 1–9 are true; only item 10 is false.

Following are three examples of great creative writing. The first is dramatic poetry, the second is the opening of a novel, and the third is part of an essay. See if you can identify each piece and explain why it is good.

Go Figure: Figures of Speech

Passage #1: Who said it? What makes it so beautiful?

> But, soft! what light through yonder window breaks?
> It is the east, and Juliet is the sun.
> Arise, fair sun, and kill the envious moon,
> Who is already sick and pale with grief,
> That thou her maid art far more fair than she:
> Be not her maid, since she is envious;
> Her vestal livery is but sick and green
> And none but fools do wear it; cast it off.
> It is my lady, O, it is my love!
> O, that she knew she were!

Source: _____

Outstanding qualities:

_____

_____

This is an excerpt from Shakespeare's *Romeo and Juliet*, of course. You know it's superb creative writing because everything Shakespeare wrote is worshipped. But look a little closer to see why his writing *deserves* to be revered—and used as a model.

Shakespeare uses a number of *figures of speech* (or *figurative language*)—words and expressions not meant to be taken literally. Figures of speech use words in fresh, new ways to appeal to the imagination. Figures of speech include similes, metaphors, extended metaphors, hyperbole, and personification. Here are just two examples that you can find in this soliloquy from *Romeo and Juliet*:

♦ *Metaphors.* These figures of speech compare two unlike things, the more familiar thing describing the less familiar one. Metaphors do not use the words *like* or *as* to make the comparison. "It is the east, and Juliet is the sun" is a metaphor.

♦ *Personification.* Here, a nonhuman subject is given human characteristics. Effective personification of things makes them seem vital and alive, as if they were human.

Words to the Wise

Figures of speech (or figurative language) are words used in fresh, new ways to appeal to the imagination. Figures of speech include similes, metaphors, extended metaphors, hyperbole, and personification.

Shakespeare personifies the sun and moon when he writes: "Arise, fair sun, and kill the envious moon,/Who is already sick and pale with grief,/That thou her maid art far more fair than she."

Using figures of speech in your own creative writing enables you to describe people, places, and things with precision and lyric beauty. This helps you create memorable images that stay in your readers' minds long after they have finished reading your words.

On the Straight and Narrow: Parallelism and Repetition

Passage #2: Can you identify this creative writing?

It was the best of times, it was the worst of times, it was the age of wisdom, it was the age of foolishness, it was the epoch of belief, it was the epoch of incredulity, it was the season of Light, it was the season of Darkness, it was the spring of hope, it was the winter of despair, we had everything before us, we had nothing before us, we were all going direct to Heaven, we were all going direct the other way—in short, the period was so far like the present period, that some of its noisiest authorities insisted on its being received, for good or for evil, in the superlative degree of comparison only.

Source: _____

Outstanding qualities:

_____

_____

This is the opening from Charles Dickens's classic novel of revolution, *A Tale of Two Cities*. Here, Dickens uses two other writing secrets to create powerful, memorable writing: *parallelism* (or *parallel structure*) and *repetition*. Much of the power of formal prose like this novel comes from the repetition of words and phrases and the connections between them.

Parallel Bars

You can create balance by pairing two related words, such as "men and women," or two related compounds, such as "best of times and worst of times." This balance in construction is called parallelism or parallel structure. It's matching words, phrases, and clauses. Notice how Dickens begins each sentence with the same phrase, *It was the* and follows with an adjective, preposition, and noun.

All the Write Stuff

When you use parallelism, repeating or adding words creates emphasis and rhythm; leaving out conjunctions creates tension. Dickens creates tension by leaving out the coordinating conjunction *and* between the following two complete sentences: "It was the best of times, it was the worst of times." The sentence normally would read: "It was the best of times, *and* it was the worst of times."

Dickens also uses parallelism to create humor: "We were all going direct to Heaven, we were all going direct the other way." Dickens's use of parallelism creates memorable phrases; it's no surprise that the opening of *A Tale of Two Cities* is one of the most famous passages in literature.

Speaker of the House

Parallelism and repetition are key elements in many of our most famous speeches, such as John F. Kennedy's inaugural address. In that speech, parallelism and repetition capture the cadences of natural speech to create one of the most memorable lines of the twentieth century: "And so, my fellow Americans, ask not what your country can do for you—ask what you can do for your country."

Words to the Wise

Parallelism (or **parallel structure**) is matching words, phrases, or clauses. **Repetition** is using the same sound, word, phrase, line, or grammatical structure over and over. Authors use repetition to link related ideas and emphasize key points.

Abraham Lincoln built the "Gettysburg Address" on parallelism and repetition, drawn from his deep knowledge of biblical rhythms: "But in a larger sense, we cannot dedicate—we cannot consecrate—we cannot hallow—this ground." Notice the repetition of the parallel phrase *we cannot.*

Proper Words in Proper Places: Diction

Passage #3: What makes this essay so effective?

These are the times that try men's souls: The summer soldier and the sunshine patriot will in this crisis, shrink from the service of his country; but he that stands it NOW, deserves the love and thanks of man and woman. Tyranny, like hell, is not easily conquered; yet we have this consolation with us, that the harder the conflict, the more glorious the triumph. What we obtain too cheap, we esteem too lightly:—'Tis dearness only that gives everything its value. Heaven knows how to put a proper price upon its goods; and it would be strange indeed, if so celestial an article as freedom should not be highly rated.

Source: _____

Outstanding qualities:

_____

_____

You've heard it, maybe even quoted it, but can you identify it? It's the opening of Thomas Paine's *The American Crisis*, a series of essays to convince people to support American independence from English rule. Before the Revolution, Paine had lived an inconspicuous life, working at a series of unimpressive jobs ranging from corset maker to grocer. The revolution called forth his brilliant prose. *The American Crisis* was a colonial best-seller, and with good cause. It's great writing.

Paine selects the precise words he needs to make his point and reach his audience. For example, notice the implications in the descriptions "summer soldier" and "sunshine patriot." Paine's words suggest that these are the people who support you only when it is convenient. Using "celestial" to describe *freedom* conveys the priceless quality of independence.

The words you select make up your *diction*. Your diction affects the clarity and impact of your message. Diction is measured from high to low, high being multisyllabic tongue-twisters and low being slang and vernacular. Neither is intrinsically good or bad; rather, each is appropriate in different writing situations.

- *Elevated diction.* Here's some elevated diction from philosopher Ralph Waldo Emerson: "Whoso would be a man, must be a nonconformist. He who would gather immortal palms must not be hindered by the name of goodness, but must explore if it be goodness."

- *Vernacular.* Here's some plain speaking from Mark Twain: "I do wonder what in the nation that frog throw'd off for—I wonder if there ain't something the matter with him—he 'pers to look mighty baggy, somehow."

Words to the Wise

The **denotation** of a word is its exact meaning. The **connotation** of a word is its emotional overtones.

How would you describe the level of Paine's diction in the preceding essay?

Denotation and Connotation

To be successful at choosing exact words for each particular context, you have to understand the *denotation* and *connotation* of words. Every word has a denotation, its explicit meaning. You can find the denotation of a word by looking it up in a dictionary. For example, if you look up the word *fat* in the dictionary, it will say, "having too much adipose tissue."

Some words also have *connotations*, or emotional overtones. These connotations can be positive, negative, or neutral. For example, *fat* has a negative connotation in our fitness-obsessed society. Being sensitive to a word's denotation and connotation is essential for clear and effective creative writing. It can also help you use the right word and so avoid getting your nose punched out because you insulted someone. Finally, you can use these connotations to create an emotional response in your reader.

Wrong Turn

Don't discount the importance of context and connotation (a word's emotional overtones). Words carry different connotations depending on how they are used, especially where gender is concerned. For example, an *aggressive* man and an *aggressive* woman are often perceived as two different animals: the former as an achiever, the latter as a word that rhymes with *witch* and *rich*.

Chart It!

Check out your understanding of connotation and denotation by completing the following chart. Write a plus (+) next to any word with a positive connotation or a dash (–) next to any word with a negative connotation.

When would you use each of these words? Why?

Word	Connotation
1. Paunchy	6. Loyal
2. Chubby	7. Reckless
3. Cheap	8. Bold
4. Thrifty	9. Gaunt
5. Stubborn	10. Slender

Answers

All odd-numbered words have a negative connotation; all even-numbered words have a positive connotation.

How to Write Well: Get Some Style

"Every style that is not boring is good," wrote French writer Voltaire. All good writing shares one common quality: it has *style*. Some modern American writers celebrated for their lucid style include Truman Capote, James Thurber, Dorothy Thompson, Joan Didion, John McPhee, Tracy Kidder, and E. B. White. Mr. White, a long-time essayist and short story writer for *The New Yorker*, oozed so much style that he even co-authored a famous little writing manual called *The Elements of Style*. It's the *ne plus ultra* of style.

Style is a series of choices—words, sentence length and structure, figures of speech, tone, voice, diction, and overall structure. A creative writer may change his or her style for different kinds of writing and to suit different audiences. In poetry, for example, a writer might use more imagery than he or she would use in prose. Style depends on purpose, audience, and appropriateness.

Words to the Wise

An author's **style** is his or her distinctive way of writing.

Don't confuse *style* with *stylishness*. The latter is faddish; the former, eternal. Stylishness is go-go boots, hula-hoops, and spandex; style is wing-tips, baseball, and pure wool. Stylish writing doesn't make it in the long haul: choose-your-own-ending novels, snuff fiction, and trash fiction are the literary equivalent of the Edsel, Olestra, and the new-formula Coca-Cola.

Also, don't confuse style with bizarreness or eccentricity. Style is not something you do to a text to tart it up, like slapping whipped cream over a sagging cake. Style is a beginning, not an end unto itself. Unless you're James Joyce, avoid making up words, running ideas together, and dragging out stream of consciousness.

Thrift, Thrift, Thrift

In every fat book there is a thin book trying to get out. Your job is to write the thin book that says it all. Often, as much gets left out as put in. A fine writing style shows an economy of language.

Conciseness describes writing that is direct and to the point. This is not to say that you have to pare away all description, figures of speech, and images. No. It *is* to say that wordy writing annoys your readers because it forces them to slash their way through rain-forest verbiage before they can understand what you're saying. Hard and lean sentences, like hard and lean bodies, require far more effort than flabby ones. And they are so much nicer.

Follow these three easy rules to create taut, effective sentences.

1. Eliminate unneeded words.

2. Don't say the same thing twice.

3. Make passive sentences active.

Let's look at each of these rules in greater detail.

Eliminate Unneeded Words

Combine sentences to achieve clarity. Cut any words that just take up space like an unwanted house guest. Here's an example:

> **Wordy:** *The Chamber* was a best-seller. It was written by John Grisham. *The Chamber* was a courtroom thriller.

> **Better:** *The Chamber*, by John Grisham, was a best-selling courtroom thriller.

Here are some words and phrases that weigh down your writing. They can always be eliminated to better effect.

Wrong Turn

Repetition is a good thing, redundancy is not. When you use repetition, you deliberately repeat words and phrases to create rhythm and emphasis. Redundancy, in contrast, adds unnecessary bits and pieces that need to be trimmed like fat from the federal budget.

Words and Phrases to Cut

as a matter of fact	because of the fact that
factor	for the purpose of
in a very real sense	in light of the fact that
in the case of	to get to the point
that is to say	what I mean to say
the point I am trying to make	

Don't Say the Same Thing Twice

Phrases such as *revert back, cover over, circle around,* and *square in shape* are redundant because they say the same thing twice. Cut! Cut! Cut!

Redundant: The editor was looking forward to the book's final completion.

Better: The editor was looking forward to the book's completion.

Make Passive Sentences Active

In the *active voice*, the subject performs the action named by the verb. In the passive voice, the subject receives the action. The *passive voice* is often far wordier than the active voice. How many unnecessary words were cut by rewriting the following sentence from the passive voice to the active voice?

Passive: Ten pages were completed in one day by the writer.

Active: The writer completed ten pages in one day.

According to the contemporary American novelist Philip Roth, a writer's voice is "something that begins around the back of the knees." *Voice* is the writer's unique personality. As a result, voice lets you tell stories that are uniquely your own. Good creative writing has a sense of life that forces the reader to keep going. There's the sense that a real person wrote the text. That's voice. It's a crucial part of a writer's creativity and originality.

Beginning creative writers are often afraid to let their voice emerge. They start with someone else's voice and hope it will yield original material. It rarely does. Getting to know your voice can be a perilous process, because in so doing you are revealing much of yourself. But you cannot adopt another personae until you find your own.

Find Your Voice!

You can turn off all the lights, sacrifice a few goats, and wait for your voice to come to you. Or you can try a few of the following 10 suggestions to see if you can cultivate voice without angering the ASPCA.

1. Be outrageous. Experiment. The more freedom you feel, the more willing you will be to release your voice.

2. Write in the dark or with your eyes closed.

3. Dress all in one color and write.

4. Activate odors that move your spirit. Try cinnamon, pine, or vanilla.

5. Try writing outdoors.

6. Surround yourself with special, evocative objects as you write.

7. Play music as you write. Change the music and see what happens.

8. Lose yourself in colors and shapes. Draw pictures; finger paint.

9. Write with the opposite hand.

10. Write fragments: dialogue, description, poetry. Don't worry about how everything will fit together.

Wit

Wit is like a Ginsu knife: fast, sharp, and merciless. Wit stays sharp, too, even when it's cut a hundred times. Like an Armani suit, you know wit when you see it: Oscar Wilde, Dorothy Parker, and Tom Stoppard are witty. Groucho Marx, Jay Leno, and Rosie O'Donnell are funny, maybe even acerbic—but not witty. Joan Rivers is too nasty; Dave Letterman is too idiotic. (Sorry, Dave, but you did it to yourself with those stupid pet tricks.) *Vanity Fair* has moments of wit; so does *The New Yorker*.

Here are some examples from Dorothy Parker's "Pig's Eye View of Literature." The first poem turns on Wilde's reputation for creating memorable epigrams; the second, on Carlyle's temper.

Oscar Wilde

If, with the literate I am
Impelled to try an epigram,
I never seek to take the credit;
We all assume Oscar said it.

Thomas Carlyle

Carlyle combined the lit'ry life
With throwing teacups at his wife,
Remarking, rather testily,
"Oh, stop your dodging, Mrs. C.!"

Wit comes from an Anglo-Saxon word that means "mind, intelligence, and reason." By the Renaissance, it referred to a clever remark, especially one that was unexpected or paradoxical. By the 1700s, wit came to mean eloquence and precision. Writers in the 1800s didn't much go for wit. They preferred the term *imagination* and all its connotations.

Today, saying it fast and funny is back. Like rock-hard abs and overpriced goat cheese, wit is in. See if it works for you.

The Least You Need to Know

◆ Figures of speech use words in fresh, new ways to appeal to the imagination.

◆ Parallelism and repetition create powerful, memorable writing.

◆ Select the precise words (diction) you need to make your point and reach your audience. Watch for the connotation (implied meaning) of words.

◆ Create style through your choices: words, sentence length and structure, figures of speech, tone, voice, diction, and structure.

◆ Be concise, direct, and to the point.

◆ Cultivate your writer's voice, through wit, if you choose.

Chapter 7

Writing Narratives

In This Chapter

- ◆ Survey the history of the short story
- ◆ Define the *well-made* short story
- ◆ Understand the *slice-of-life* short story
- ◆ Preview the elements of short narratives: plot, point of view, characters, dialogue, conflict, setting, and mood

"The four requirements for a good short story are brevity, a religious reference, a sexual reference, and a conflict," the writing teacher instructed his class.

The next day a student handed in a story that read in full: "My God," said the duchess. "Take your hand off my knee!"

Well, writing a short story isn't quite that easy (and the story itself isn't quite that short), but after you've finished this chapter, I have no doubt that you'll have a good overview of the process. This will make it easier for you to decide how to frame your own stories.

In this chapter, you'll first get some background on the short story. This will help you understand its development and various formats. Then you'll explore the two main types of short stories, the *well made* and the *slice of life*. The chapter concludes with a preview of the elements of the short story: plot, point of view, characters, dialogue, conflict, setting, and mood.

Let's start with a brief history of the short story.

What a Short Story Is ... and Isn't

Every time I teach a seminar in short story writing, the first question I get is, "What exactly *is* a short story?" Good question.

For starters, the term *short story* tells us that we're dealing with a brief narrative, a kind of writing that tells a fictional tale. Short story writer Stephen Vincent Benét said that a short story "can be read in an hour and remembered for a lifetime." That gets to the heart of the matter, but we need a little more to go on.

We know that the short story is one of the oldest forms of writing. The earliest known short stories, Egyptian tales inscribed on papyrus, date from the year 3000 B.C.E. Since these narratives were found in tombs, we can tell that the ancient Egyptians realized the importance of having some good reading material for the afterlife.

Other countries also added to the short story's rich legacy. From India came the Jatakas, the teachings of Buddha, around the year 500 B.C.E., and the Panchatantra, Hindu beast fables. In these fables, animals talked like human beings to make moral points. Aesop, the Greek slave who lived in the sixth century B.C.E., originated similar fables that were written down in the first and second century C.E.

The Bible also contributed to the development of the short story. The Old Testament abounds in examples of short stories; the tales of Ruth, David and Goliath, and Esther are all cases in point. In the New Testament, Christ's parables can be classified as brief narratives because they tell a story.

The Middle Ages saw the appearance of many short narrative forms. Chaucer's *Canterbury Tales* (1387–1395) are famous examples. If you're looking for a good model story as well as a good read, try Chaucer's "Miller's Tale."

The Arabian Nights, a series of romantic tales, dates back to the eighth century, but they were first published in French in 1704. The modern short story really begins with the growth of the mass market and the rise of commercial magazines in the nineteenth century.

Washington Irving (1783–1859) is regarded by many critics as the father of the modern short story. He saw the purpose of fiction as entertainment, not instruction, and entertain he did by combining American and European history and folklore, social observation and humor.

There are two basic types of short stories—the *well-made* short story and the *slice-of-life* short story. We'll examine each in turn so you can decide which version suits your interests and taste.

Write Angles

Using old German folktales as his base, Irving created a series of remarkable short stories. His 1820 publication of "Rip Van Winkle" and "The Legend of Sleepy Hollow" catapulted him to fame. Both stories became international sensations in large part because of their main characters: Rip, whose "great error was an insuperable aversion to all kinds of profitable labor," and Icabod Crane, a fellow so skinny that one might mistake him for the image of "famine descending upon the earth, or some scarecrow eloped from a cornfield."

The Well-Made Short Story

The American writer and literary critic Edgar Allen Poe (1809—1849) created what has come to be called the well-made short story. Washington Irving may be the father of the short story, but Edgar Allan Poe did all the heavy lifting, shaping the story into its familiar form.

Poe penned the classic definition of the short story, what we think of when we think of a short story. He wrote that the short story should have a single and unique effect and that every word, every sentence, should matter. Here are his exact words:

> A skillful literary artist has constructed a tale. If wise, he has not fashioned his thoughts to accommodate his incidents; but having conceived, with deliberate care, a certain unique or single effect to be wrought out, he then invents such incidents—he then combines such events as may best aid him in establishing this preconceived effect …. In the whole composition there should be no word written, of which the tendency, direct or indirect, is not to the one preestablished design.

The key here is "single effect" and "preconceived design." According to Poe, a short story, like a good outfit, is all of a piece. Further, Poe asserted, this unity must be established from the very beginning of the story; if a writer's "very initial sentence tends not to the outbringing of this effect, then he has failed in his first step." When we finish reading a well-made short story, we can infer a message about life, the *theme*.

Poe's rules were rigid in other regards, too. He felt that for unity of effect the ideal short story should be read without pause. For this reason, he limited the length of the story to one- to two-hours' reading time. The effect that Poe sought to create was terror, passion, or horror—or "a multitude of other such effects."

Words to the Wise

Theme is the main idea of a literary work, its general statement about life. You can state the theme outright in the work, or make readers infer it from details in the plot, characters, and setting.

Poe is responsible for the emergence of the short story as a popular and respected literary form. Here's how he did it in "The Cask of Amontillado."

To achieve his revenge for a minor slight, Montressor tricks his enemy Fortunato into a wine cellar by playing on his vanity about his knowledge of fine sherry. The story starts this way …

It was about dusk, one evening during the supreme madness of the carnival season, that I encountered my friend. He accosted me with excessive warmth, for he had been drinking much.…

I said to him, "My dear Fortunato, you are luckily met. How remarkably well you are looking today! But I have received a pipe of what passes for Amontillado [a type of sherry], and I have my doubts."

"How?" said he. "Amontillado? Impossible! And in the middle of the carnival!"

Drunk as a skunk, Fortunato falls for the bait and follows Montressor into the wine cellar/catacomb. Montressor lures him deeper and deeper into the damp cavern. When they reach the end of the tunnel, Montressor springs forward and chains him to the granite. Fortunato is too astounded to resist. In a flash, Montressor has uncovered the pile of stone and mortar he had conveniently stashed there earlier and with chilling industry walls his friend in.

By the time the second tier is built, Fortunato is moaning; by the fourth, he's screaming and clanking his chains. Nonetheless, Montressor keeps working. By midnight, he's just about done. Right before he lays the last brick to entomb his "friend" alive, Fortunato screams out, *"For the love of God, Montressor!"* "Yes," Montressor replies, "for the love of God!"

The story ends …

I hastened to make an end of my labor. I forced the last stone into its position; I plastered it up. Against the new masonry I re-erected the old rampart of bones. For the half of a century no mortal has disturbed them. In pace requiescat! ["May he rest in peace!"]

The total effect is chilling horror and delicious suspense.

The Slice-of-Life Short Story

Although the Russian writer Anton Chekhov's plays—*The Cherry Orchard, The Three Sisters, The Seagull*—established him as one of the greatest dramatists of the twentieth century, his hundreds of short stories have also had a significant impact on writing, immensely influencing the art of fiction.

Chekhov (1860–1904) had a different take on the short story: He saw it as a succession of little scenes composed like a mosaic or the dots on an Impressionistic painting. Compared to Poe's stories, Chekhov's stories seem to lack a plot, a cohesive story.

Further, the characters usually don't speak to each other in the conventional give-and-take of dialogue. Instead, they engage in brief little speeches that often don't seem linked to the situation at hand. No one appears to listen to what anyone else is saying. The characters are in their own little world. Readers get the impression that it's every character for himself, people isolated on the stage of life. When we finish reading a slice-of-life short story, we don't come away with a clear message about the meaning of the experience, either.

So what holds these stories together? It's the character's moment of realization, the *epiphany*. Made famous by the Irish writer James Joyce, the epiphany is our payoff when everything we have read in the story comes together.

As late as 1950, short stories meant narratives with well-defined plots—the well-made story. Now, however, the slice-of-life plotless story is popular because it closely mirrors the seeming aimlessness and alienation of modern life. Pick up this month's issues of *The New Yorker, The Atlantic, Playboy* (yes, I know that you get it for the excellent fiction), and smaller literary magazines for examples of the slice-of-life short story.

A few notable writers are staging a revolt against the slice-of-life story and returning to the well-made tale. These writers include Elmore Leonard, Stephen King, Michael Chabon, and Michael Crichton. This is great news for you, because it means that both types of stories are in vogue!

Similarities Between the Well-Made and Slice-of-Life Narratives

Whether you're writing a well-made short story or a slice-of-life short story, most short stories share the following characteristics: A short story …

♦ Is a prose narrative (this means it's not poetry).

♦ Has fewer than 10,000 words. On average, a short story tends to run between 2,000 to 7,000 words.

♦ Describes one main event that tells a story.

♦ Features a small cast of characters, usually no more than one or two main characters.

♦ Takes place during a limited time frame. The action might take place in a day, a week, or a month, for example. There are some exceptions, but usually the action doesn't last for years.

♦ Often shows a character undergoing an event that changes him or her. This event reveals one facet of human nature.

As with designer water, we even have specialized kinds of short stories today. A *short short* story can be between 1,000 and 1,500 words. There's even a micro-mini story, called a *flash*, that runs about 750 words. So how long should *your* short story be? Make it just long enough to tell what you need it to tell. No more, no less.

All the Write Stuff

Fiction is writing based on the writer's imagination, so it contains made-up characters and events. However, even though fiction is made up, it has firm roots in reality. Virginia Woolf has written: "Fiction is like a spider's web attached ever so lightly perhaps, but still attached to life at four corners."

I've heard novice writers declare that they plan to write short stories for a few years before they tackle a novel. They figure a short story is easier to write than a novel because it's shorter. "I'll learn to walk before I learn to dance," they argue. Bad move. It's like saying you're going to learn the cha-cha before attempting pole vaulting.

Learning to write a short story isn't easier than learning to write a novel—it's just different. As a result, it doesn't necessarily take more time to become a proficient novelist than it does to become a proficient short story writer.

Elements of a Short Story

Read the following narrative and decide whether it qualifies as a short story—and why.

> Joanne is having a relationship with a sentence. It is a beautiful sentence, and she loves it very much. They met in Haiti, when Joanne was on vacation, a number of years ago. The sentence was in French then, but Joanne didn't mind. Even through a language barrier, she knew what it was saying to her. She could see that the two of them were meant to be together.
>
> The sentence was translated into English, and Joanne happily brought it back to America with her. She read it every day, mooning over every word, admiring her sentence's delicate phrasing. She knew she had the most perfect sentence in the whole world. And it was good to her because it made her life complete.
>
> Joanne told all her friends about her new lover. They were all shocked and confused, and told her she was crazy. But she knew they were jealous, because they didn't have a sentence like hers. No one else did. She was the only person in the world who felt this way. She never let them near her sentence, much less read it. It was too good for petty people like them.
>
> The sentence spent almost a year translated into German for political reasons. Joanne worried about it every day. When it got back, would it still be the same sentence she had known before? She waited, and worried, and sure enough, it returned to her—a little different, perhaps, but what did semantics matter? It was still the sentence she knew and loved.
>
> Years passed. Joanne and her sentence led very happy, fulfilled lives. They lived together, traveled together, and grew old together. Then, one day, Joanne read her sentence as she had in her youth. To her dismay, she discovered she no longer understood it. She had no idea what the sentence meant anymore.
>
> Joanne is having a relationship with a sentence. But she no longer thinks it a beautiful sentence, and she no longer loves it. Now, all she has is a scrap of paper and a dependent clause.
>
> —by Charles Rozakis

This *is* a short story (although a very short one!) because it has the elements of a short story: plot, conflict, point of view, characters, dialogue, setting, and mood. Time to explore these elements more closely.

Start with the Plot

To paraphrase E. M. Forster, if an author writes, "The king died and the queen died," that's a *story*. By writing, "The king died and the queen died *of grief*," the author has established a *plot*. You've already learned that a short story is a prose *narrative*. This means that it tells a story. The *plot* is the sequence of events that make up the story.

Plot is the arrangement of events in a work of literature. Plots have a beginning, middle, and end. The writer arranges the events of the plot to keep the reader's interest and convey the theme. An effective plot draws the reader into the characters' lives and helps us understand the choices they made.

In many well-made narratives, the events of the plot can be divided as follows:

◆ *Exposition:* introduces the characters, setting, and conflict.

◆ *Rising Action:* builds the conflict and develops the characters.

◆ *Climax:* shows the highest point of the action.

◆ *Resolution:* resolves the story and ties up all the loose ends. The resolution is also called the *denouement*.

Create Conflict

In a narrative, a *conflict* is a struggle or fight. Conflict makes a short story interesting because readers want to discover the outcome. The conflict sets up action and leads to suspense. Both conflict and suspense are necessary to make a successful short story.

There are two kinds of conflict: *external* and *internal*. Short stories often contain both external and internal conflicts.

◆ External conflict: Characters struggle against a force outside themselves, such as another character or a natural force such as a hurricane or tornado.

◆ Internal conflict: Characters battle a force within themselves, such as moral scruples.

Choose a Point of View

A car and a truck collide. In addition to the two drivers, there's a slew of witnesses: three passengers, four kids playing on the sidewalk, a man getting his mail, a woman with a videocamera who happened to be filming close by, and a hang glider flying overhead. This gives us a total of 12 different points of view. Most likely, that means we'll get 12 different descriptions of the accident.

As any insurance agent or police officer can tell you, who tells the story and how it is told are critical to the story that emerges. The same is true with fiction. The reader's vantage point—the point of view—determines what we see and how it's interpreted. A story's tone and even its meaning can change radically depending on the point of view.

Below are the main points of view you can select from as you write your short stories:

- First-person point of view: The narrator is one of the characters in the story and explains the events through his or her eyes.

- Third-person limited point of view: The narrator tells the story through the eyes of only one character, using the pronouns *he*, *she*, and *they*.

- Omniscient point of view: The narrator looks through the eyes of all the characters and is thus "all-knowing."

Develop Realistic Characters

A *character* is a person in a narrative. Main characters have important roles in the literary work; minor characters have smaller parts. Memorable characters—whether main or minor—come alive for your readers. Even though they're fictional, these creations seem to really exist. Characters can be categorized in different ways, as the following chart shows:

Description	Definition
Protagonist	The main character
Antagonist	The person in conflict with the main character
Static character	Stays the same throughout the story
Dynamic character	Grows and changes during the story

Write Sizzling Dialogue

Dialogue is the conversation in fiction or drama. It is the exact words a character says. In a short story or novel, quotation marks are used to point out the dialogue. Effective dialogue not only sounds realistic, it also helps develop the plot and reveal the characters' personalities.

Here's an example from Washington Irving's short story "Rip Van Winkle." Rip has just awakened to discover that he's overslept by 20 years. Trying to figure out what has happened, he approaches a woman for information. As you read, see how Irving uses the dialogue to build the plot to its climax:

"What is your name, my good woman?" asked he.

"Judith Gardenier."

"And your father's name?"

"Ah, poor man, his name was Rip Van Winkle; it's twenty years since he went away from home with his gun, and has never been heard of since—his dog came home without him; but whether he shot himself, or was carried away by the Indians, nobody can tell. I was then but a little girl."

Rip had but one question more to ask, but he put it in a faltering voice: "Where's your mother?"

"Oh, she too had died but a short time since, she broke a blood vessel in a fit of passion at a New-England peddler."

Words to the Wise

Dialogue is a speaker's exact words. A **conflict** in a narrative is a struggle or fight.

There was a drop of comfort, at least, in this intelligence. The honest man could contain himself no longer. He caught his daughter and her child in his arms. "I am your father!" cried he. "Young Rip Van Winkle once—old Rip Van Winkle now!—Does nobody know poor Rip Van Winkle!"

Paint a Setting

The *setting* of a story is the time and place where the events take place. Sometimes you will state the setting outright: "It was a sunny, clear September, with a nip in the air." Other times, however, you'll have readers infer it from details in the story. You'll plant clues in the characters' speech, clothing, or means of transportation.

Mold a Mood

Mood is the strong feeling we get from a literary work. The mood is created by characterization, description, images, and dialogue. Some possible moods include: terror, horror, tension, calmness, and suspense. Mood is also called *atmosphere*.

I've presented the elements of narrative in a specific order, but there's no saying that you have to follow this order as you develop your story. For example, a snatch of dialogue might spark the entire story and so you'll write pages of conversation before you know just where it's going. Or you may start with a character and spin the story out from there. The choice is completely yours.

The Least You Need to Know

- The *well-made* short story has a single effect, a clear plot, and a theme. It should be of a length to be read in one sitting.

- The *slice-of-life* short story provides a glimpse into a life, seemingly without a structured plot or evident theme.

- Both forms of the short story are prose (not poetry), have fewer than 10,000 words, describe one main event, feature a small cast of characters, and take place during a limited time frame.

- All short stories have these elements: plot, point of view, characters, dialogue, conflict, setting, and mood.

Chapter 8

What's the Problem? Plotting Your Story

In This Chapter

◆ Understand plot

◆ Deconstruct a plot

◆ Learn how to plot a story

◆ Write a plot (or two!)

As you learned in Chapter 7, *plot* is the arrangement of events in a work of literature. Your plot can be as formal as the exposition → rising action → climax → resolution format of the *well-made* story or as seemingly random as the *slice-of-life* story. Regardless of the format you choose, your stories must have a structure, the plot. That's what we'll cover in this chapter.

Build Me Up, Buttercup: Plot Structure

The plot of a story can be as loose as modern morality, but there must be something there to keep the reader reading. The story needs something more than the mere list of events or the writer's deep insight into the human condition. What keeps us reading, what holds the words together, is like the melody in music. It's the *structure*, and it allows the conflict and suspense to build.

As you learned in the previous chapter, traditional short stories follow a very specific structure. They open by introducing the *setting* (time and place), *characters*, and *conflict*. As the story unfolds, the action builds (or rises) to the point of highest interest, the *climax*. Next, the events wind down through the falling action. The rising action is longer than the falling action to allow the writer to eke out that last drop of suspense and tension. Last, the writer ties up all the loose ends in the resolution or denouement. Here's how a traditional short story plot looks in diagram form:

The structure of a well-made story.

Setting, Characters, Conflicts   Climax   Denouement

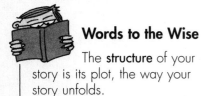

Words to the Wise

The **structure** of your story is its plot, the way your story unfolds.

This three-part structure—beginning/middle/end—dominated short story writing for centuries before experimental writers began to shake it up. As a result, in contemporary fiction, the structure of a short story can vary. For example, a single story can be narrated by several different characters. The story can begin with the end and end with the beginning. But whatever the arrangement of parts, there has to be a structure to hold it all together.

Plot and Meaning: A Match Made in Heaven

The plot structure must reinforce the content and its meaning. As a result, you will vary the structure of your plots depending on the story you're telling. For example, in a mystery story, consider withholding plot exposition until later in the tale to build suspense and tension.

As you plan the plot of each story, ask yourself, "How can I arrange the story elements to tell the story in the best possible way?" You want the story clear but also suspenseful. You want to control the reader's emotional responses.

It All Comes Out in the End

Your readers will hate you if your story's resolution isn't logical. Don't depend on coincidence to resolve the conflict. None of this "Thank goodness we won the lottery and saved the farm!" stuff. Nix also on "So you're the long-lost cousin I've been searching for all this time?"

And deep-six the infamous "And then they woke up and it was all a dream" stuff, too. It's just plain lazy and cheats the reader.

Analyze a Model

As I've emphasized throughout this book, one of the best ways to become a more creative writer is to study models of recognized literary merit. In addition to seeing how the masters do it, studying models helps you decide what techniques suit your personal style—and which ones don't.

Mark Twain's "The Celebrated Jumping Frog of Calaveras County," first published in a New York newspaper in November 1865 and quickly reprinted around the country, is justly famous for its clever plot. It's also a peachy story for its use of ...

- ◆ *Vernacular.*
- ◆ Exaggeration.
- ◆ Humor.
- ◆ A deadpan narrator.

Critics agree that "The Jumping Frog" is likely the best humorous sketch ever produced in America.

Words to the Wise

Vernacular is the ordinary language of people in a particular region. Twain, as with many other writers, used vernacular to create realistic characters and an informal tone. So can you!

Words to the Wise

A **tall tale** is a wildly exaggerated folktale. Tall tales often contain outrageous events and unbelievable occurrences.

"The Celebrated Jumping Frog of Calaveras County" is a *tall tale*, a folktale that exaggerates the main events or the characters' abilities. Originally an oral tradition that included such American folk heroes as Paul Bunyan and his blue ox Babe, John Henry, and Mike Fink (the Mississippi riverman), the tall tale eventually found its way into the American literary tradition around the middle of the nineteenth century. The tales likely started as entertainment during the long and lonely nights on the frontier. Through exaggeration and outright lies, each speaker would try to top the last one with outrageously farfetched yarns. "The Celebrated Jumping Frog of Calaveras County" is based on a tall tale Twain heard in a mining camp. That just goes to show that inspiration comes from all around!

Before you begin your analysis, remember these definitions that you learned in Chapter 7:

◆ *Exposition:* The introduction, in which the writer gives background information about the characters, setting, and basic situation.

◆ *Rising Action:* The main part of the story in which the main character struggles to overcome obstacles to achieve a goal.

◆ *Climax:* The high point of interest or suspense in the story.

◆ *Resolution:* The point in the story in which the central conflict is ended. In many stories, the climax and the resolution are the same because the climax resolves the action.

As we have discussed, short stories have a small cast of characters. "The Celebrated Jumping Frog of Calaveras County" has only four characters—three people and an amphibian:

◆ The Narrator: name withheld to protect the innocent

◆ Simon Wheeler: as windy as Chicago; a blow-hard blatherer

◆ Jim Smiley: a gambler who will gamble on *anything*

◆ Dan'l Webster: a frog

The Exposition

The unnamed narrator, a stranger in town, calls on Simon Wheeler to ask about Leonidas W. Smiley, a friend of a friend. The narrator soon learns that he's been set up: Leonidas W. Smiley doesn't exist. Wheeler then backs the narrator into a corner and launches into a tale of a man named Jim Smiley, whose love of gambling is rivaled only by Imelda Marcos's love of shoes. The story of Jim Smiley starts this way:

> There was a feller here once by the name of Jim Smiley, in the winter of '49—or may be it was the spring of '50—I don't recollect exactly, somehow, though what makes me think it was one or the other is because I remember the big flume wasn't finished when he first came to the camp; but any way, he was the curios-est man about always betting on any thing that turned up you ever see, if he could get any body to bet on the other side; and if he couldn't, he'd change sides. Any way that suited the other man would suit him—any way just so's he got a bet, he was satisfied. But still he was lucky, uncommon lucky; he most always come out winner. He was always ready and laying for a chance; there couldn't be no solitry thing mentioned but that feller'd offer to bet on it, and

take any side you please, as I was just telling you. If there was a horse-race, you'd find him flush, or you'd find him busted at the end of it; if there was a dog-fight, he'd bet on it; if there was a cat-fight, he'd bet on it; if there was a chicken-fight, he'd bet on it; why, if there was two birds setting on a fence, he would bet you which one would fly first; or if there was a camp-meeting, he would be there reg'lar, to bet on Parson Walker, which he judged to be the best exhorter about here, and so he was, too, and a good man. If he even seen a straddle-bug start to go anywheres, he would bet you how long it would take him to get wherever he was going to, and if you took him up, he would foller that straddle-bug to Mexico but what he would find out where he was bound for and how long he was on the road. Lots of the boys here has seen that Smiley, and can tell you about him. Why, it never made no difference to him—he would bet on any thing—the dangdest feller. Parson Walker's wife laid very sick once, for a good while, and it seemed as if they warn't going to save her; but one morning he come in, and Smiley asked how she was, and he said she was considerable better—thank the Lord for his inf'nit mercy—and coming on so smart that, with the blessing of Prov'dence, she'd get well yet; and Smiley, before he thought, says, "Well, I'll risk two-and-a-half that she don't, any way."

Notice how Twain stretches the reader's credulity as the bets get more and more exaggerated.

Smiley is especially proud of his "fifteen-minutes nag" who always makes it to the finish line first, despite her asthmatic wheezing. Smiley delights in conning the spectators into giving the nag a huge head start, even though the glue-factory reject always makes it in first.

The Rising Action

In the same way, Smiley's ornery bull pup, named Andrew Jackson after the tenacious president, always manages to win dog fights. The little dog waits until all the bets are on the table. Then it grabs onto an opponent's hind leg …

jest by the j'int of his hind leg and freeze to it—not chew, you understand, but only jest grip and hang on till they throwed up the sponge, if it was a year. Smiley always come out winner on that pup, till he harnessed a dog once that didn't have no hind legs, because they'd been sawed off by a circular saw, and when the thing had gone along far enough, and the money was all up, and he come to make a snatch for his pet holt, he saw in a minute how he'd been imposed on, and how the other dog had him in the door, so to speak, and he 'peared surprised, and then he looked sorter discouraged-like, and didn't try no more to win the fight, and so he got shucked out bad. He give Smiley a look, as much as to say his heart was broke, and it was his fault, for putting up a dog that hadn't no hind legs for him to take holt of, which was his main dependence in a fight, and then he limped off a piece and laid down and died. It was a good pup, was that Andrew Jackson, and would have made a name for hisself if he'd lived, for the stuff was in him, and he had genius ....

The Climax

Soon after, Smiley "ketched a frog one day, and took him home, and said he cal'klated to edercate him; and so he never done nothing for three months but set in his back yard and learn that frog to jump." Dan'l Webster, the talented frog named after the silver-tongued orator and diplomat, learns his lessons well and captures the admiration of the local gamblers. One day the proverbial stranger strolls into town and Smiley sets him up for the sting—or so he thinks. Here's how it goes down:

> Well, Smiley kept the beast in a little lattice box, and he used to fetch him down town sometimes and lay for a bet. One day a feller—a stranger in the camp, he was—come across him with his box, and says: "What might it be that you've got in the box?"
>
> And Smiley says, sorter indifferent like, "It might be a parrot, or it might be a canary, may be, but it ain't—it's only just a frog."
>
> And the feller took it, and looked at it careful, and turned it round this way and that, and says, "H'm—so 'tis. Well, what's he good for?"
>
> "Well," Smiley says, easy and careless, "He's good enough for one thing, I should judge—he can outjump any frog in Calaveras county."
>
> The feller took the box again, and took another long, particular look, and give it back to Smiley, and says, very deliberate, "Well, I don't see no p'ints about that frog that's any better'n any other frog."
>
> "May be you don't," Smiley says. "May be you understand frogs, and may be you don't understand em; may be you've had experience, and may be you ain't only a amateur, as it were. Anyways, I've got my opinion, and I'll risk forty dollars that he can outjump any frog in Calaveras county."
>
> And the feller studied a minute, and then says, kinder sad like, "Well, I'm only a stranger here, and I ain't got no frog; but if I had a frog, I'd bet you."

Smiley, no rocket scientist, leaves Dan'l with the stranger while he goes off to the swamp to fetch another amphibious opponent. The stranger thinks to himself for a moment and then "took a teaspoon and filled him full of quail shot pretty near up to his chin and set him on the floor." Smiley returns with a choice frog and the race begins.

> The new frog hopped off, but Dan'l give a heave, and hysted up his shoulders—so—like a Frenchman, but it wan't no use—he couldn't budge; he was planted as solid as an anvil, and he couldn't no more stir than if he was anchored out. Smiley was a good deal surprised, and he was disgusted too, but he didn't have no idea what the matter was, of course.

> The feller took the money and started away; and when he was going out at the door, he sorter jerked his thumb over his shoulders—this way—at Dan'l, and says again, very deliberate, "Well, I don't see no p'ints about that frog that's any better'n any other frog."

> Smiley he stood scratching his head and looking down at Dan'l a long time, and at last he says, "I do wonder what in the nation that frog throw'd off for—I wonder if there ain't something the matter with him—he 'pears to look mighty baggy, somehow." And he ketched Dan'l by the nap of the neck, and lifted him up and says, "Why, blame my cats, if he don't weigh five pound!" and turned him upside down, and he belched out a double handful of shot. And then he see how it was, and he was the maddest man—he set the frog down and took out after that feller, but he never ketched him. And …

The Resolution

Simon Wheeler gets interrupted and the narrator attempts a hasty retreat. But Simon buttonholes the man with a new tale of a "yaller one-eyed cow that didn't have no tail, only jest a short stump like a bannanner, and …"—but the stranger makes good his escape.

All the Write Stuff

Twain created humor by relating wildly exaggerated stories in a deadpan tone, which underscores the humor because it implies that the narrator is unaware of the story's absurdity.

In Literature as in Life

"Write about what you know" is classic advice for beginning fiction writers—and with good reason. The richest source for ideas is your own life. Unfortunately, it's also the most sensitive.

Most writers want to write about their own lives. Brutal childhoods, not-so-brutal childhoods, painful teen years, prom queen thrills, lost loves, found loves—they all make good pickings for the creative writer. But no one wants to read a short story in which the thinly disguised narrator moans about how his thinly disguised parents made him walk 10 miles to school, uphill both ways, in the snow, barefoot, and so on *ad nauseum.*

By far the most common experience is a writer who tries to entertain and move readers without taking any personal risks. Some experts will advise you to spill your guts as freely as you spill ink. I don't agree with either of these viewpoints.

Only you can judge your level of comfort. There's a not-so-fine line between truth and dare. I question the motives of writers who claim to "tell the truth" about their lives. It often seems to me that they are doing little more than getting revenge. My advice: Mine your own life freely for your fiction, but mind your motives, too.

So you're stuck in a cab and the driver offers you a plot idea. "I'd rather chew glass than take his idea," you mutter deep into your collar. Later that week, your hairdresser offers you another intriguing plot idea. Because she's holding a sharp pair of scissors, you are exceedingly polite. Nonetheless, you're thinking, "Don't give up your day job, kiddo."

Conventional wisdom sneers at narrative ideas drawn from ordinary people. Don't sneer so fast. I believe that you should listen to everyone. Many of the best plots come from suggestions and everyday events.

For example, famous novelist Joseph Conrad (1857–1924) drew many of the plots of his stories and novels from his own experience. His novel *Lord Jim* is based on the story of the pilgrim ship *Jeddah,* which set out from Singapore in 1880 with 950 passengers bound for the holy lands. Conrad heard the story (probably from a rickshaw driver) when he disembarked in Singapore in 1883, although he didn't write the novel for another 15 years.

Theodore Dreiser's classic *An American Tragedy* is based on the true story of Chester Gillette, who murdered his pregnant girlfriend when she stood in the way of his ascension into high society. Dreiser read the story in the newspaper. Truman Capote got the idea for his "nonfiction novel" *In Cold Blood* from another real-life murder case.

Plan Your Own Story

Your plan can be long or short, simple or complex. It can be anything *you* want, as long as it helps you figure out the plot—where you're going with a particular story.

Many writers find it helpful to use a checklist as they create their plots. The checklist lays everything out in a linear fashion, making it easier to follow. Try the following checklist as you plot your stories:

❏ What story am I telling? What plot format will help me tell my story with clarity and suspense?

❏ Do I want to arrange the event in chronological (time) order, one after the other?

❏ Do I want to use a *flashback* to recount an earlier episode? Flashbacks help fill in missing information, explain the characters' actions, and advance the plot.

❏ Do I want to use a *flashforward* to recount an event that has not yet taken place?

❏ Do I want to open my story *in medias res*—the middle of the action—and later show how the plot arrived at that point?

❏ Do I want to have the events take place externally, or do I want to have some take place in the characters' minds?

Words to the Wise

A **flashback** is a scene that breaks into the story to show an earlier part of the action. A **flashforward** is a scene that breaks into the story to show a later part of the action. **In media res** is beginning a story in the middle of the action.

Asked and Answered

Asking and answering questions is another good technique for plotting a story. Try it now. Answer each of the following questions to narrow down your story and build its structure:

Who? Characters

_____

What? Conflict

_____

When? Time

_____

Where? Place

_____

Why? Characters' motivation

_____

How? Resolve conflict

_____

Write Angles
If you submit a short story, novel, or script to an agent or editor, you'll most likely be asked to provide the *premise:* the basis of your story. In your premise, you'll trace how specific actions lead to specific results. Think of the premise as the "teaser" to get the readers' attention and make them want to read the entire narrative.

Story Triangle

The *story triangle* is a very creative way to generate plot ideas. It's quick and easy, too, so why not try it now? Follow these directions:

1. Name of main character

2. Two words describing the main character

3. Three words describing the setting

4. Four words describing the main problem

5. Five words describing first problem

6. Six words describing second problem

7. Seven words describing third problem

8. Eight words describing the solution

Now complete the worksheet on the next page to get your story humming.

Plot Diagrams

According to writer Peter De Vries, "Every narrative should have a beginning, a muddle, and an end." How can you avoid having a "muddle" in the middle of your story? I recommend that you start by plotting the basic idea of your story with a simple diagram. These diagrams can help you establish causation—having each event build to the one that follows.

Following are two diagrams that work well. Select the one that best suits your audience, purpose, and tone.

The first diagram gives you a simple way to plot your short story. You may wish to use this diagram when you're brainstorming the basics of your plot. Jot down ideas in each of the second diagram (boxes) to arrange the events in the order you choose.

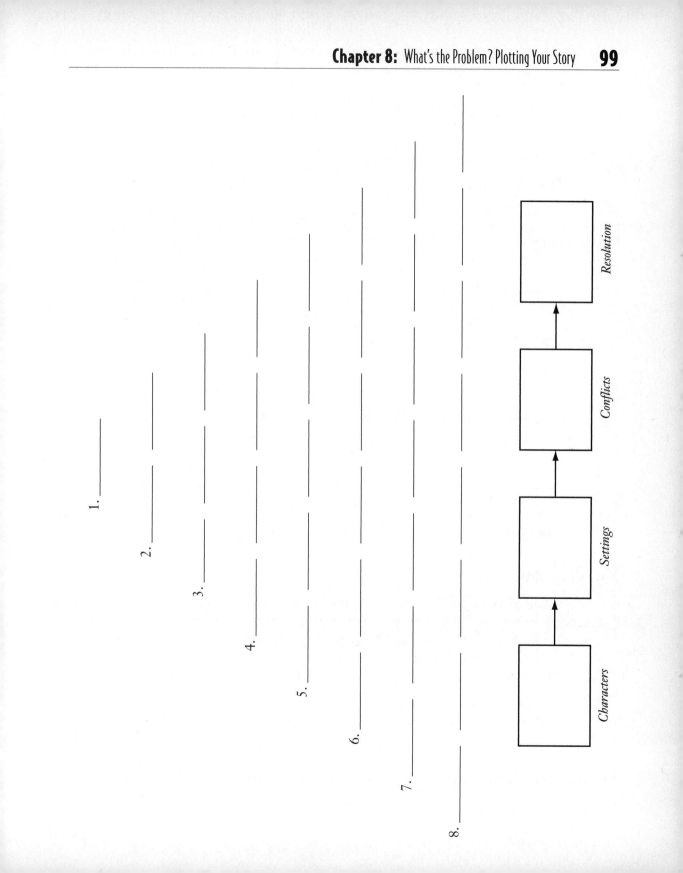

1. _____

2. _____

3. _____

4. _____

5. _____

6. _____

7. _____

8. _____

| Characters | → | Settings | → | Conflicts | → | Resolution |

Let's take it one step further.

Complete the following worksheet to arrange the framework of your story.

Main Characters: _____

_____

_____

Minor Characters: _____

_____

_____

Settings: _____

_____

_____

Conflict: _____

_____

Events: _____

_____

_____

_____

Resolution: _____

_____

Draft Your Story

Now, how do you actually sit down and start to turn all your ideas into a unified whole? There's no one right way to write a short story. The important thing is to find the method that works with your personality. Here are some methods you may wish to try:

Drafting Method 1: Use your charts, webs, other visuals, and notes as a framework for your first draft. Adhere very closely to these notes. Start at the beginning and work through everything. Try to write at a steady pace until you reach a natural breaking point, such as the end of a page or incident.

Drafting Method 2: Read through all your planning material and then set it aside. Try to write your story in one sitting to maintain a single impression or effect, but feel free to jump around the manuscript as different ideas occur.

Drafting Method 3: Write without notes and visuals. Instead, just start freewriting by letting your ideas flow without brakes. Then look for links among ideas and explore these ideas.

Remember, you're not under any obligation to use all or even part of your first draft. This realization can free you to explore new directions as you write.

"Call Me Ishmael": First Lines

First impressions count. Great first lines have entered our consciousness like first kisses. So now you're thinking, "If I can't write the perfect beginning, how am I going to make it through the entire story?"

If you're stuck for an opener, skip it. You heard me, just skip it. Draw some lines in your manuscript and move on. By the time you're halfway through your story, you'll have come up with a great opening.

Plot a Tall Tale

Did you hear the one about the fish that got away? That fish was the size of a 747. What about the man who ate 30 hot dogs at one sitting? (Or was that 300 hot dogs?)

Plot your own tall tale. Start with a real incident or a make-believe one and then exaggerate specific elements to create interest, suspense, or humor. Use any of the methods you learned in this chapter or any that work for you. Plan your plot on a separate piece of paper. Then describe your plot on the following lines.

The Least You Need to Know

◆ *Plot* is the structure of your story, the way the events unfold.

◆ Traditional plots have an *exposition* (introduction), *rising action* (unfolding action), *climax* (high point), and *resolution* (end of conflict).

◆ The plot structure must reinforce the content and its meaning.

◆ Study models of fine stories to learn how to plot your own stories.

◆ Plot a story by jotting down ideas, using a checklist, asking and answering questions, and/or making a diagram.

Chapter 9

Friction in Fiction: Creating Conflict

In This Chapter

◆ Understand conflict in narration

◆ Examine the two types of conflict: internal and external

◆ Analyze conflict in a short story

◆ Create some fictional conflict of your own

Two kids were trying to figure out what game to play. One said, "Let's play doctor."

"Good idea," said the other. "You operate, and I'll sue."

Monkey see, monkey do! In real life, conflict is strife between opposing forces. Sometimes the disagreement is resolved with words, as this funny little anecdote about the two kids shows. Other times, however, the discord involves fists or even firearms.

As we briefly discussed in Chapter 7, *conflict* has the same meaning in fiction as it does in life—opposition between two forces. Conflict is one of the primary elements in narration because most plots develop from conflict.

As a result, you have to understand conflict to construct a compelling short story or other narrative.

In this chapter, you'll explore conflict in detail. First, we'll do an in-depth exploration of conflict in narration. This includes an analysis of the two types of conflict: internal and external. Then you'll identify the conflict in some famous fiction and a full-length professional short story. By the end of the chapter, you'll be ready to create a story conflict of your own—and I'll give you a clever way to spark your creativity!

People Who Need People or Things = Conflict

Conflict makes a narrative interesting because readers want to discover the outcome of the struggle. The process looks like this:

> Conflict → sets up action → leads to suspense

Both action and suspense are necessary to make a successful narrative. If nothing happens in a story, readers yawn. Conflict keeps 'em awake and eagerly turning the pages.

Words to the Wise

Conflict in narrative writing is a struggle or fight between opposing forces.

Conflict does not necessarily mean violence. In your stories, your main character will have a specific need, goal, or purpose that he or she wants to attain, but something is standing in the way. The main character struggles to overcome the opposition. He or she may win or lose. It's the struggle that engages your readers.

Frequently, the conflict is resolved by the end of the work, although in many "slice-of-life" modern short stories, the conflict is left unresolved.

Contemporary short story writer Garrison Keillor focuses on deceptively simple, everyday conflicts in a small town in Minnesota. A typical conflict in a Keillor story is whether the men of the family will watch football on TV at Thanksgiving or not, for example. Shockmeister Edgar Allan Poe, in contrast, wrote about a crisis of conscience over a murder in "The Telltale Heart." Lots of juicy internal conflict there. His other horror stories are equally gruesome.

Conflicts to Consider

Following are some broad categories of conflict you can adapt for your short stories. As you write, you will narrow each of these conflicts to target your audience, purpose, and tone.

- Cultural misunderstandings, as children of immigrants struggle to keep or reject the values of their parents' culture, for instance

- Disagreements over food

- Generational rifts, as parents and children clash

- Problems with health issues

- Problems with physical safety

- Strife over shelter

- Issues with approval and esteem

- Misunderstandings in a friendship

- Fights between lovers

- Battles between people and nature, such as a protagonist being caught in a storm, earthquake, and so on

- Antagonism sparked by philosophical or spiritual crises of conscience

There are two basic types of conflict. In an *external conflict*, characters struggle against a force outside themselves. In an *internal conflict*, characters battle a force within themselves. Narratives often contain both external and internal conflicts as characters struggle with outside forces or people and with their own desires. Let's examine these conflicts more closely.

External Conflicts

The primary external conflicts are just what you'd expect:

- Person versus person (or many people)

- Person versus nature

For example, in the novel *Carrie* by Stephen King, the conflict is between Carrie and her fellow teenagers. The resulting bloodbath is so exciting that you can't put the book down. In the short story "To Build a Fire" by Jack London, the main character fights the extreme cold of the Yukon to stay alive. Who wins: man or nature? Read on to find out!

Jack London (1876–1916) saw conflict in stark terms:

> Mercy did not exist in the primordial life. It was misunderstood for fear, and such misunderstanding made for death. Kill or be killed, eat or be eaten, was the law.

> —*Call of the Wild*

"To Build a Fire," first published in 1902, starts out this way: Ignoring the advice of a more experienced man, a rookie prospector in the Yukon attempts a long journey on foot during an intense cold spell with only his dog as his companion. The prospector is not the sharpest knife in the drawer, unfortunately.

When the rookie gets wet, he stops to build a fire to restore his circulation. He succeeds at first, but snow falls from a tree onto the fire and extinguishes it. He tries to get a new fire going, but he is too numb and clumsy. Panicked, the man starts running toward the camp where his partners are waiting for him, but he doesn't have the strength to go far. He eventually collapses in the snow, falls asleep, and dies. The dog remains until the man is dead, then, seeking warmth, heads toward the camp.

Final score: Nature 1, Man 0.

Internal Conflicts

There's only one internal conflict: Person versus himself or herself. In an internal conflict, the character struggles to resolve a serious issue. It may be a moral choice, a physical choice, a social choice. Whatever the decision, it involves some major heavy lifting in the character's soul.

For instance, in the short story "The White Heron" by Sarah Orne Jewett, the protagonist Sylvia struggles between her eagerness to please a young stranger and her desire to protect a white heron. In "The Interlopers" by Saki, the main characters Ulrich and Georg experience an internal conflict as they decide whether to become friends. In *The Adventures of Huckleberry Finn*, Huck battles with his conscience over whether or not to turn Jim into the slave hunters.

Kate Chopin (1851–1904) published the scandalous novel *The Awakening* in 1899. A stunning study of a young woman whose deep personal discontents lead to adultery and suicide, the story concerns Edna Pontellier's doomed attempt to find her own identity through passion. Edna is a young married woman with attractive children and an indulgent and successful husband, but she's not into the mothering gig. During a summer vacation, Edna "begins to realize her position in the universe as a human being, and to recognize her relations as an individual to the world within and about her."

Edna gives up her family, money, respectability, and eventually her life in search of self-realization. The internal conflict is too great and Edna takes her own life by drowning herself. The novel ends with Edna's suicide:

> The foamy wavelets curled up to her white feet, and coiled like serpents about her ankles. She walked out. The water was chill, but she walked on. The water was deep, but she lifted her white body and reached out with a long, sweeping stroke. The touch of the sea is sensuous, enfolding the body in its soft, close embrace ....

> She thought of Léonce [her husband] and the children. They were a part of her life. But they need not have thought that they could possess her, body and soul. How Mademoiselle Reisz would have laughed, perhaps sneered, if she knew! "And you call yourself an artist! What pretensions, Madame! The artist must possess the courageous soul that dares and defies."

> **Write Angles**
>
> Folktales and fairy tales often use conflicts about unfulfilled wishes. Think of Cinderella and her Prince. Think of Pinocchio longing to be a real boy.

Identify the Conflict

The following short story by Floyd Dell contains both internal and external conflict. As you read the story, look for each type of conflict.

The Blanket

Petey hadn't really believed that Dad would be doing it—sending Granddad away. "Away" was what they were calling it. Not until now could he believe it of Dad.

But here was the blanket that Dad had that day bought for him, and in the morning he'd be going away. And this was the last evening they'd be having together. Dad was off seeing that girl he was to marry. He'd not be back till late, and they could sit up and talk.

It was a fine September night, with a silver moon riding high over the gully. When they'd washed up the supper dishes they went out on the shanty porch, the old man and the bit of a boy, taking their chairs. "I'll get me fiddle," said the old man, "and play ye some of the old tunes." But instead of the fiddle he brought out the blanket. It was a big, double blanket, red, with black cross stripes.

"Now, isn't that a fine blanket!" said the old man, smoothing it over his knees. "And isn't your father a kind man to be giving the old fellow a blanket like that to go away with? It cost something, it did—look at the wool of it! And warm it will be these cold winter nights to come. There'll be few blankets there the equal to this one!"

It was like Granddad to be saying that. He was trying to make it easier. He'd pretended all along it was he that was wanting to go away to the great brick building—the government place, where he'd be with so many other old fellows having the best of everything. But Petey hadn't believed Dad would really do it, until this night when he brought home the blanket.

"Oh, yes it's a fine blanket," said Petey, and got up and went into the shanty. He wasn't the kind to cry, and, besides, he was too old for that, being eleven. He'd just come in to fetch Granddad's fiddle.

The blanket slid to the floor as the old man took the fiddle and stood up. It was the last night they'd be having together. There wasn't any need to say, "Play all the old tunes." Granddad tuned up for a minute, and then said, "This one you'll like to remember."

The silver moon was high overhead, and there was a gentle breeze playing down the gully. He'd never be hearing Granddad play like this again. It was as well Dad was moving into that new house, away from here. He'd not want, Petey wouldn't, to sit here on the old porch of fine evenings, with Granddad gone.

The tune changed. "Here's something gayer." Petey sat and stared out over the gully. Dad would marry that girl. Yes, that girl who'd kissed him and slobbered over him, saying she'd try to be a good mother to him, and all. His chair creaked as he involuntarily gave his body a painful twist.

The tune stopped suddenly, and Granddad said: "It's a poor tune, except to be dancing to." And then: "It's a fine girl your father's going to marry. He'll be feeling young again, with a pretty wife like that. And what would an old fellow like me be doing around their house, getting in the way, an old nuisance, what with my talk of aches and pains! And then there'll be babies coming, and I'd not want to be there to hear them crying at all hours. It's best that I take myself off, like I'm doing. One more tune or two, and then we'll be going to bed to get some sleep against the morning, when I'll pack up my fine blanket and take my leave. Listen to this, will you? It's a bit sad, but a fine tune for a night like this."

They didn't hear the two people coming down the gully path, Dad and the pretty girl with the hard, bright face like a china doll's. But they heard her laugh, right by the porch, and the tune stopped on a wrong, high, startled note. Dad didn't say anything, but the girl came forward and spoke to Granddad prettily: "I'll not be seeing you leave in the morning, so I came over to say good-by."

"It's kind of you," said Granddad, with his eyes cast down; and then, seeing the blanket at his feet, he stopped to pick it up. "And will you look at this," he said in embarrassment, "the fine blanket my son has given me to go away with!"

"Yes," she said, "it's a fine blanket." She felt of the wool, and repeated in surprise, "A fine blanket—I'll say it is!" She turned to Dad, and said to him coldly, "It cost something, that."

He cleared his throat, and said defensively, "I wanted him to have the best."

The girl stood there, still intent on the blanket. "It's double, too," she said reproachfully to Dad.

"Yes," said Granddad, "it's double—a fine blanket for an old fellow to be going away with."

The boy went abruptly into the shanty. He was looking for something. He could hear that girl reproaching Dad, and Dad becoming angry in his slow way. And now she was suddenly going away in a huff. As Petey came out, she turned and called back, "All the same, he doesn't need a double blanket!" And she ran up the gully path.

"Oh, she's right," said the boy coldly. "Here, Dad"—and he held out a pair of scissors. "Cut the blanket in two." Both of them stared at the boy, startled. "Cut it in two, I tell you, Dad!" he cried out. "And keep the other half!"

"That's not a bad idea," said Granddad gently. "I don't need so much of a blanket."

"Yes," said the boy harshly, "a single blanket's enough for an old man when he's sent away. We'll save the other half, Dad; it will come in handy later. I'll give it to you, Dad—when you're old and I'm sending you—away."

There was a silence, and then Dad went over to Granddad and stood before him, not speaking. But Granddad understood, for he put out a hand and laid it on Dad's shoulder. Petey was watching them. And he heard Granddad whisper, "It's all right, son—I knew you didn't mean it." And then Petey cried.

But it didn't matter—because they were all three crying together.

Fill out the following worksheet with the conflicts you see in this story.

External conflicts:

_____

_____

_____

_____

_____

_____

Internal conflicts:

_____

_____

_____

_____

_____

One of the best parts of reading narrative is finding your own meaning. You can then adapt these insights to your own creative writing to express your individuality. Here's how I look at the story. Your interpretation might differ.

External conflicts:

1. Petey versus his father over his father's decision to send Granddad to the old age home.

2. The girl versus Dad over his decision to buy an expensive blanket for his father.

3. Petey versus the girl over her false concern for his welfare.

Internal conflicts:

1. Petey versus himself over his sorrow at his grandfather's departure.

2. Dad versus himself over his guilt for sending his father away.

All the Write Stuff

Dell used the term "china doll" to describe the girl because her "hard, bright face" reveals her true nature—cold and heartless. He also uses the symbol of the scissors to represent severing the bonds of love, duty, respect. The theme (or main idea) can be stated: "There is no real 'generation gap': We will all be old someday" or "Unintentionally, we all do cruel and unpleasant things."

Conflict: The Spice of Stories

Inspiration comes from many places, some of them so obvious that we may overlook them because they're staring us in the face. One key to creative writing is to notice the important in the obvious and transmute it into art.

For the noted short story writer Flannery O'Connor (1925–1964), inspiration once came from a slogan: "The life you save may be your own." This slogan, popular a number of years ago, urged motorists to drive carefully to avoid killing themselves. In O'Connor's story of the same name, the slogan about reckless driving becomes a metaphor for selfishness. The conflict concerns a mother trying to marry off her daughter to a shiftless man.

Create your own story with an external conflict, and internal conflict, or both. Use a slogan as inspiration. Here are some ideas to get you started.

♦ Start by thinking of a slogan with deeper implications than might strike the average person.

♦ Develop a conflict which expresses these inferences.

♦ Work the slogan into the story at some point and use it as the story's title.

♦ As you think and write, remember that often the best way to become more creative is to loosen up and stop worrying about being "perfect."

Here are some slogans to consider:

♦ "Can you hear me now?"™

♦ "We never stop working for you"™

♦ "Reach out and touch someone"™

♦ "Where's the beef?"™

♦ "Blondes have more fun"™

♦ "It takes a strong man to make a tender chicken"™

♦ "All the news that's fit to print"™

♦ "I can't believe I ate the whole thing"™

Begin your short story on the lines below and attach as many separate sheets of paper as you need. At this point, don't get bogged down with concerns about grammar and usage. Instead, focus on hammering out the first draft of your story. Save this story to reread and perhaps revise later.

_____

_____

_____

_____

_____

_____

_____

_____

_____

_____

_____

_____

The Least You Need to Know

♦ In fiction, a *conflict* is a struggle or fight. Conflict makes a short story interesting because readers want to discover the outcome of the struggle.

♦ In an *external conflict*, characters struggle against a force outside themselves.

♦ In an *internal conflict*, characters battle a force within themselves.

♦ Narratives often contain both external and internal conflicts as characters struggle with outside forces or people and with their own desires.

What a Character!

In This Chapter

- ◆ Distinguish between protagonists and antagonists
- ◆ Learn about round characters, flat characters, dynamic characters, and static characters
- ◆ Explore different types of characterization
- ◆ Learn about indirect and direct characterization
- ◆ Develop realistic characters for your stories

Washington Irving describes Icabod Crane, the main character in "The Legend of Sleepy Hollow," as …

> tall, but exceedingly lank, with narrow shoulder, long arms and legs, hands that dangled a mile out of his sleeves, feet that might have served for shovels, and his whole frame most loosely hung together. His head was small, and flat at top, with huge ears, large green glassy eyes, and a long snipe nose, so that it might have been mistaken for a weathercock perched upon a spindle neck, to tell which way the wind blew. To see him striding along the profile of a hill on a windy day, with his clothes bagging and fluttering about him, one might have mistaken him for the genius [image] of famine descending upon the earth, or some scarecrow eloped from a cornfield.

Icabod Crane is unquestionably a fictional creation, but because of Washington Irving's vivid description of his character, the lanky schoolteacher has leaped off to page right into the American imagination. In this chapter, you'll discover the techniques that Washington Irving and other master storytellers use to create unforgettable characters. Then you'll practice some of these techniques to begin creating realistic characters for your own stories.

Protagonists and Antagonists

Who are the people in your story? Why do they act as they do? How can you make them seem like real people? Start with the basics: the good guy and the bad guy.

Most short stories have a main character, also called a *protagonist*. The *protagonist* is the most important character in your story. He, she, or it is at the center of the conflict and the focus of the reader's attention. The protagonist is usually a person, but may be an animal or even a force of nature. The protagonist is often heroic and admirable but does not have to be especially nice, heroic, or larger than life. I've called the protagonist the "good guy" to help you remember that he or she is the focus of the story.

Here are some examples of protagonists:

- Jean Val Jean in *Les Miserables.* The hero of the novel and play, Jean Val Jean steals bread to feed his starving family and is thrown into jail for his "crime."

- The big game hunter Rainsford in "The Most Dangerous Game" is the focus of our attention after he is shipwrecked on a very unusual island where he must fight for his life.

- Henpecked Walter Mitty is the main character in "The Secret Life of Walter Mitty" as he daydreams heroic fantasies to escape from his wife's orders and demands.

Words to the Wise

The **protagonist** is the main character in a work of fiction. An **antagonist** is the force or person in conflict with the main character.

The *antagonist* is the force or person in conflict with the main character. An antagonist can be another character, a force of nature, or society as a whole. The antagonist can even be something within the character blocking him or her from success. Here are some examples:

- Inspector Javert in *Les Miserables.* The villain, he relentlessly hunts Jean Val Jean to throw him back into jail.

◆ Bored with hunting animals, General Zaroff hunts Rainsford in a pursuit to the death.

◆ Walter Mitty's wife is the antagonist in the story as she conflicts with her mousy husband.

Types of Characters

Characters are classified in different ways:

◆ *Round characters* show many different traits, faults as well as virtues. They may be generous, hard-working, and jealous, for example.

◆ *Flat characters* are one-dimensional figures. They lack depth or resonance. Often, they function as types or stereotypes, such as the tightfisted husband, the seductress, or the spoiled child.

◆ *Dynamic characters* develop as people throughout the story. They grow and change as real people do.

◆ *Static characters* do not change. They remain the same at the end of the story as they were in the beginning.

These categories aren't exclusive. For example, a round character can be dynamic. Further, one type of character isn't better than the other. Rather, each has a special function to fulfill in a narrative. For example, the flat characters often serve as foils or background for the dynamic character. In a similar way, a static character often helps to underscore the changes the dynamic character experiences.

Don't be fooled: Major characters don't have to be dynamic. Also, you might create a major character who doesn't even appear in the story. The story might revolve around the reactions of the other characters to this one individual.

Words to the Wise

Round characters show many different traits, while flat characters are one-dimensional. Dynamic characters grow and change, while static characters do not change.

Methods of Characterization

You create unforgettable characters through *characterization*, the different ways that you tell your readers about characters. Here are some elements of characterization:

♦ The character's physical appearance and traits. For instance, is the character emotional, principled, open-minded, caring—or rational, unprincipled, obstinate, and cold?

♦ The character's actions.

♦ The character's background: his or her hometown, childhood, education, past experiences, and so on.

♦ The reaction of the other characters to the character's physical appearance and actions.

♦ The character's speech (his or her dialogue).

♦ The character's thoughts, feelings, and desires. What motivates the character to act and speak in a certain way?

♦ The comments made by other characters about this person.

♦ The thoughts, feelings, and actions of other characters.

♦ The narrator's direct comments about a character's nature and personality.

Words to the Wise

Characterization is the process of creating and developing a character.

If your story is to come alive on the page, your characters must seem to be alive. Your reader has to be able to visualize your characters. This doesn't mean that your characters have to be based on real people; neither does it mean that we have to like your characters. But if your readers aren't interested in your characters, they won't want to read your story.

The following chart provides some examples. Use them as models as you frame your own characters.

Method of Characterization	Examples
Description of the character's appearance	"He was a man of perhaps thirty, very tall and thin, and his face, too, was thin, with a big hawklike nose and a strong jutting chin." —*Banner in the Sky* by James Ramsey Ullman
The character's own thoughts, and feelings	"When my turn came, I was very dialogue, confident." —*The Joy Luck Club* by Amy Tan
The dialogue, thoughts, and feelings of other	"He put a red-hot boiled potato down my back," explained Bill, "and then mashed it with his characters foot." —"The Ransom of Red Chief" by O. Henry

Method of Characterization	Examples
The narrator's direct comments about a character	"Alfonso sat on the porch trying to push his crooked teeth to where he thought they belonged. He hated the way he looked." —"Broken Chain" by Gary Soto

Sometimes you tell about characters directly. This is called *direct characterization.* Other times, you might decide to let readers reach their own decisions by showing the comments, thoughts, and actions of the other characters. This is called *indirect characterization.*

Direct Characterization

In direct characterization, you state a character's traits outright. Here are some examples of direct characterization.

> "Rainsford's first impression was that the man [General Zaroff] was singularly handsome: his second was that there was an original, almost bizarre quality about the general's face. He was a tall man past middle age, for his hair was a vivid white; but his thick eyebrows and pointed military mustache were as black as the night from which Rainsford had come. His eyes, too, were black and very bright. He had high cheekbones, a sharp-cut nose, a spare, dark face, the face of a man used to giving orders."

> —"The Most Dangerous Game" by Richard Connell

This description directly tells readers what General Zaroff looks like.

> "My mother believed you could be anything you wanted to be in America."

> —*Joy Luck Club* by Amy Tan

This comment tells us that the narrator's mother is convinced that America is the land of limitless opportunity.

> "I was so scared that my stomach heaved, empty as it was."

> —"The Day the Sun Came Out" by Dorothy M. Johnson

This dialogue directly tells readers how the character felt—terrified!

 **All the Write Stuff**

Remember, if you are writing a traditional story, your task is to place believable characters in a vividly imagined setting and then set the characters in motion.

Indirect Characterization

With indirect characterization, you let readers infer a character's traits from his or her appearance, actions, or speech. You also provide the reactions of other characters to help readers draw conclusions about a character. Here are some examples of indirect characterization:

> He knew that when he kissed this girl, and forever wed his unutterable visions to her perishable breath, his mind would never romp again like the mind of God. So he waited, listening for a moment longer to the tuning-fork that had been struck upon a star. Then he kissed her. At his lips' touch she blossomed for him like a flower and the incarnation was complete.
>
> —*The Great Gatsby* by F. Scott Fitzgerald

From this description, we can infer that Jay Gatsby is an idealistic dreamer who has made this girl—Daisy Buchanan—the idealization of his dreams.

> "If you won't take me, I'll travel with any wagon who will."
>
> —"The Day the Sun Came Out" by Dorothy M. Johnson

This comment suggests that the speaker is brave and determined.

> "I didn't want to harm the man. I thought he was a very nice gentleman. Soft-spoken. I thought so right up to the moment I cut his throat."
>
> —*In Cold Blood* by Truman Capote

From this snatch of dialogue, we can draw the conclusion that the speaker is a cold-blooded killer, inhuman in his viciousness.

Words to the Wise

In **direct characterization,** you tell readers what characters are like. In **indirect characterization,** you reveal characters through their appearance, speech, or actions.

As the storyteller, you have the option of describing your characters outright, obliquely, or both. No one method is "better" than the other. Choose the method or combination of methods that best helps you appeal to your readers.

The more you know about your characters, the easier it will be for you to make your readers feel like they know them as well. Following are two ways that you can create realistic, believable characters that will hook your readers so you can reel 'em in.

Getting to Know You

One of the best and easiest ways to flesh out your characters is by creating a "character trait web." Photocopy the following graphic organizer so you have one for each character. Feel free to modify the number of traits as necessary to fit the character and the story. Examples can come directly from details you will include in the story or be based on inferences that readers will make.

Start by writing the character's name in the middle of the web. Then add details and examples.

Stuck for character traits? Here are some to get you started:

- ◆ Ambitious
- ◆ Brave
- ◆ Cruel
- ◆ Lazy
- ◆ Generous
- ◆ Dishonest
- ◆ Patriotic
- ◆ Cowardly

- ◆ Selfish
- ◆ Gloomy
- ◆ Loving
- ◆ Honest
- ◆ Humble
- ◆ Bold
- ◆ Shy
- ◆ Loyal

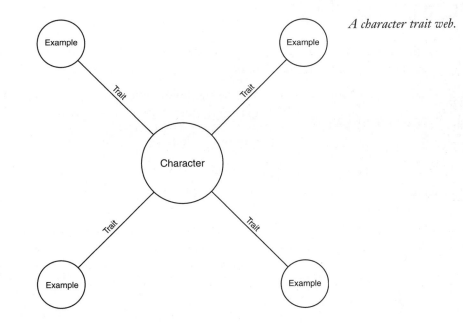

A character trait web.

What's in a Name?

What's in a name? A lot. Look what happened to Romeo and Juliet because of *their* names. The significance of names is deeply embedded in our consciousness. Some Native Americans believe that knowing a person's name gives you power over them; some Christians take a new name when they are confirmed. As a writer of fiction, you should pick your characters' names carefully because readers relate to characters according to their names.

Find names that convey a sense of each character's personality. Think how the names sound, their connotations. For example, "Daisy" suggests flowerlike vulnerability, while "Butch" conveys a hulk. "Dexter" is a geek, "Amber" is a beauty queen, "Martha" is virtuous but dull. Margaret Mitchell originally planned to call the protagonist of *Gone with the Wind* "Pansy," but wisely decided that "Scarlett" (as in scarlet woman) certainly described her strong-willed heroine much better.

In general, avoid using the names of real people. There are too many lawyers in the world who don't have enough work and would love to sue your butt off. If you get your characters' names from a telephone book, use the first name of one person and the last name of another.

Name only your main characters. Identify the one-shot gas station attendant as "gas station attendant" and the walk-through store clerk as "store clerk." Most of us have filled up our brains already, so why clutter them with unnecessary details?

Just the Facts, Ma'am

Another effective way to create realistic and believable characters is by constructing a character chart. Here, you profile your characters by inventing their history. The following worksheet is a handy way to build their lives. Photocopy this worksheet and use one for your protagonist and one for your antagonist.

Character Worksheet

Name:_____

Physical description:

Age: _____

Height and weight: _____

Eyes: _____

Hair: _____

Special abilities: _____

Personal data:

Education: _____

Occupation: _____

Social class: _____

Religion: _____

Ethnicity: _____

Hobbies: _____

Marital status: _____

Children: _____

Friends: _____

Ambitions: _____

Family:

Place in family: _____

Immediate family members: _____

Pets: _____

Personality:

Main personality traits: _____

Disposition: _____

Self-image: _____

A Capsule Portrait

In a capsule portrait, you write a biography of your main character(s). Actors often use this technique as they prepare to embody a fictional person. In addition to describing the character's appearance, likes and dislikes, and habits, they provide the character's history, the so-called "backstory."

Try it yourself. Invent a character and write a brief bio of him or her. Consider these questions as you write:

1. What are the character's key traits? How are they related to each other? To the character's actions?

2. How do you feel about this character? What makes this character appealing? Unappealing?

3. What are the key incidents in the character's past?

4. What forces in the character's past shaped this character into the person he or she is today?

5. Does the character change or grow? If so, how? If not, why not?

Write your character sketch on the following lines. Try not to exceed this space. Remember: You're providing a brief history!

The Least You Need to Know

◆ The *protagonist* is the main character in a work of fiction. An *antagonist* is the force or person in conflict with the main character. A story needs both a protagonist and an antagonist to have conflict.

◆ *Round characters* show many different traits, while *flat characters* are one-dimensional. *Dynamic characters* grow and change, while *static characters* do not change. One type of character is not better than another.

◆ *Characterization* is the process of creating and developing a character.

◆ In *direct characterization*, you tell readers what characters are like. In *indirect characterization*, you reveal characters through their appearance, speech, or actions. Most stories use a mix of direct and indirect characterization.

I've Looked at Life from Both Sides Now: Point of View

In This Chapter

- ◆ Define point of view

- ◆ Explore different points of view: first person, third-person limited, third-person omniscient, stream of consciousness, and multiple points of view

- ◆ Understand the effect of point of view

- ◆ Experiment with point of view

- ◆ Create compelling and realistic dialogue

As you have learned, *narration* is telling a story. A literary work that tells a story is called a *narrative*. Both fiction and nonfiction can be narratives, as long as there's a story involved. For example, a short story and a novel are fictional narratives; a memoir and an autobiography are nonfiction narratives. (Still with me?)

Every narrative has a speaker or a voice. Not surprisingly, this voice is called the *narrator*. The narrator's perspective is the story's *point of view*.

The point of view determines who will tell the story and what details the story will include. This makes point of view a crucial element in fiction.

In this chapter, you'll learn the different vantage points from which you can tell your story, both fiction and nonfiction. You'll discover the strengths and weaknesses of each point of view and explore how each one can change your narrative. Then I'll show you how to craft authentic dialogue so your characters sound like real people.

What Is Point of View?

Point of view is the position from which a story is told. You have three main choices:

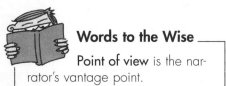

Words to the Wise

Point of view is the narrator's vantage point.

- ◆ The first-person point of view
- ◆ The third-person limited point of view
- ◆ The third-person omniscient point of view

Let's look at each point of view in detail.

First-Person Point of View: Me, Myself, and I

In the *first-person point of view*, the narrator is one of the characters in the narrative and explains the events through his or her own eyes, using the pronouns *I*, *me*, *my*, and *mine*. Unless the narrator is Carnack the Magnificent, he or she doesn't know the other characters' thoughts.

Ben Franklin used the first-person point of view for his *Autobiography* (1771), as the following excerpt shows. Using the first-person vantage point enables Franklin to create a slightly mocking tone to poke fun at the earnest adolescent he had been. The first-person point of view also helps readers experience Franklin's individual voice and personality vividly, crucial for a memoir.

> It was about this time I conceived the bold and arduous project of arriving at moral perfection. I wished to live without committing any fault at any time; I would conquer all that either natural inclination, custom, or company might lead me into.

Edgar Allan Poe also used the first-person point of view for his short story "The Black Cat," as the following excerpt shows. This vantage point enabled him to show that the narrator was barking mad. In the passage below, the narrator kills his wife when she tries to prevent him from killing their cat. (I know it's crazy; I could make this up?)

One day she [the narrator's wife] accompanied me, upon some household errand, into the cellar of the old building which our poverty compelled us to inhabit. The cat followed me down the steep stairs, and, nearly throwing me headlong, exasperated me to madness. Uplifting an ax, and forgetting in my wrath the childish dread which had hitherto stayed my hand, I aimed a blow at the animal, which, of course, would have proved instantly fatal had it descended as I wished. But this blow was arrested by the hand of my wife. Goaded by the interference into a rage more than demoniacal, I withdrew my arm from her grasp and buried the ax in her brain. She fell dead upon the spot without a groan.

Write Angles

Poe did such a convincing job of creating vividly insane first-person speakers that many readers became convinced that he was as nuts as his narrators. Not so: The original hard-luck kid was sane. Orphaned by age three and adopted soon after, he never bonded with his new father. Set adrift, he suffered from a case of terminal poverty. He looked so bad when he personally submitted the manuscript of "The Raven" to *Graham's Magazine* that even though the editors rejected the poem, they took up a collection of $15 to give him.

The following excerpt is the polar opposite: a completely sane narrator telling about the inciting incident in the story. (Don't worry: It's not a murder or even the acquisition of a pet.) This is a narrator we can trust.

I received one morning a letter written in pale ink, on glassy, blue-lined notepaper, and bearing the postmark of a little Nebraska village. (Willa Cather)

Third-Person Limited Point of View: Standing in the Hall

In the *third-person limited point of view*, the narrator tells the story through the eyes of only one character, using the pronouns *he, him, she, her, they,* and *them*. Thus, the narrator knows what one character thinks and feels but only what the others say and do. The third-person limited point of view, in contrast to the first-person point of view, allows the writer to achieve distance and some measure of objectivity.

Henry Adams decided on the third-person limited point of view for his classic memoir, *The Education of Henry Adams* (1918). Notice how much more formal and distant the tone is from Franklin's writing:

As the boy grew up to ten or twelve years old, his father gave him a writing-table in one of the alcoves of his Boston library, and there, winter after winter, Henry worked over his Latin Grammar and listened to these four gentlemen discussing the course of politics.

Anne Beattie also used the third-person limited point of view in her short story "Imagined Scenes." We see the events through the eyes of the female narrator. This point of view enables the author to show how the couple is drifting apart.

When she wakes from a dream, David is already awake. Or perhaps he only wakes when she stirs, whispers to him. He doesn't sound sleepy; he's alert, serious, as though he'd been waiting for a question. She remembers last year, the week before Christmas.

Third-Person Omniscient Point of View: Knowing It All

In the *third-person omniscient point of view*, the narrator looks through the eyes of all the characters and is not a character in the novel. As a result, we say that the narrator is "all-knowing." As you would expect, the narrator uses the pronouns *he, him, she, her, them,* and *they.* This point of view gives the narrator the greatest distance from the events in the story.

Here's an example from Flannery O'Connor's short story "The Life You Save May Be Your Own." As you read, see how the narrator is standing outside the action, looking in. This enables the narrator to explain what each character is doing.

The old woman and her daughter were sitting on their porch when Mr. Shiftlet came up their road for the first time. The old woman slid to the edge of her chair and leaned forward, shading her eyes from the piercing sunset with her hand. The daughter could not see her in front of her and continued to play with her fingers.

Words to the Wise

Stream of consciousness is a narrative technique that attempts to capture the way the mind works by showing the unpredictable, natural movement of a character's thoughts and feelings.

In the following excerpt from the short story "Power" by Jack Cope, the narrator is a voice that tells the story. The narrator observes the events but does not take any part in them.

When his mother came to say goodnight to him he turned his face over into his pillow and would not kiss her. It was something he had never done before and it was because he was angry with them both. His mother patted his back and ruffled his white hair and said, "Goodnight, darling." But he gritted his teeth and did not answer.

Stream of Consciousness

Stream of consciousness is a narrative technique that presents thoughts as if they were coming from a character's mind. Since thought is not linear, the words in stream-of-consciousness narration are not arranged in time order. Instead, the events of the story jump around, mixing with the character's emotions and memories just as they might spontaneously occur in real life. Use stream-of-consciousness narration if you want to reveal a character's complex psychology and present it in realistic, compelling detail.

Katherine Anne Porter used this technique in her short story "The Jilting of Granny Weatherall" to show Granny's thoughts as she is dying. As you read the following passage, find the three different events Granny recalls. Write them on the chart that follows:

> Granny felt easy about her soul. Cornelia, where are your manners? Give Father Connolly a chair. She had her secret comfortable understanding with a few favorite saints who cleared a straight road to God for her. All as surely signed and sealed as the papers for the new Forty Acres. Since the day the wedding cake was not cut, but thrown out and wasted.

Event #1: _____

Event #2: _____

Event #3: _____

Answers

Event #1: Granny realizes that Father Connolly is visiting.

Event #2: Granny recalls buying the land, forty acres.

Event #3: Granny recalls being jilted.

Try some stream-of-consciousness narration yourself. Start by thinking about a single person, place, or thing that you would like to include in a narrative. Freewrite your associations with this inciting incident. Let your mind roam freely, disregarding formal punctuation.

Inciting incident: _____

Stream of consciousness: _____

_____

_____

_____

_____

Multiple Points of View

In multiple viewpoints, the author chooses two or three characters from whom readers learn what is happening. Each character can only know what he or she learns by witnessing something or being told. John Fowles' novel *The Collector,* for example, is written half from the kidnapper's point of view and half from the victim's.

Nobel laureate William Faulkner (1897–1962) was the Big Daddy of multiple points of view. In addition to multiple narrators, Faulkner also experimented with such narrative techniques as …

- ◆ Stream of consciousness.

- ◆ Interior monologues.

- ◆ Discontinuous time.

Faulkner's novel *The Sound and the Fury* tells the same story through four different viewpoints: that of the three Compson brothers—Benjy, Quentin, and Jason—and their black servant Dilsey. Explaining his decision to go with multiple narrators in this novel, Faulkner wrote:

> "I tried first to tell it with one brother, and that wasn't enough. That was Section One. I tried it with another brother, and that wasn't enough. That was Section Two. I tried the third brother, because Caddy [one of the characters] was still to me too beautiful and too moving to reduce her to telling what was going on, that it would be more passionate to see her through somebody else's eyes, I thought. And that failed and I tried myself—the fourth section—to tell what happened, and I still failed."

Here's how it sorts out.

Section 1: April 7, 1928

The first section is told from the point of view of Benjy Compson, a mentally retarded 33-year-old man. Even though Benjy's thoughts are recorded in short sentences with simple words, reading this section is extraordinarily difficult because Benjy has no concept of time or place. The entire section is written in stream of consciousness; here, the thoughts of a retarded man. As a result, random stimuli from the present (a word, a smell, a taste) propel him to the past, instantly and without warning.

Since this is confusing stuff to follow, Faulkner changes the typeface from Roman to italic every time Benjy shifts from the present to the past. Consider using a similar font change if you decide to experiment with stream-of-consciousness narration.

The Sound and the Fury Section 2: June 2, 1910

The second section tells the same story from Quentin Compson's point of view on the day he commits suicide. A student at Harvard University, he is wandering around Boston preparing to take his life. Although his thoughts are obviously more intelligent than Benjy's, they are no less easy to follow, since he is deranged.

The Sound and the Fury Section 3: April 6, 1928

This section is seen through the eyes of the third Compson brother, Jason, and takes place on Good Friday. The voice is very different from the two that came before: Unlike his brothers, Jason is neither retarded nor suicidal. Rather, he's hopping mad. The opening sentence establishes his anger: "Once a bitch always a bitch, what I say."

The Sound and the Fury Section 4: April 8, 1928

Everything comes together in the final section, told from the third-person limited viewpoint, Dilsey. She is a reliable observer, so readers finally get an objective view of events. The novel ends:

> [Benjy's] broken flower drooped over Ben's fist and his eyes were empty and blue and serene again as cornice and facade flowed smoothly once more from left to right, post and tree, window and doorway and signboard each in its ordered place.

In 1945, Faulkner added a fifth viewpoint to the same events: "I should have done this when I wrote the book," he remarked. "Then the whole thing would have fallen into pattern like a jigsaw puzzle when the magician's wand touched it."

Choosing a Point of View

Each point of view has its advantages. Your choice depends on your …

- ◆ Purpose.
- ◆ Audience.
- ◆ Topic.

For example, if you are writing a historical romance story for women, you might use the third-person omniscient point of view to give the story a panoramic feel. On the other hand, if you are writing a memoir for a general readership, you might choose the first-person point of view to make your story personal and immediate. This will help readers identify with your experiences.

When you select a point of view, consider what plot events you want to reveal and which ones you want your readers to infer. Also consider if you want to create a reliable narrator or an unreliable one. Another consideration is whether you want the narrator to give an objective or a subjective account of the story's events. Here's the difference:

♦ An *objective narrator* presents the facts and allows readers to draw their own conclusions.

♦ A *subjective narrator* presents his or her own opinions along with the facts. The reader must be careful to separate the two.

Choose the *first-person point of view* when you want to:

♦ Give your story a sense of immediacy and reality.

♦ Make the story feel very personal.

♦ Look inside one character's mind.

♦ Withhold information to create tension and suspense.

♦ Make it seem like the narrator is talking directly to readers.

♦ Make sure that readers know only as much as the narrator knows.

♦ Create an unreliable narrator to call into question his or her interpretation of events. This technique is especially useful in horror stories, mysteries, and science fiction.

All the Write Stuff

If you do decide to switch point of view midstream, be sure to leave a one-line break or change the typeface for every switch in narrator. This way, your reader will have a guidepost to follow.

Choose the *third-person limited point of view* when you want to:

♦ Provide readers with more information about the characters and events than you can give them through a first-person narrator.

♦ Show the events through the eyes of one character.

♦ Encourage readers to identify with that character.

♦ Keep a distance between the reader and events.

♦ Use a voice rather than an identifiable character to tell the story.

Choose the *third-person omniscient point of view* when you want to:

◆ Give a full view of all events and characters.

◆ Show what everyone thinks and feels.

◆ Use a voice rather than an identifiable character to tell the story.

◆ Keep a distance between the reader and events.

◆ Create a wide-angle view.

Presto! Change-O!

One of the best ways to learn to write creatively is to practice, so here's a chance to make your chops. Below are two passages from literature. Both are written in the first person. Rewrite each one as directed. Then decide which version you prefer and why.

> John Reed was a schoolboy of fourteen years old; four years older than I, for I was but ten; large and stout for his age, with a dingy and unwholesome skin; thick lineaments in a spacious visage, heavy limbs and large extremities. He gorged himself habitually at table, which made him bilious, and gave him dim and bleared eyes and flabby cheeks.

Rewrite from the third-person omniscient point of view:

_____

_____

_____

_____

> I unwound his long scarf and helped him out of his coat. As I got him settled in his desk, Mother arrived with my other brown shoe. I jammed my foot into it with all the children watching.

Rewrite from the third-person limited point of view, from the teacher's viewpoint:

_____

_____

_____

_____

Write Now

Now start from scratch by writing a brief snatch of narrative for each of the following scenarios.

1. Using the first-person point of view, explain how a 55-year old man feels on his wedding day. It is his first marriage.

_____

_____

_____

_____

2. Using the third-person limited point of view, describe the same scene from his mother's vantage point.

_____

_____

_____

_____

3. Using a third-person omniscient point of view, describe the wedding.

_____

_____

_____

_____

 **All the Write Stuff** _____

If your writing stalls, trying switching the point of view. Laura Ingalls Wilder, for example, originally wrote the first novel in her famous _Little House_ series in the first person. It didn't allow her the distance she needed, however, so on the advice of her editor, Wilder retold the story from the third-person omniscient. This change in point of view transformed memories into story.

Using Dialogue and Dialect

Dialogue is the conversation in fiction or drama, the exact words a character says. Quotation marks are used to point out the dialogue. Dialogue should be easy to read.

For this to work, don't run several characters' dialogue all in one paragraph. Begin a new paragraph for each exchange or reply. This also helps eliminate the repetitive "he said" and "she replied."

Dialogue not only draws you immediately into the story, but it's one of the best ways to reveal character. Dialogue helps you show your characters' ...

- ◆ Educational level.

- ◆ Geographic background.

- ◆ Ethnic background.

- ◆ Emotional state.

- ◆ Motives.

You reveal these characteristics by the level of diction, slang, accent, euphemisms, jargon, and punctuation you use. You can also use *dialect*, the way people speak in a certain region or area. In a dialect, certain words are spelled and pronounced differently. Dialects help you describe your characters and setting more fully. Here's an example from Stephen Crane's novella *Maggie, A Girl of the Street.*

> "Smash 'im, Jimmie, kick deh damn guts out of 'im," yelled Pete, the lad with the chronic sneer, in tones of delight.
>
> The small combatants pounded and kicked, scratched and tore. They began to weep and their curses struggled in their throats with sobs. The other little boys clasped their hands and wriggled their legs in excitement. They formed a bobbing circle about the pair. A tiny spectator was suddenly agitated.
>
> "Cheese it, Jimmie, cheese it! Here comes yer fader," he yelled.

The dialect "'im" for *him*, "deh" for *the*, "yer" for *your*, and "fader" for *father* help readers visualize the street urchins. The contrast between their street dialect and the speaker's elevated diction (as in "A tiny spectator was suddenly agitated") establishes an ironic distance between the narrator and the story he tells.

Here's another example from *The Adventures of Huckleberry Finn*. Notice how Twain captures Huck's character through his speech.

> You don't know about me without you have read a book by the name of *The Adventures of Tom Sawyer*; but that ain't no matter. That book was made by Mr. Mark Twain, and he told the truth, mainly. There was things which he stretched, but mainly he told the truth. That is nothing. I never seen anybody but lied one time or another, without it was Aunt Polly, or the widow, or maybe Mary. Aunt

Polly—Tom's Aunt Polly, she is—and Mary, and the Widow Douglas is all told about in that book, which is mostly a true book, with some stretchers, as I said before.

Rewrite Huck's dialect into standard American English. See how the change in language affects your perception of his character.

_____

_____

_____

_____

_____

_____

_____

Craft dialogue that not only reveals character but also advances the plot, as shown in these examples.

The Least You Need to Know

- ◆ Point of view, the narrator's perspective, determines who tells the story and what details the story includes.

- ◆ Stream of consciousness is a narrative technique that narrates events as if they were coming from a character's mind.

- ◆ In multiple viewpoints, the author chooses two or three characters from whom readers learn what is happening.

- ◆ Choose a point of view depending on your audience, purpose, and topic.

- ◆ Create realistic dialogue to reveal character and advance the plot.

Chapter 12

Last Licks: Setting, Theme, and Titles

In This Chapter

- ◆ Understand the importance of setting
- ◆ Create a vivid setting and mood
- ◆ Weave in a theme
- ◆ Choose a title
- ◆ Show—don't tell—through details

Setting is an important element in all your fiction, whether you're writing a short story, a novella, or a novel. In some instances, the setting serves as a supporting player in your narrative, but in other stories, it can assume center stage. In fact, setting can become so important that it functions as a character in the narrative.

In this chapter, you'll discover how to choose a setting that reinforces your plot, conflict, characters, and theme. Then I'll show you how to add the finishing touches to your stories: working in the theme and the title. Let's start by analyzing the effect of setting.

Location, Location, Location: Setting

Would you like to visit the following setting? Why or why not?

> One day that Tom Walker had been to a distant part of the neighborhood, he took what he considered a short cut homeward, through the swamp. Like most short cuts, it was an ill-chosen route. The swamp was thickly grown with great gloomy pines and hemlocks, some of them ninety feet high, which made it dark at noonday and a retreat for all the owls of the neighborhood. It was full of pits and quagmires, partly covered with weeds and mosses, where the green surface often betrayed the traveler into a gulf of black, smothering mud; there were also dark and stagnant pools, the abodes of the tadpole, the bullfrog, and the water-snake, where the trunks of pines and hemlocks lay half-drowned, half-rotting, looking like alligators sleeping in the mire.
>
> —"The Devil and Tom Walker"

From this description, Washington Irving establishes a feeling of foreboding and impending doom. Which phrases warn you that something frightening will happen to Tom Walker in the woods? For me, it's these phrases:

◆ "Gloomy pines and hemlocks"

◆ "Made it dark at noonday"

◆ "Pits and quagmires"

◆ "Gulf of black, smothering mud"

◆ "Dark and stagnant pools"

◆ "Watersnake"

◆ "Half-drowned, half-rotting, looking like alligators sleeping in the mire"

You know that something eerie and weird is going to happen in this isolated place—and you eagerly read on to find out what it is. As you can tell from this example, an effective setting drives the plot just as a dramatic conflict does.

The *setting* of a story is the time and place where the events take place. In addition to such factual details as geographical location, place names, and historical references, setting includes the following elements:

◆ Date of the week, month, year

◆ Time of day

- Season

- Weather conditions

- Sensory details about the place

- Physical buildings, rooms, and objects

- Names of people

- Social environment

- Characters' dress, manners, and customs

Words to the Wise

Setting is the time and place where the events in a narrative take place.

You can use the story's setting to …

- Make a story more realistic.

- Act as a force against which the protagonist struggles, even the source of the central conflict.

- Symbolize ideas that you wish to convey.

- Reinforce other story elements, such as the theme.

- Contrast other story elements, such as the character's emotions.

- Help establish the story's mood (more on this later).

Ways to Create a Story's Setting

Sometimes you will state the setting outright, as in the famous opening of Snoopy's short stories: "It was a dark and stormy night." Below is a longer example from Ann Petry's story "Doby's Gone."

> That spring when Sue was six they moved to Wessex, Connecticut—a small New England town whose neat colonial houses cling to a group of hills overlooking the Connecticut River.

The description of the setting introduces the story's location. It also helps readers infer important information about the characters' backgrounds and social class. The detail of the "neat colonial houses" implies social order; the river view implies an affluent community.

Often, creative writers use sensory details to paint the setting vividly. This helps readers visualize the setting and make it come alive in their minds. The details appeal to the sense of sight, smell, taste, touch, and sound. Reread the excerpt from Washington

Irving's short story "The Devil and Tom Walker" earlier in this chapter. You'll see that Irving uses details that appeal to sight, touch, and sound.

See how writer Jane Yolen uses vivid sensory imagery in the following description of setting from her short story "Greyling":

> Once upon a time when wishes were aplenty, a fisherman and his wife lived by the side of the sea. All that they ate came out of the sea. Their hut was covered with the finest mosses that kept them cool in the summer and warm in the winter.

To appreciate Yolen's artistry and understand how she creates a vivid setting, isolate the details and arrange them on a chart like this:

Sight

1. _____

_____

2. _____

_____

Taste

3. _____

_____

Touch

4. _____

_____

Answers

Sight

    1. A fisherman and his wife lived by the side of the sea

    2. Their hut was covered with the finest mosses

Taste

    3. All that they ate came out of the sea

Touch

    4. … Finest mosses that kept them cool in the summer and warm in the winter

Other times, however, you will not describe the setting in great detail. Instead, you will have readers infer the setting from details in the story. You'll plant clues in the characters' speech, clothing, or means of transportation. This is an especially effective technique for increasing suspense and compelling your audience to read on. Consider using this method of creating setting when you are writing a mystery story or science fiction tale, for instance.

All the Write Stuff

These same techniques for creating a vivid setting by using sensory detail work equally well when you write a memoir or other nonfiction work that entails descriptions of time and place.

Setting Takes Center Stage

Some settings are more important than others, functioning almost as another character in the conflict. In these instances, the conflict must take place during a specific time and place. This is true of the short stories of Jack London, for example, where the frozen North is as important a character as the prospectors. Here's an excerpt from London's famous short story "To Build a Fire." The main character, an unnamed prospector in the Yukon, freezes to death because he doesn't take the setting seriously enough, as you learned in a previous chapter. As the following passage shows, the story could not have taken place anywhere else to the same effect.

> As he turned to go, he spat speculatively. There was a sharp, explosive crackle that startled him. He spat again. And again, in the air, before it could fall to the snow, the spittle crackled. He knew that at fifty below spittle crackled on the snow, but this spittle had cracked in the air. Undoubtedly it was colder than fifty below—how much colder he did not know. But the temperature did not matter.

Of course, London is being ironic here: The temperature matters very much. In fact, the temperature is the cornerstone of the story because by disregarding it, the prospector perishes.

Setting is also crucial in Nathaniel Hawthorne's classic stories of Puritan sin and guilt, as shown in his allegorical tale "Young Goodman Brown." Here is an excerpt:

> With this excellent resolve for the future, Goodman Brown felt himself justified in making more haste on his present evil purpose. He had taken a dreary road, darkened by all the gloomiest trees of the forest, which barely stood aside to let the narrow path creep through, and closed immediately behind. It was all as lonely as could be; and there is this peculiarity in such a solitude, that the traveler knows not who may be concealed by the innumerable trunks and thick boughs overhead; so that with lonely footsteps he may yet be passing through an unseen multitude.

In this story, elements of the setting function symbolically. The "forest" stands for evil, the temptations of the world; the "narrow path" represents the way of righteousness. Those who stray from the "path" fall victim to wickedness and all manner of licentiousness. As the story continues, we see Young Goodman Brown ("Mr. Everyman") fall off the path and succumb to sin. Not an easy read, but it surely shows how a master can make setting reinforce the theme.

How to Create the Setting

Speaking of the importance of setting, writer Eudora Welty said:

> Every story would be another story, and unrecognizable if it took up its characters and plot and happened somewhere else. Fiction depends for its life on place. Place is the crossroads of circumstance, the proving ground of What happened? Who's here? Who's coming?

Setting is created by language. How many—or how few—details you include is completely your decision. You may want to describe the setting in great detail or leave much of it up to the reader's imagination. As I've stressed, the best way to learn a writing technique is by studying models. Let's apply this method here.

In William Faulkner's "A Rose for Emily," for example, the narrator carefully describes the house that Miss Emily lives in because it's vital to the story. This description helps readers visualize the shabby Mississippi town in the post–Civil War South. The house becomes a symbol for Miss Emily's decay and her inability to deal with change, as the following passage suggests:

> It was a big, squarish frame house that had once been white, decorated with cupolas and spires and scrolled balconies ... set on what had once been our most select street. But ... only Miss Emily's house was left, lifting its stubborn and coquettish decay above the cotton wagons and the gasoline pumps—an eyesore among eyesores.

The phrase "that had once been white" refers to Miss Emily's reputation as well as her house. She had an affair with a Northern day laborer (and later killed him, but that's another matter), which sullied her reputation. The decay of the house symbolizes the decay of Miss Emily; the house has fallen apart just as Miss Emily has collapsed under the weight of despair and disappointment. In her disgrace, she is as much an eyesore as the house.

How can you tell how important the setting should be in your short story? The setting will be a major player if the main character is ...

♦ Challenging the elements.

♦ Attempting to conquer the environment.

♦ Escaping from a specific place.

♦ Staying alive in a dangerous place.

Setting and Mood

Even when it doesn't play a leading role, setting can be used to create mood, and the location doesn't have to be specific. Aspects of the setting also help determine the story's mood—the emotion it conveys. The *mood* (or *atmosphere*) is the strong feeling we get from a piece of writing. The mood is created by characterization, description, images, and dialogue. Some possible moods include terror, horror, cheerfulness, elation, calm, and suspense. Recall the ominous mood of "The Devil and Tom Walker," for instance.

Try it yourself. Read the following details from these settings. Identify the mood suggested by each one. Explain which details create the mood you identified.

1. From "The Fall of the House of Usher" by Edgar Allan Poe

During the whole of a dull, dark, and soundless day in the autumn of the year, when the clouds hung oppressively low in the heavens, I had been passing alone, on horseback, through a singularly dreary tract of country, and at length found myself, as the shades of evening drew near, within view of the melancholy House of Usher.

_____

_____

_____

_____

2. From "Occurrence at Owl Creek Bridge" by Ambrose Bierce

Farquhar dived as deeply as he could. The water roared in his ears like the voice of Niagara, yet he heard the dulled thunder of the volley and, rising again toward the surface, met shining bits of metal, singularly flattened, oscillating slowly downward.

_____

_____

_____

_____

3. From "The Open Boat" by Stephen Crane

None of them knew the color of the sky. Their eyes glanced level, and were fastened upon the waves that swept toward them. These waves were the hue of slate; save for the tops, which were of foaming white, and all the men knew the colors of the sea. The horizon narrowed and widened, and dipped and rose, and at all times its edge was jagged with waves that seemed thrust up in points like rocks.

_____

_____

_____

_____

Possible responses:

1. The mood is gloomy and depressed, created by such details as "dull, dark, and soundless day," "autumn of the year," "clouds hung oppressively low in the heavens," "singularly dreary tract of country," "the shades of evening," and "melancholy."

2. The mood is dramatic and mysterious, created by such details as "The water roared in his ears like the voice of Niagara," and "shining bits of metal, singularly flattened, oscillating slowly downward."

3. The mood is dismal and terrifying, created by such details as "None of them knew the color of the sky," "These waves were the hue of slate," "all the men knew the colors of the sea," and "its edge was jagged with waves that seemed thrust up in points like rocks."

Weave in the Theme

The *theme* of a narrative such as a short story is its main idea, a general statement about life. The theme is often based on the way the characters act.

While the theme can be stated outright in a story, writers usually have readers infer it from details about plot, characters, and setting. Unless you're writing a fable, the theme of your story shouldn't teach or preach. Rather, it should present a universal truth or your view of life.

Words to the Wise

The **theme** of a narrative is its main idea, a general statement about life.

For example, the theme of Eudora Welty's short story "A Worn Path" suggests the power of love. This is conveyed through Phoenix Jackson's difficult journey to get medicine for her grandson. Welty deliberately set the story at Christmas, to reinforce the theme of love and self-sacrifice.

How can you create the theme in your short stories? While plot, setting, and characters combine to make the theme apparent, use the following three time-honored techniques from the writer's tool bag:

◆ Repeat key patterns and symbols

◆ Make allusions to a well-known place, event, person, work of art, or other work of literature

◆ Insert key details that suggest larger meanings

Don't worry too much about theme; readers will discover whatever meaning they want in your stories. Further, their interpretation often adds levels of meaning and richness you might have alluded to only subconsciously.

A Note on the Creative Process

Creativity is an elusive thing. Some stories flow smoothly, like silky yarn being woven into a beautiful tapestry. Others are knit together in fits and starts over many months or even years.

I've treated theme late in the process of writing a story, but you may just as easily begin with your theme. Remember, you do not have to write your stories in the order in which I've suggested, but when you're first starting off, it's handy to have a method that works for many writers. As you get more experience, vary the order in which you create each element. You may wish to start with an intriguing character or spooky setting, for instance. You can then build your stories around these elements.

Go with whatever works best for you.

What's in a Name? Add a Title

Like a sign above the door, a title is your first chance to grab your readers. A title should tantalize your readers and leave them panting for more. The famous British mystery writer Agatha Christie once used a snatch of overheard conversation—"Why didn't they ask Evans?"—for a title. So keep your ears open. Take this as your license to snoop.

There are five main types of titles for narratives:

◆ Labels

◆ Statements

◆ Questions

◆ Commands

◆ "Combo Platters" (such as a statement that functions as a label)

Sometimes a story is sparked by a title; other times, you'll add the title last, as you would icing on a delicious cake. Whether you start with the title or finish with it, the following suggestions will help you craft memorable titles:

◆ Try to keep it brief. Some writers argue that a title should be no more than six words long. I say: Make your title as long or as short as you need, but shorter is usually more effective because it is catchier.

◆ Make it enticing. Create titles that make your readers want to dive right into your story.

◆ Explore different forms. If one format seems flat, try another format. For example, change a statement title into a question or a label into a command.

Below are the titles of some famous short stories. You can use these as models, but be sure to read the stories!

Story	Author
"Hands"	Sherwood Anderson
"Looking for Mr. Green"	Saul Bellow
"The Demon Lover"	Elizabeth Bowen
"Babylon Revisited"	F. Scott Fitzgerald
"Araby"	James Joyce
"The Rocking-Horse Winner"	D. H. Lawrence
"The Magic Barrel"	Bernard Malamud
"Shiloh"	Bobbie Ann Mason
"Shooting an Elephant"	George Orwell
"The Open Window"	Saki
"Act of Faith"	Irwin Shaw
"Flight"	John Steinbeck
"Everyday Use"	Alice Walker
"Roman Fever"	Edith Wharton
"The Mark on the Wall"	Virginia Woolf

Show, Don't Tell!

"Show, don't tell!" Make this your storytelling mantra. As we've discussed in this chapter, bring the characters, conflict, and setting to life in your narratives by using sensory details:

◆ Describe how things taste, smell, look, feel, and sound.

◆ Use concrete details that help readers form vivid mental images.

◆ Breathe life into the characters, conflict, and setting by using your personal, unique writing style.

Here's an example:

Weak style, lacking sensory details:

Nick enjoyed walking through country graveyards on fall afternoons. He enjoyed looking at the marble tablets with their ornate, old-fashioned inscriptions. They made him remember how sad he felt when his grandfather had died last year.

Strong style, with specific details:

I remember my grandfather's funeral, the hurried cross of sand the minister drew on the coffin lid, the whine of the lowering straps, the lengthening cleanly cut sides of clay, the lack of air forever in the close dark lined pink satin.

—John Updike

Let's isolate the details in the second passage that make it more effective than the first passage:

Sense	Detail
sight	"the lengthening cleanly cut sides of clay"
sound	"the whine of the lowering straps"
smell	"the lengthening cleanly cut sides of clay"
feel	"cross of sand the minister drew on the coffin lid; the lack of air forever in the close dark lined pink satin."

Are We There Yet?

Are you ready to write your narrative? Ready or not, here you go! Use this checklist to make sure you've included everything you need to pen a prize-winning short story.

❏ Have you decided what type of short story you're writing (a mystery story, a horror story, a love story, etc.)?

❏ Have you worked out the conflict?

❏ Do you have a protagonist and an antagonist?

❏ Have you structured your story with a clear beginning, middle, and end?

❏ Have you established the time and place for the action?

❏ Is the conflict resolved in a logical way?

❏ Have you identified your audience? Is every detail aimed at your audience?

❏ Did you "show, not tell" by using description?

❏ Did you create a tantalizing title?

❏ Did you revise and edit your writing so it is the best that you can do?

Some short story writers claim they never know where the story will go when they start it. I don't doubt this technique works well for them, but then again, I also believe Richard Nixon wasn't a crook, the check is in the mail, and there's another train right behind this one. I'll argue that writers who claim they don't plan *on paper* have done a great deal of planning *in their heads* before they started putting pen to paper. They also tend to gloss over all their false starts and wasted time.

Experiment with the suggestions I've given you. See what works for your personal style. Here's the key: Roll with the punches. Be flexible. Don't get yourself boxed into your planning notes. Think about what you want to achieve in your story and then choose the best way to accomplish your aim.

The Least You Need to Know

◆ Use setting to make your story more believable, to symbolize key ideas, and to reinforce important story elements.

◆ Use sensory details to paint the setting in vivid details and create the mood.

◆ Weave in the theme, your message about life.

◆ Add a title to entice readers.

◆ Show, don't tell, and look both ways before crossing the street.

Chapter 13

Meet the Fiction Family

In This Chapter

◆ Define "fiction"

◆ Learn about the different types of fiction, including the novel, the "Bildungsroman," epistolary fiction, gothic horror novels, picaresque fiction, the roman à clef, romance novels, and transgressive fiction

◆ Write a one-sentence novel

◆ Get into the groove

It was the best of times, it was the worst of times, it was the age of wisdom, it was the age of foolishness, it was the epoch of belief, it was the epoch of incredulity, it was the season of Light, it was the season of Darkness, it was the spring of hope, it was the winter of despair, we had everything before us, we had nothing before us, we were all going direct to Heaven, we were all going direct the other way—in short, the period was so far like the present period, that some of its noisiest authorities insisted on its being received, for good or for evil, in the superlative degree of comparison only.

—*A Tale of Two Cities* by Charles Dickens

Dickens was comparing two eras, but he could just as easily have been talking about fiction: "Fiction is dead, fiction has never been more alive; everyone reads good fiction, no one reads good fiction; fiction is getting worse every day, fiction is breaking new ground every day …." You get the idea.

The debate about the role of fiction rages on, as it has done for centuries. Fortunately, fiction is very much alive and more exciting than ever. And best of all, this type of creative writing offers many variations and options that you're sure to find exciting.

This chapter describes the different types of fiction so you can find the niche that's perfect for your special talents.

What Is Fiction?

Fiction is writing that tells about made-up events and characters. Fiction offers something for every writer. That's because fiction, like lovers, comes in many forms. In previous chapters, you learned all about brief fiction, the short story, so in this chapter, we'll concentrate on longer works of fiction.

Which type (or types) of longer fiction do you want to write? Use this checklist to make note of them. Starred entries are explained later in this chapter.

_____ adult books	_____ picaresque novels*
_____ adventure novels	_____ realistic fiction
_____ Bildungsroman*	_____ roman à clef*
_____ children's storybooks	_____ romance novels*
_____ comic novels	_____ satiric novels
_____ epistolary novels*	_____ science fiction
_____ gothic horror novels*	_____ transgressive fiction*
_____ historical novels	_____ young adult fiction
_____ mysteries	_____ westerns

Words to the Wise

Fiction is writing that tells about made-up events and characters. Novels and short stories are examples of fiction.

Let's take a closer look at some of the different forms that fiction can take. See which ones suit your unique interests and abilities.

The Novel

"Oh! It is only a novel!" exclaims a character in Jane Austen's novel *Northanger Abbey*. In short, it's only "some work in which the most thorough knowledge of human nature, the happiest delineation of its varieties, the liveliest effusions of wit and humor are conveyed to the world in the best chosen language." It is a creed that all modern novelists (down to our own Stephen King and Anne Rice) have tried to live up to. And now the mantle has passed to you.

All books are a monument to the human spirit, but the novel is a particularly admirable feat because of its length and breadth. The story of a good novel resonates within us as something more real than life itself. Who can forget Oliver Twist's wrenching plea for a little more gruel, Rhett Butler's slamming the door on Scarlett, and Huck Finn's "lighting out for the territory ahead of the rest." And even though novelists may sometimes use real-life people as their inspiration, successful characters end up as unique creations, greater than the sum of their parts. Fierce Captain Ahab, proud Hester Prynne, and sinister Michael Corleone are among the most notable.

A *novel* is a long work of fiction. There is no specific required length that sets the novel apart from its cousins the short story or the *novelette*, a work of fiction usually between 50 to 100 pages. If you're going to push me to the edge, as a general rule, a novel is more than 50,000 words.

Words to the Wise

The **novel** is a long work of fiction.

All novels have a fairly specific setting (the time and place of the action). If the setting includes real historical figures and becomes as a character in the story, you're dealing with a historical novel. Charles Dickens's *A Tale of Two Cities* and Robert Grave's *I, Claudius* are both historical novels. Fiction that contains imaginary situations and characters that are very similar to real life is called *realistic fiction*.

The "Bildungsroman"

So you want to describe how the hero escaped his lousy childhood to become a mensch? Then the *Bildungsroman* is the form for you. German for "novel of development," this fictional form deals with maturation, wherein the hero becomes civilized. No, this does not mean that he finally puts his socks in the hamper and remembers that the treadmill is not an extension of his closet. Rather, in these novels, the hero becomes aware of himself as he relates to the objective world outside of his subjective consciousness. Famous examples include:

Words to the Wise

The **Bildungsroman** is a fictional story that deals with maturation. **Epistolary fiction** recounts the story in a series of letters.

◆ Thomas Mann's *The Magic Mountain*

◆ Samuel Butler's *The Way of All Flesh*

◆ James Joyce's *A Portrait of the Artist as a Young Man*

Take a Letter, Maria: Epistolary Fiction

If you've read Alice Walker's contemporary novel *The Color Purple*, you'll recall that Walker uses letters between her characters to advance the story. By using this form of the novel, Walker is drawing on a long literary history. The 1700s were the heyday of the epistolary novel. Samuel Richardson's epistolary novel *Pamela*, for instance, concerns a young woman of virtue and her seducer.

Generally considered the first modern novel, *Pamela* was published in 1740 and immediately became the talk of London. Here's the plot in a nutshell: Pamela Andrews becomes a lady's maid at age 12 when her family suffers financial reverses. Upon the death of her mistress three years later, Pamela comes to the attention of her mistress's son, "a young gentleman of free principles, who … attempted, by all manner of temptations and devices, to seduce her." Pamela manages to tame his base advances and become his wife—the goal of any good eighteenth-century gal.

Here's an example from *Pamela* to use as a model as you explore this form of fiction:

Letter I

Dear Father and Mother,

I have great trouble, and some comfort, to acquaint you with. The trouble is, that my good lady died of the illness I mentioned to you, and left us all much grieved for the loss of her; for she as was a dear good lady, and kind to all us her servants. Much I feared, that as I was taken by her ladyship to wait upon her person, I should be quite destitute again, and forced to return to you and my poor mother, who having enough to do to maintain yourselves …. My master said, I will take care of all of you, my good maidens; and for you, Pamela (and took me by the hand; yes, he took my hand before them all), for my dear mother's sake, I will be a friend to you, and you shall take care of my linen ….

Letter II

Dear Pamela,

Your letter was indeed a great trouble, and some comfort to me and your poor mother. We are troubled, to be sure, for your good lady's death, who took such care of you, and gave you learning, and, for three or four years past, has always been giving you clothes and linen, and everything that a gentlewoman need not be ashamed to appear in …. Everybody talks how you have come on, and what a genteel girl you are; and some say you are very pretty; and indeed, six month since, when I saw you last, I should have thought so myself, if you was not our child. But what avails all this, if you are to be ruined and undone!—Indeed, my dear Pamela, we begin to be in great fear for you ….

All the Write Stuff

The excerpts from *Pamela* can also serve as a model for a romance novel set in the eighteenth century because it gives the flavor of the period: the diction, manners, and customs.

Most epistolary novels depend on an exchange of correspondence: You write to me, I write back, and so on. But the rule is carved in sand, not granite. Mary Shelley's *Frankenstein*, for example, is a one-way letter.

Gothic Horror Fiction

We have the Gothic tradition to thank for such gems as *Sorority Girl Slashers at the Bowl-a-Rama* and *Abbott and Costello Meet the Bride of Frankenstein*. First popular in the late eighteenth century and the early nineteenth, Gothic lit is chock-full of mystery, horror, violence, and terror. Gothic writers accomplish this through …

- Decapitations.
- Undead dead.
- Premature entombment.
- Spooky castles.
- Rattling chains.
- If you're really lucky, even a little perverted sex.

The Spirit of the Public Journals, a 1797 pamphlet, gives the following "recipe" for the Gothic novel. Among the "ingredients" listed are an old castle, a long gallery with secret doors, three freshly murdered bodies, assorted skeletons, and "noises, whispers, and groans."

All the Write Stuff

Notice that I keep citing all these classic writers? There's a method to my madness. To write the best, you have to read the best. Fortunately, they're not all dead white guys. The classic honchos come in all varieties and offer something for everyone.

Long before Stephen King, the trendsetters were the following shockmasters:

♦ Horace Walpole (*The Castle of Otranto*, 1764)

♦ Clara Reeve (*The Champion of Virtue*, 1777)

♦ Ann Radcliffe (*The Mysteries of Udolpho*, 1794)

♦ Mary Wollstonecraft Shelley (ol' Zipperneck himself, *Frankenstein*, 1818)

♦ Edgar Allan Poe (many short stories, mid-1800s)

Picaresque Fiction

A travelogue with a twist: the *picaresque* (pronounced *pick-are-ESK*, not *picturesque*) describes the exploits of a rogue. "Picaresque" comes from the Spanish word *picaro*, which means "rogue." Not surprisingly, it's a Spanish genre. (Can we conclude that there are more rogues in Spain than there is coal in Newcastle?)

All the Write Stuff

Picaresque fiction tells the story of an appealing scoundrel. A **roman à clef** (pronounced *roman ah clay*) represents real events and characters under the guise of fiction.

The form originated in sixteenth-century Spain as a kind of parody of tales of chivalric adventures. As a result, the picaresque novel has an episodic structure, as the hero experiences a series of wild adventures.

The rogue's adventures can be sexual, but they don't have to be. Among the most famous picaresque novels are Henry Fielding's *The History of Tom Jones* (risqué) and Mark Twain's *The Adventures of Huckleberry Finn* (not a drop of sex in it). The movie *Goodfellas* can also be considered a picaresque story because of its portrayal of mobster Henry Hill.

Below is a tantalizing nibble from *Tom Jones* to serve as a model as you frame your own picaresque fiction. Before you read this passage, you should know what the great Dr. Johnson said when he first read *Tom Jones:* "Shocking! I scarcely know of a more corrupt work." The amorous antics of a passionate young rogue made *Tom Jones* a hit in its own day and the book has lost none of its appeal, as the following passage shows.

Though Mr. Blifil was not yet ready to eat every woman he saw, yet he was far from being destitute of that appetite which is said to be the common property of all animals. Now the agonies which affected the mind of Sophia rather augmented than impaired her beauty; for her tears added brightness to her eyes, and her breasts rose higher with her sighs.... Nor was his desire at all lessened by the aversion which he discovered in her to himself. On the contrary, this served rather to heighten the pleasure he proposed in rifling her charms, as it added triumph to lust. The rivaling poor Jones, and supplanting him in her affections, added another spur to his pursuit, and promised another additional rapture to his enjoyment.

Fiction with a Key

A *roman à clef* uses contemporary historical figures as its chief characters, but they are cloaked with fictitious names. One of the most recent and notorious examples is Joe Klein's *Primary Colors*, a thinly disguised account of the Clinton administration. Reaching a little further back through the curtains of time, there's *Valley of the Dolls*, Jackie Susann's account of pill-popping among Hollywood's leading ladies. On a less sensational plane, the main character in Aldous Huxley's *Point Counter Point*, Mark Rampion, is modeled on fellow novelist D. H. Lawrence.

Love Makes the World Go 'Round: Romance Novels

Put an innocent young woman in an isolated mansion. Throw in a devilishly handsome, brooding young man. On page 22, have the hero say, "Good morning." For the next 10 pages, the heroine wonders what he meant. Add some heaving breasts, flowing hair (male and female), and passionate whoopee. Don't you wish it were that easy to write a *romance novel?*

Romance novels have come a long way, baby. Today, these stories of love and passion range from the tame to the tempestuous. Perhaps in the entire history of book publishing, there has never been such a phenomenon as the apparently limitless success of romance novels. They total nearly 40 percent of all paperback novels sold in America. *Harlequin Publishers* alone sold nearly 200 million romances in one year, averaging a book per second.

Because the romance novel follows a formula (a set of strict guidelines about characters, plot, setting, and length), it may be easier for the first-time author to write. If you're interested in this type of novel, you can get more information from these resources:

- *How to Write Romances* by Phyllis Taylor Pianka
- *Writing and Selling the Romance Novel* by Sylvia K. Burack
- *How to Write Romance Novels that Sell* by Marilyn M. Lowery
- *You Can Write a Romance and Get It Published!* by Yvonne MacManus

If you decide to write a romance novel, send for the author's guidelines from a publisher *before* you start writing. Otherwise, you could end up trashing a whole lot of manuscript. You can get the publisher's address from *Literary Market Place* (in the reference section of the library) or from the inside cover of any romance novel.

Transgressive Fiction

The term *transgressive fiction* was coined less than a decade ago by a writer in the *Los Angeles Times* to describe fiction that graphically explores nasty stuff like aberrant sexual practices, urban violence, dysfunctional family relationships, and drug use. Words used as compliments to describe these novels include "subversive," "avant-garde," "bleak," and "pornographic."

Words to the Wise

Romance novels are stories of love and passion almost always aimed at a female audience. **Transgressive fiction** is bleak, modern, and often pornographic.

Transgressive fiction has its roots in the novels of William Burroughs and the Marquis de Sade. Its contemporary practitioners include Dennis Cooper, the author of *Try*, a novel whose main character is a sexually abused teenager with a heroin-addicted buddy and an uncle who makes pornographic videos. The genre is also characterized by distinctive visuals, such as undersized formats, the whole text set in italics, and bizarre cover art. Write at your own risk.

Do-It-Yourself Adventure Novel

I can't ask you to write an entire novel, but I *can* ask you to write a one-sentence version! Here's how to do it.

Take one or more phrases from each column to create your own premise for an adventure novel. Keep it to one sentence. (When you have time, you can expand it into a longer novel.)

Setting	Heroes
Amidst virgin forests,	Manly pioneers
Amidst heaving oceans,	Manly Native Americans
Amidst besieged forts,	Demure blond debs
Amidst Lake Glimmerglass,	Brunette spitfires
Amidst burned-out bunkers,	Clean-cut American soldiers

Villains	Weapons
Confront dastardly guerrillas	Armed with hand grenades.
Confront dastardly sailors	Armed with swords.
Confront dastardly rebels	Armed with cannons.
Confront dastardly Nazis	Armed with machine guns.
Confront dastardly soldiers	Armed with bows and arrows.

Write your one-sentence novel here:

_____

_____

_____

_____

You *Can* Get There from Here

Okay, so you've decided what type of long fiction to write. Perhaps you'll start with a romance; maybe sci-fi is your bag. No matter: Now it's time to get crackin'. "I don't have the time to write a novel," you whine. Not to worry; the journey of 50,000 words starts with a single sentence. Follow these eight suggestions to get started on your novel—*today*.

All the Write Stuff

Writing Mysteries, a handbook by the Mystery Writers of America (edited by Sue Grafton), offers detailed advice for writing gripping whodunits.

1. *Make yourself a "writing appointment."* Set aside a block of time during which you will write—and only write. Start with 10 minutes a day and build up. As your novel takes shape, you'll want to write more and more.

2. *Schedule breaks.* Breaks help you clear your mind and generate ideas. Keep the breaks brief. I recommend a half-hour walk or jog.

3. *Delegate, delegate, delegate.* One way to give yourself more time is to pay someone else to do the things that are keeping you from writing. Obviously, this only makes sense if you can afford it. You don't need a staff of seven. Instead, consider getting someone to mow the lawn, clean the place, and watch the kids.

4. *Set priorities.* Let the houseplants die. A little dust never hurt anyone. Who needs home-baked cookies?

5. *Reward yourself.* Reward yourself for finishing a certain number of pages, for writing for a specific length of time, or just for work well done. Do lunch with a friend, buy a silly trinket, stop and plant the flowers.

6. *Deal with interruptions.* Get an answering machine (if you don't already have one). Use the answering machine to monitor your calls. Take the call only if it's really important. For example: Your agent calls to say your novel has been sold—and optioned for a movie.

7. *Avoid isolation.* Writing a novel is not the same as taking religious vows. You don't have to become the life of the party as you write, but neither do you have to go native in greasy sweatpants and ratty slippers.

8. *Believe in yourself.* The people who write novels are not necessarily the most witty, brilliant, or well educated. They aren't even the most deserving, compassionate, or likable. They are, however, the most relentless, patient, and thick-skinned. Stick with it!

The Least You Need to Know

- Fiction is writing that tells about made-up events and characters. Like frozen desserts, fiction comes in many forms.

- The novel is a long work of fiction. The Bildungsroman is a fictional story of maturation. Epistolary fiction recounts the story in a series of letters.

- Picaresque fiction tells the story of an appealing scoundrel. A roman à clef describes real events and characters under the guise of fiction.

- Romance novels are stories of love and passion. Transgressive fiction is bleak, modern, and often pornographic.

- Fiction comes in so many forms—short as well as long—that you're sure to find some that suit your special talents.

Nonfiction

"I don't care what's written about me as long as it isn't true," 1930s wit Dorothy Parker claimed. We'll stick pretty close to the truth here, Ms. Parker—after all, nonfiction is writing that describes real people and events.

Nonfiction can take many forms: memoirs, magazine articles, and instruction. Each form has its own structural requirements, but their basis is the same—writing that sets up a proposition, defends it, and proves it. That's what you'll learn here … and a whole lot more—including how to write poetry!

Chapter 14

Writing Nonfiction

In This Chapter

- ◆ Survey nonfiction
- ◆ Explore *creative nonfiction*
- ◆ Discover four types of personal essays
- ◆ Learn techniques for writing personal essays
- ◆ Write a personal essay

Nonfiction can take many forms: articles, autobiographies, biographies, creative nonfiction, essays, humorous pieces, instruction, inspiration, magazine articles, memoirs, newspaper features, letters, reference books, research papers, and textbooks.

Make no mistake about it: Each of these types of writing is creative in its own way and calls for special techniques and talents. Nonfiction is not fiction's neglected stepsister—quite the contrary is true. Nonfiction was around long before fiction appeared on the scene and thus has a noble heritage and reputation.

Here I'll show you how to apply your artistry to writing essays, likely the most basic and useful nonfiction form (as well as one of the most often read). We'll save other forms of nonfiction—memoirs, articles, and poetry—for their own chapters.

Reality Is Stranger Than Truth: Creative Nonfiction

One of the most popular—and controversial—types of nonfiction has been dubbed *creative nonfiction.* A relatively new form of writing, creative nonfiction blurs the line between fiction and nonfiction by adopting the fiction writer's techniques, such as creating dialogue, writing scenes from memory, and imagining scenes outright. As Dave Eggers explains in his creative nonfiction work *A Heartbreaking Work of Staggering Genius:*

> All events described hercin actually happened, although on occasion the author has taken certain, very small liberties with chronology, because that is his right as an American.

The first well-known example of creative nonfiction is Truman Capote's 1965 book *In Cold Blood,* described in Chapter 1.

Today, there's a noisy controversy over whether writers of creative nonfiction can make up facts, create composite characters, or invent composite scenes. As a nonfiction writer, you make a deal with the reader to tell the truth—but what happens if the truth becomes more "true" by the addition of fictional elements? That's what Edmund Morris claimed he did in his 1999 biography of Ronald Reagan, *Dutch,* by creating a fictional narrator (also named "Edmund Morris") who supposedly knew Reagan since his youth. "I used it [the invented character] primarily because I needed to have a close observer of Reagan from his peer group," Morris said, "so the fictional observer is a literary embodiment of the biographer's own persona." Other writers have judged Morris's invention harshly, however, believing that it crosses too far over the line from nonfiction to fiction.

In the flourishing realm of creative nonfiction, it's often difficult to tell where truth ends and invention begins. Below are some recent books that have been classified as creative nonfiction. Read a few to see how you might adapt this form of nonfiction to your story. The techniques of creative nonfiction are increasingly common in memoir.

Words to the Wise

Creative nonfiction is a type of nonfiction writing that includes elements of fiction, such as invented dialogue.

- *The Fabulist* by Stephen Glass
- *Love Me* by Garrison Keillor
- *I Should Be Extremely Happy in Your Company* by Brian Hall
- *Invisible Eden* by Maria Flook
- *San Remo Drive* by Leslie Epstein
- *Dutch* by Edmund Morris

Types of Personal Essays

As we discussed in Chapter 1, an *essay* is a brief writing on a specific subject. Like any other kind of creative writing, essays can be on any topic at all. When you write a personal essay, you address your readers about your own experiences and emotions. The essay's slant reflects your attitude and taps your creativity.

Your purpose will determine how you write about the topic. Remember the four purposes for writing: narrative, persuasive, descriptive, and expository. Suppose you are planning to write an essay on your local library. For a narrative essay, you might tell a story about the library; for a persuasive essay, you might convince your readers to support the library bond issue or visit the library more often. For a descriptive essay, give sensory details about the library's atmosphere; for an expository essay, you could explain how the online card catalog system works.

Narrative Essays

Remember that *narration* is writing that tells a story. Narrative essays can be developed in many ways, including chronological order (time order), as you would construct a story. The difference, of course, is that an essay is nonfiction rather than fiction. Narrative essays can also be developed through cause and effect, comparison and contrast, and definition. Let's focus on developing a narrative essay through definition.

Here are some ways to construct a definition passage or essay:

◆ List characteristics of a thing beyond what you need to just identify it.

◆ Define the whole by naming its parts.

◆ Define the object by tracing its origins.

◆ Give synonyms for the concept or object being defined.

The following brief narrative essay uses the history of "Melba toast" to define the term:

Toast of the Town

Have you ever wondered how Melba toast got its name? It was named after Nellie Melba, a famous Australian soprano of the late nineteenth and early twentieth century. The prima donna was staying at the Savoy Hotel in London and following a stringent diet. According to the legend, she was living on almost nothing but toast. Normally she was served her meals by the famous French chef and food writer Auguste Escoffier, but on one particular occasion, the master chef was busy elsewhere so the great lady's toast had to be prepared by one of the sous chefs. Probably more used to preparing timbales than toast, the assistant bungled the job. When the hapless waiter served the toast to Nellie Melba, the head steward rushed forward to offer his heartfelt apologies at the debacle. But before the head steward could reach her, Nellie exclaimed, "How clever of Escoffier! I have never tasted such lovely toast!" Ever since then, these crisp, thin slices of toast have been known as "Melba toast."

Persuasive Essays

You learned in Chapter 1 that *persuasive writing* moves readers to action or belief. Aristotle, the Big Greek Daddy of Persuasion, believed that argument meant discovering all the available ways of persuasion in a situation where the truth was up for grabs.

Aristotle settled on three ways that people could convince others to adopt a certain point of view or approve a course of action. Broadly stated, he identified these three elements as …

1. *Logos.* The appeal to the audience's reason.

2. *Pathos.* The appeal to the audience's emotions.

3. *Ethos.* The degree of confidence that the speaker's character or personality inspires in readers.

The goal of these three appeals is the same, although each one takes a different approach. Each appeal can be used separately, or they can be combined to increase the persuasive mojo. When you argue a point in an essay, you analyze a subject, topic, or issue in order to persuade your readers to think or act a certain way. Here's an example from one of America's most famous essays.

> When in the course of human events, it becomes necessary for one people to dissolve the political bands that have connected them with another, and to assume among the powers of the earth, the separate and equal station to which the laws of nature and of nature's God entitle them, a decent respect to the opinions of mankind requires that they should declare the causes which impel them to the separation.

> We hold these truths to be self-evident: that all men are created equal; that they are endowed by their Creator with certain unalienable rights; that among these are life, liberty, and the pursuit of happiness; that to secure these rights, governments are instituted among men, deriving their just powers from the consent of the governed; that whenever any form of government becomes destructive of these ends, it is the right of the people to alter or abolish it, and to institute new

government, laying its foundation on such principles and organizing its powers in such form, as to them shall seem most likely to effect their safety and happiness.

—Thomas Jefferson, The Declaration of Independence (1776)

Expository Essays

Recall that *exposition* is writing that explains, shows, or tells about a subject. As a result, many essays are often developed through exposition. The following example is developed through cause and effect. The cause is *why* something happens; the effect is the *result, what happens* due to the cause. Therefore, cause-and-effect essays establish a relationship between events.

As you read the following passage, identify the topic that the writer is explaining. Also notice how the details make the essay lively and interesting.

The potato has had a major historical impact on Ireland. In the eighteenth and nineteenth century, the average Irish citizen planted potatoes and ate about ten pounds of potatoes a day—and little else. Potatoes are nourishing: on this diet, the Irish population nearly tripled from the middle of the eighteenth century to just about the middle of the nineteenth century. But depending on only one food was dangerous. When the potato blight hit Europe in 1845, the results were devastating in Ireland. There, the potato famine meant more than starvation that year. It meant no seed potatoes to use to grow the next year's crop. It meant that the pig or cow that would usually have been sold to pay the rent had to be slaughtered, because there was nothing to fatten it on. No pig or cow meant no rent. No rent meant eviction. As a result, homelessness and disease followed on the heels of hunger. Almost a million Irish people died as a result of the potato blight. Another million moved to the United States.

Descriptive Essays

Remember that *description* is a kind of writing that creates a word picture of what something or someone is like. Description is made up of sensory details that help readers form pictures in their minds.

The following passage describes a pivotal scene from George Orwell's famous essay "Shooting an Elephant." Orwell, the pen name of Eric Blair (1903–1950) is famous not only for his grim novels *Animal Farm* (1945) and *1984* (1948), but also for his passionate defense of the integrity of the English language. His essay "Shooting an Elephant" focuses on the use and abuse of power. Notice how Orwell draws on the sense of touch and hearing as well as sight:

When I pulled the trigger I did not hear the bang or feel the kick—one never does when a shot goes home—but I heard the devilish roar of glee that went up from the crowd. In that instant, in too short a time, one would have thought, even for the bullet to get there, a mysterious, terrible change had come over the elephant. He neither stirred nor fell, but every line of his body had altered. He looked suddenly stricken, shrunken, immensely old, as though the frightful impact of the bullet had paralyzed him without knocking him down …

You can use description in all your essays in the following ways:

- To make scenes realistic and memorable

- To help readers experience an emotion

- To share your feelings more clearly

- To bring characters to life

- To convey key ideas, especially complex ones

- To help readers feel like they're on the scene

Follow these six guidelines when you write descriptive essays:

1. Start by deciding on a method of organization. Spatial organization, for example, works especially well if your details are mainly visual. If you're describing an incident, consider chronological order.

2. Then select a point of view, the vantage point from which you will relate events or details in your essay.

3. Clearly identify the subject (no guessing games, please).

4. Use details to create a strong mood or feeling about the subject.

5. As you write, draw on all five senses: sight, touch, hearing, taste, smell.

6. Consider including *figures of speech*, those imaginative comparisons that evoke feelings in your readers.

Writing Personal Essays

Whether your purpose in your essays is to narrate, persuade, explain, or describe (or some combination thereof), following the five easy steps can help you get started.

1. Write what you want to write. Yes, I know that you've likely gotten this advice before, and with good cause: It really holds true. Choose a topic that really matters to you. Since you're writing a personal essay, you want to choose something that touches your soul. Otherwise, you'll likely have trouble mustering the passion you need.

2. Determine your purpose and audience. Your purpose will determine how you write about the topic. For instance, if you write a narrative essay, your purpose is to entertain. As a result, your essay is likely to be light and charming. An expository essay, in contrast, is designed to explain or instruct. It may still be amusing, but its primary purpose is to teach 'em.

3. Gather information. You can do this informally by tapping your memories and jotting down notes. Or, you could do some formal research by interviewing people, reading online sources, or checking reference books. Be sure you have the facts you need to make your essay interesting to your readers.

4. Write the essay. Decide how many paragraphs your essay will have. A brief essay of 350–500 words will usually have an introduction, a body (three-to-five paragraphs), and a conclusion. Then get your ideas down on paper.

5. Revise and edit. Let your essay sit to "cool down" a few hours or a few days, if you have the time. Then reread your essay and decide what to keep and what to change. Don't be discouraged! It takes time to whip your essay into the form you want. I published the following essay in a local newspaper. It took five drafts until I was satisfied.

Wrong Turn _____

Don't forget to narrow your topic to fit your parameters. For example, if you want to submit a 500-word essay to a newspaper, don't write about all extreme sports; instead, take a small slice of the topic, enough to cover in detail in the space you have.

Study a Personal Essay

I wrote the following essay for a newspaper column on Long Island experiences. I wanted to explore my feelings about my home and convey those feelings to my readers. As you read, think about whether or not you agree with my main idea: that living on Long Island is worth the hassle.

When I was young, time seemed to stand still. But as I plunge kicking and screaming into my middle years, time compresses and I find myself thinking about eternity. No, not mortality, spirituality, or perfume; rather, I'm talking about the unique meaning "eternity" has for Long Islanders.

To empty-nesters left contemplating the remains of an Easter feast once the guests have rolled out the door, eternity is two people and a ham. To my single female friends, eternity is waiting for Mr. Right to appear on their doorstep and in their arms. To a long-married man, eternity is shopping for shoes with his wife.

To Long Islanders, however, eternity takes on a whole new meaning. My train-going friends claim that eternity is the Long Island Railroad loudspeaker squawking during rush hour, "LIRR delays through Jamaica, delays through Hicksville, delays on the Ronkonkoma branch...." Why not just drive? You know the answer to that question if you've ever been westbound on the Southern State in the fall, as the sun sets on the highway and you're blinded for six straight miles. Traffic grinds to a standstill as everyone fumbles with their sun visors and squints into their windshield. You know what eternity is when you travel from New York City to the Hamptons on a Friday night in August. They don't call it "Long" Island for nothing.

Long Islanders who revel in our natural, shopping, and cultural wonders see eternity as trying to leave the Point Lookout parking lot on July fourth after the fireworks. No one disagrees that it's an exercise in endless time trying to get into Jones Beach on a glorious Saturday in July. Or escape from the Roosevelt Field, Sunrise Mall, or Smithhaven Mall parking lots anytime in December. Ever been stuck in the parking lot after a concert at the Tilles Center at C.W. Post, the Staller Center at SUNY Stony Brook, or Westbury Music Fair? We've all had a little taste of eternity trying to leave the Nassau Coliseum after a concert, Islanders' hockey game, or pet show, too.

A few years ago, I visited my in-laws in Meadville, PA. Life is slow and easy in Meadville. You get your Dairy Queen cone in two seconds flat. No traffic jams on their highways and you can always get a parking spot at the Super-8. There's never a line at the carp farm, either. You can see those carp any time you want. It's so different from Long Island, where it's hurry up and wait. No one seems to be pushing, shoving, or tapping their foot impatiently in Meadville—unlike on Long Island.

So why do Long Islanders wait on line for an eternity to get season's tickets for the Long Island Ducks? Why don't we explode in road rage when we're trying to find a parking spot at the mall the week before Christmas? Why do we stand in line at Home Depot to buy one screw while the customer in front of us is buying everything he needs to build a house?

I think Long Islanders are unique in their calm acceptance of waiting. It's not that we're any more patient than people in Los Angeles, Chicago, Dallas, or Boston—crowded places all. It's not that we like waiting: after all, Long Islanders are busy, busy, busy.

Here's the reason why we put up with an eternity of waiting on Long Island's highways, shopping malls, beaches, and cultural venues: it's worth it. It's so crowded on Long Island because everyone wants to live on Long Island. We may not have the widest highways, the biggest malls, the bluest ocean, or the hottest cultural attractions, but when you put it all together, we do have it all. Whatever you want, you can get it on Long Island. Long Island's concert halls offer classical music, heavy metal, and blues. We've got restaurants and delis that sell food from around the world; colleges and universities that offer degrees in teaching and technology and every other subject you can imagine. The North Shore has the mildness of the sound; the South Shore has the wildness of the ocean.

And if you're patient enough, you might even get there while you're still young enough to enjoy it all.

All the Write Stuff

You've probably also heard that you should write what you know. Yes and no. On the upside, writing what you know often gives your writing an authenticity because you are an expert. On the downside, it can often be boring to write what you know because you do know it so well. Why not take a risk and write something you have to research and discover fresh?

Essay This

Write your own personal essay on a topic that is interesting or important to you. You can use my topic—the positive aspects of living in your region greatly outweigh the negative ones—or come up with your own topic. Keep your essay about the same length as mine, no more than 700 words.

Here are some ideas to get you started.

Brainstorm a Topic

If you have trouble coming up with a topic, write the letters of the alphabet down the left-hand side of your paper. Next to each letter, write a word that starts with that letter. For example, write "apples" next to A, "Bermuda" next to B, "cats" next to C, and so on. Write as many words as you can for each letter. Use these words as springboards for topics.

Pick a Purpose

Once you have a topic, decide if the essay will be narrative, persuasive, descriptive, or expository. You may wish to combine two purposes, such as narrative and expository, by using a story as a springboard for your explanation, for instance.

No one method of development is better or worse than the other; choose the method that suits your topic, purpose, and audience.

Give Credit Where Credit Is Due

Be sure to give credit for any research that you use. Here's how I did it in an essay I wrote for a library newsletter. You'll see the source at the end of the paragraph. This tells readers that the entire paragraph came from this source.

> People said the invention of the airplane would destroy train travel. They were wrong.
>
> People said the invention of television would destroy radio. They were wrong.
>
> People said the invention of the Internet would sound the death knell for libraries. Wrong, wrong, wrong.
>
> In a recent poll, 91% of the total respondents believed libraries will exist in the future, despite all the information available on the Internet. The same number of people believe libraries are changing and dynamic places with a variety of activities for the whole family. Nearly all the people polled agreed libraries are unique because they offer patrons access to nearly everything on the Web or in print, as well as personal service and assistance in finding materials. Over 80% believe libraries and librarians play an essential role in our democracy and are needed now more than ever.
>
> *[Source: March 2002 KRC Research and Consulting survey for the American Library Association.]*

Write a Thesis Statement

Writing a clear statement of purpose helps you focus your ideas and stay on target. You don't have to use the statement in your essay (you likely won't because it *is* so obvious), but keeping it in front of you helps you avoid drifting off.

Use this format:

> In this essay I am going to *prove that* ...
>
> In this essay I am going to *tell a story about* ...

In this essay I am going to *explain that* …

In this essay I am going to *explain how* …

In this essay I am going to *explain why* …

In this essay I am going to *describe* …

Write your essay on these lines. Attach separate sheets of paper as you need them.

_____

_____

_____

_____

_____

_____

_____

_____

_____

_____

_____

_____

_____

_____

_____

_____

_____

_____

_____

_____

The Least You Need to Know

- ◆ Nonfiction can take many forms, and each type is creative in its own way and calls for special techniques and talents.

- ◆ *Creative nonfiction* is a type of nonfiction writing that blurs the line between nonfiction and fiction.

- ◆ Essays can be developed through narration, exposition, persuasion, and/or description.

- ◆ No one method is better or worse than the other; choose the method that suits your topic, purpose, and audience.

Chapter **15**

Writing Memoirs

In This Chapter

- ◆ Define *memoir*
- ◆ Explore the advantages of writing a memoir
- ◆ Learn how to get started and follow through
- ◆ Read a model memoir

Your memories are like the squares of a beautiful and unique quilt, stitched with love and care. How long have you promised yourself or your family that you would write your memoirs? Let me help you get started.

First, I define *memoir* and then explain why you should be writing one. Then I'll take you step-by-step through the writing process. Last, you'll find a brief sample memoir that you can use as a model.

What Is a Memoir?

Speaking of her memoir, the mystery writer Agatha Christie once wrote: "Autobiography is too grand a term. It suggests a purposeful study of one's whole life. It implies names, dates, and places in a tidy chronological order. What I want is to plunge my hand into a lucky dip and come up with a handful of assorted memories."

Memoir is autobiography, a life story. It's your personal and family history, the real-life story of your past. But no matter how closely you try to hew to the "truth," memoir is by nature a combination of fiction and nonfiction because no one's memory is perfect. Everyone remembers events a little bit differently. Further, we intentionally craft the story of our life to make it compelling reading. As a result, we tweak events to make them better reading. These "tweaks" bring in elements of fiction.

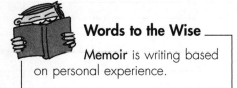

Words to the Wise

Memoir is writing based on personal experience.

Memoir is built on the following fundamentals:

Element	Explanation
Plot	Your story
Structure	How you choose to arrange events
Description	Details that appeal to the five senses
Dialogue	A speaker's exact words
Characterization	Telling and showing what characters are like
Point of view	The vantage point from which the story is told
Voice	The writer's unique personality

Since most successful memoirs read like short stories or novels, you'll want to shape your story to make it compelling. Using the techniques of fiction can help you accomplish this.

Why Write a Memoir?

Everyone has wonderful stories to tell. By sharing these stories in writing, we enrich everyone's life. This is true not only for the teller, but also for those who have the privilege of reading our memoirs.

Why not just share your memories orally? As wonderful as it is to talk with family and friends, the stories will be half-forgotten or lost altogether if you don't write them down. When you write the story of your life, you take sharing to another level. Your memoirs are valuable because they ...

- ◆ Preserve the people, places, and events of the past.
- ◆ Comfort, caution, console, and cheer people.
- ◆ Often inspire other family members to preserve their own memories.
- ◆ Are a priceless historical document.

Preserving your memories means honoring individual lives, experiences, and relationships. It means celebrating the joys and treasured memories as well as passing on the hard-earned lessons and challenges you faced. Sharing your stories strengthens your entire community as well as your individual family. Writing is a vehicle for exploring the what and the why of life and making sense of it. As a result, writing a memoir often leads to dramatic insights and personal growth as well.

Whether the audience is just you, your family members, co-workers, or the world at large, your story deserves to be told. Now that I've convinced you to invest a little time in a writing project that promises rich rewards, let's get started!

It's Just Too Big a Job!

When I say, "Why not write your memoirs?" people think they have to write about their entire life. They have to describe *everything* that ever happened, every person, place, thing, and conversation. Relax—you don't have to do that at all!

Since your life story is *your* life story, you can put in or take out whatever you want. *You* make the rules and you can change them as you go along. Here are some ideas for parameters:

◆ Write a complete history. Document all the major events in your life. If you decide to go this route, perhaps you'll want to start by describing your early childhood and move into your adult experiences.

◆ Choose a key event in your life. For instance, focus on your high school graduation, your wedding day, or the day you retired. Describe just one of these incidents, weaving in other stories only if they fit and you want to.

◆ Choose an everyday event that had special significance. Perhaps you want to write about a memorable conversation, meeting, or chance encounter.

All the Write Stuff

Keep a copy of the daily newspaper the day your child is born. I also save that week's newsmagazines (*Time, Newsweek, U.S. News & World Report*) and a *TV Guide*. My kids love to look through these historical documents from the day and week they were born. Perhaps they'll use these documents when they write their memoirs.

Remember, the scope of your memoir is your decision, so choose only the areas that interest you.

Getting Started (It's Easy!)

I often run workshops on writing memoirs, and the number-one question I get is "How do I get started?" It's surprisingly easy to begin a memoir. That's because there are many ways to start. Here are a series of ideas that my students and I have used with great success:

Ask yourself: "What are my earliest memories?" Recalling your early memories often opens the floodgate of memory.

You may wish to start with one of the highlights of your life, such as a memorable day, a close call, a key childhood memory, a challenge you met with assurance. Here are some other ideas:

- An illness or a death in the family
- The birth or arrival of a sibling
- A disaster (fire, flood, tornado, automobile accident)
- A relationship with an older person, or a peer
- A failure or a success at school
- Boyfriends/girlfriends, deciding to marry or not to marry
- Career choices
- Religious and spiritual experiences

Find a Focus with a Worksheet

Having trouble deciding what events really mattered in your life so far? Use the following worksheet to help you decide where to place your emphasis.

Narrow Your Ideas

1.   Has my life turned out as I imagined it would? Why or why not?

_____

_____

---

2.   What's been my greatest accomplishment so far?

_____

_____

3.   What's been my greatest challenge, disappointment, or frustration?

_____

_____

4.   What's the most important thing in my life right now? Why?

_____

_____

5.   What would I have done differently, if I'd known then what I know now?

_____

_____

6.   What are my goals now? What do I hope to accomplish next?

_____

_____

7.   If I could do anything I wanted to do, what would it be?

_____

_____

8.   What is my philosophy of life?

_____

_____

9.   What role does religion play in my life?

_____

_____

10.   What advice would I give people about love, marriage, raising children, handling money?

_____

_____

Tap Sensory Memories

For many people, the smallest sensory experience can send off waves of memory. It might be a whiff of perfume, the sweet melting of cotton candy on your tongue, the smell of musty autumn leaves.

That's the case for one of the most famous memoirs of all times, *Remembrance of Things Past* by Marcel Proust (1871–1922). Although this groundbreaking literary memoir is an enormous seven volumes, the inciting moment is almost comically tiny: a cookie. Nibbling on a madeleine (a small, rich cookie), Proust suddenly has an overwhelming feeling of happiness. He soon associates his joy with his memory of having tea with his Aunt Leonie. He realizes the value of a spontaneous memory, which sets the tone for his entire memoir.

All the Write Stuff

The more details you get down on paper as you brainstorm, the more specific facts you'll have to work with as you write. This will make it easier for you to be descriptive and detailed in your memoir.

After tasting the cookie, Proust writes:

> But when from a long-distant past nothing subsists, after the people are dead, after the things are broken and scattered, taste and smell alone, more fragile but more enduring, more unsubstantial, more persistent, remain poised a long time, like souls, remembering, waiting, hoping, amid the ruins of all the rest, and bear unflinchingly, in the tiny and almost impalpable drop of their essence, the vast structure of recollection.

You can often tap sensory memories by listing ideas. Here are some ideas for items to list. Choose as many—or as few—as you need:

- Favorite foods
- Comfort foods
- Favorite places
- Clothes you wore
- Hobbies
- Favorite books
- Favorite sports
- Holiday foods
- The smells of important places
- The fragrances of friends
- Cars you've owned
- Good smells
- Childhood pets
- Childhood skills

Then make some notes about anything that comes to mind from the items on the list. Writing down your memories triggers other thoughts and helps keep your focus.

Tap Visual Sources

If you're a visually based person, try drawing a map of your neighborhood as it appeared when you were a child. Add other sketches as well, perhaps your grade-school building, family garden, childhood home, the barracks where you had boot training, your lake cabin, the local shopping mall. Don't worry if you're not Rembrandt; the sketches are designed to help jog your memory, not hang on a museum wall.

You can also browse through old photograph albums, scrapbooks, and video tapes. There's a wealth of biographical information in these sources. Seeing a picture of yourself wearing a favorite outfit or standing with a childhood friend often unleashes a torrent of memories. Study the pictures closely for details, such as …

- The paintings and other artwork on the wall.
- The curtains and drapes.
- The furniture.
- The knickknacks around the room.
- What people are wearing.
- The way you and others wore their hair.
- The look on people's faces.
- Body language—how people are standing, sitting, and so on.

What memorabilia do you have? Do you save theater programs, ticket stubs, campaign buttons, promotional items, and personal treasures that have meaning only to you? Did you save a bottle of sand from the first time you saw the ocean? Sort through your memorabilia to find the story behind each object. Here are some additional items you might use as inspiration:

- Cards, letters, e-mail
- Foreign money
- Dog tags
- Report cards
- Yearbooks

You can also visit places that were special to you in the past. If you're fortunate to live near the area where you spent your childhood or teen years, it's easy to drive by some of the places that were important in your life. These might include your childhood house, grade school, athletic fields, and so on. Seeing the actual site or building can often help to bring back memories. When you see your elementary school playground, for instance, you'll be amazed at how small everything is! The jungle gym seems so large when you are a child.

Stroll Down Memory Lane

Reading through library archives is another great source of inspiration. Most major libraries and historical societies have old newspapers, photographs, magazines, and objects that are available to the public. Find the ones that pertain to your childhood and adolescence. You'll find yourself spending hours looking at these because they conjure up so many memories. And it's usually possible to get copies of these documents. Libraries also have a variety of city directories and maps, as well as genealogical material like census records and so on.

You may also find it helpful to go to historical museums or antique shops. These are wonderful places to see items that are now considered collectible but were once everyday objects in our life. After all, how many people have kept old cereal boxes, cookie tins, or 78 rpm records? A friend uses the iron pots and pans her grandmother cooked with around the turn of the century in Germany. Imagine my friend's astonishment when she saw the same type of pots and pans on display at the Immigration Museum on Ellis Island!

All the Write Stuff

Skim a timeline of world events from your childhood and adolescence. Look especially for events that are linked to your life events. You can find world event time-

You can also interview family members and friends. They're a real gold mine of memories. If you're fortunate to still have living parents, grandparents, or aunts and uncles, talk to them. You'll be delighted at the stories they'll recall of your childhood. Here are some ideas:

- Silly things you said or did
- Places you visited as a family
- Your personality as a child
- Family secrets you were too young to know
- A description of a long-ago family party or reunion

Friends are another great way to stimulate some great memories. Think of the "remember whens" you could trigger with old school buddies or next-door neighbors.

Getting Organized

You may wish to arrange your topics in time order to organize your memories. Just start with a list of the important dates. Let's give it a whirl now. Fill in this timeline with some key milestones from your life.

Event	Date	Key Memories
birth	_____	_____
first day of school	_____	_____
school events	_____	_____
HS graduation	_____	_____
first job	_____	_____
military service	_____	_____
courtship	_____	_____
wedding	_____	_____
birth of children	_____	_____
subsequent jobs	_____	_____
important trips	_____	_____
honors and awards	_____	_____

Then add unusual events, such as …

- The time you caught the prize fish.

- The day you bought your first pet.

- The time your mother made you wear that ugly outfit.

- Your first date. Who was the lucky person? What did you do? (What *didn't* you do?)

- The day your two-year-old swallowed the crayons (coins, battery, etc.).

Congratulations! You've created a plan of action, so you're ready to write the story of your life. Add vivid details, dialogue, and description and you've created a memoir. Read on for some useful hints and ideas to make your writing easier and more enjoyable.

Drafting

Memoirs are unique because they are such personal writing. After all, you're telling your own true story, not a story you made up. Therefore, write in your own style, in a manner that's natural for you. Don't worry about perfect grammar or spelling on your first draft; remember, you'll correct all problems as you revise, edit, and proofread.

1. Outline

Before you draft, try outlining the main ideas. This can help you include everything you want to say in the correct order.

2. Use a Flow Chart

Jot down the main events of the incident you're telling, its broad strokes. Then arrange the events in chronological order, from first to last. A flow chart can help you straighten out the time tangle. Your flow chart may look like the following example from a friend's life, the first time he ran away from home. As you read this brief diagram, notice the vivid sensory details.

Age two, ran away ➡ diaper trailing and nose running ➡ ate pancakes with real maple syrup and fresh-picked berries ➡ parents found me and took me home

3. Consider Variations in the Narrative

Decide whether to use a flashback, flashforward, or straight chronology.

Words to the Wise

Flashbacks are scenes that break into the story to show an earlier part of the action. **Flashforwards** are scenes that show a later part of the action.

- A *flashback* is a scene that breaks into the story to show an earlier part of the action.

- A *flashforward* is a scene that shows a later part of the action.

Flashbacks and flashforwards help fill in missing information, explain the characters' actions, and advance the plot.

4. Use the First-Person Point of View

Use *I*, *me*, and *mine* to tell the story through your own eyes. Some memoirs are written in the third person, but I have always found these arrogant and artificial. But each to his own taste, as the cannibal said to the missionary.

5. Use Description

To bring the past to life, use images and descriptive details that appeal to the five senses. Describe sights, sounds, smells; use details that help your readers get a vivid mental picture of the person, place, or event. To get those details flowing, consider questions like these:

- What year did this take event place? How old was I? Who were my friends?

- What was the weather like?

- What was I wearing?

- What was the name of the street where we lived?

- What did that lobster roll taste like?

- How much did gas cost the summer I got my driver's license?

Wrong Turn

Warning: Painful memories do surface as you write memoirs, since writing about a disturbing experience relives that pain. The process is difficult, but it can be healing. It's also perfectly okay to avoid writing about difficult experiences.

6. Consider Memorabilia

Here are some items to consider adding at appropriate places in the memoir:

- Copies of your birth certificate, awards, honors, newspaper clippings

- Favorite family recipes

- Line drawings and illustrations

- Maps or drawings of important places

- Photographs

- Samples of your poetry, writing, calligraphy, and/or artwork

Enjoy the process. The writing should be fun, not a burden.

Don't worry about checking facts. Don't fret if you forgot someone's name or a particular date—just focus on getting the story written. You can go back later to get the details letter-perfect. Ignore spelling and grammar, too. That can all be fixed later.

Wrong Turn

You may wish to have family members and friends edit your memoir and offer comments. Decide if this will make it easier for you to write or more difficult. If it adds a layer of tension, keep the manuscript to yourself until you are ready to share it.

Start to fit the pieces together but don't worry about resolving any inconsistencies. The entire memoir can be fact-checked when you've finished drafting. Remember that everyone is human, which means that we all have flaws. Don't demand perfection of yourself, just writing.

Don't feel overwhelmed by time constraints; after all, no one says you have to finish the project this month or even this year. (And if anyone does put pressure on you, tell them to write their *own* memoir and leave you alone!)

Polishing Your Writing

As you revise and edit, make sure that your memoir has a clear focus. The nature of the experience itself may naturally indicate the focus, or you may wish to show the effects of the experience to underline its importance.

You may wish to create an editing checklist to help you focus on the key areas to revise and edit. Here's a model you can use:

- ❑ Is my writing concise but complete? The manuscript text should contain all the necessary information and details but no unnecessary words.

- ❑ Are my ideas linked in a logical way? You may wish to use transitions to connect related ideas.

- ❑ Is my writing clear? Be sure you included descriptions of each person so outsiders know who they are and why they are important to your narrative.

- ❑ Did I avoid giving the same information twice? Make your point and move on.

- ❑ Did I include sensory details, description, and dialogue to make my writing interesting? Try to include details that use all five senses.

Sharing Your Memoir

You may wish to reserve your memoir for your eyes only or share it with an audience. The choice is yours. Here are some ideas for publishing:

◆ Use a desktop word-processing program for a quick, easy, and inexpensive document. Not computer savvy? Local libraries often give free classes in using these programs. The libraries often have the computers and software available, too, for free.

◆ Photocopy your memoir yourself and bind it with a spiral spine. Many copy shops have a "drop off and pick up" service for only a few pennies more than a do-it-yourself job.

◆ Package your memoir in book form by taking the manuscript to a quick printer who can produce hardcover single copies at low cost. Many online companies offer the same "on demand" printing services.

◆ Post your memoir on your web page. You can also have it published on the Web by companies that specialize in this.

All the Write Stuff

If you give a copy of the memoir to family members and friends, you might wish to add a thank-you note to those who helped.

No matter which publishing route you choose, consider donating a copy of your memoir to your local historical society or library.

Enjoy a Model Memoir

When my first child was born 22 years ago, I started writing my memoirs. I included not only my own childhood among Long Island's potato and duck farms, but also stories from my parents, siblings, and in-laws. Here's an excerpt from the oral history I took from my father-in-law, Nick Rozakis, who was born March 9, 1915:

> I entered the Navy on May 8, 1943, and served until April 1, 1946. Since I was stationed in Chicago for the duration of the war, I tell everyone I successfully protected Lake Michigan from invasion, but I was really a fireman, a specialist F-3rd class. This isn't what I wanted to do at all, so I let a buddy talk me into taking the EDDY test for radio technician. I passed the test, but I flunked out of radio school in three weeks. I really wanted to write, so I applied to *Stars and*

Stripes. My application was approved (maybe because I said I was editor-in-chief of the high school newspaper, which wasn't true), but when I went for the interview they discovered I was a fireman so they said, "No writing for you!" Instead, I was sent to be an instructor in firefighters' school. This was the first time I got in trouble … but not the last.

My husband, a brilliant and celebrated writer, turned my fragmentary research into a brief memoir, which he delivered at his father's funeral:

"I entered the Navy on May 8, 1943, and served until April 1, 1946. Since I was stationed in Chicago for the duration of the war, I tell everyone I successfully protected Lake Michigan from invasion, but I was really a fireman, a Specialist F-3rd Class. This wasn't what I wanted to do at all … I really wanted to write, so I applied to *Stars & Stripes.* My application was approved (maybe because I said I was editor-in-chief of the high school newspaper, which wasn't true), but when I went for the interview they discovered I was a fireman, so they said, 'No writing for you!' Instead I was sent to be an instructor in the firefighters school."

So this was my father … a man who would downplay his achievements rather than boast about them … a man who would shrug off the bad things that happened and look forward to the next good thing … and a man who always had a story to tell that would make the people around him smile.

This was a man who spent 35 years in the NYC Fire Department, working at one time or another in every borough in the city, and retiring with the rank of captain. In the early 1960s, after the roof of a burning building fell on him, I read in the newspaper about "the late Louis Nicholas Rozakis" and said to him, "Doesn't this mean you're dead?" And he just looked at me and said, "Well, who are you going to believe—that newspaper or me?"

This was a man we called "Old Nas" because he took a line of Greek that roughly translates into "the red goats and the white mice should eat you" and turned it into "the Nasay Fahnay Chorus" that he got lots of his relatives to sing at weddings and other family functions.

But more importantly, this was a man who never lectured us on what to do or how to act. Instead, he taught by example and these are just a few of the lessons we learned:

If you have a responsibility, make sure you fulfill it. As a kid, I had trouble understanding why my father was always working strange hours. I mean, other dads worked from 9 to 5 Monday through Friday. Mine worked two nights and two days and sometimes weekends and invariably on Christmas or Thanksgiving.

And he was not just working in the fire department … he was working as an insurance broker and a tax accountant and a moving man … but all so that there was food on the table, clothes on our backs and a roof over our heads.

Treat everybody equally. When Clarence Williams, one of the first black men to join the NY Fire Dept, came to work, my father readily shared his locker with him. Of course, Clarence was warned not to touch the pictures of my dad's "nieces" that were hanging in the locker. By the way, I have a number of female cousins, but I've never been able to locate any of ones who posed for those scantly clad pictures.

Just "be there" for people. Without making a show of it, my father would help out relatives and friends who needed it, whether financially, physically or otherwise. He wasn't looking for glory; he just believed that it was the right thing to do.

Common sense is more important than all the rules ever written. My father liked to think of himself as a rebel, but he was much more the man who knew what the rules were and when it made sense to follow them … and when it was more practical to ignore them to get something done.

Nothing is gained by holding a grudge. No matter who did him wrong—and there were those who did over the years—my father never wasted time holding a grudge. He'd just kind of shrug it off and move on.

Smile … and make the people around you smile, too. In the past few days, I've talked with so many people whose lives my father touched and what they told me all boiled down to the same thing: He always made them smile.

And perhaps that's the most important lesson of all. My father used to say, "I don't tell lies … I tell stories." And I would reply with a quote from songwriter Mason Williams: "This is not a true tale, but who needs truth if it's dull?" My father loved to tell stories to people—and maybe the details would change a little if you heard the story more than once—but he always made you smile.

In fact, I suspect that right about now, there's probably a big backup in the line of people waiting to get into heaven. I figure my father's probably standing at the gate telling St. Peter about his adventures on the "Blind Date" radio show or when, annoyed that my brothers were fighting because one touched the other's piece of cake, he squashed every piece of the cake or about the time in the Sizzler when his shorts fell down.

And down here, we'll be missing the opportunity to hear those tales just one more time, left only to retell them in our own words. But if you believe as I do that no one truly dies until there's no one left who remembers him, well, my father's probably achieved immortality.

The Least You Need to Know

◆ *Memoir* is autobiography, a life story. It contains elements of fiction: plot, description, dialogue, characterization, and point of view.

◆ Memoirs enrich everyone's life by preserving the people, places, and events of the past.

◆ Your memoir can encompass your entire life or just a slice of it.

◆ There are many techniques for getting started and writing. Experiment with all of them and select the ones that work best for you.

Chapter 16

Glossies 101: Writing Magazine Articles

In This Chapter

◆ Discover today's sizzlin' sellers

◆ Craft lively leads

◆ Practice different methods of organizing the body of your article

◆ Learn how to write the most salable articles

Word alert! There's a magazine that needs your article right now. Why? Because you're a creative writer and magazines of all types and categories flourish in the United States. People may not make time to read books, but they sure are reading magazines. All things being equal, it's easier to publish a magazine article than a book.

According to the 2003 *World Almanac*, the best-selling magazine in 2001 (the latest year for which statistics are available) is *Reader's Digest*, with a paid circulation of 12,212,040 readers. The second-best seller, *TV Guide*, boasts nearly 10 million readers. *Better Homes and Gardens?* 7.6 million readers. *National Geographic* has sales of nearly 7 million. The *NRTA/AARP Bulletin* has a whopping circulation of nearly 22 million readers, but the magazine is given free to every member of AARP.

In this chapter, you'll first learn to write a magazine article, from top to toe, lead to conclusion. Then I focus on the most popular types of magazine articles and show you how to write each one. Next I describe different ways to develop your articles. You'll learn methods that apply to virtually every magazine article you write.

The Hit Parade

Below are the 25 magazines that boast the top paid circulation. Based on this list, what trends do you see? How many of these magazines and trends match your writing style and interests?

1. *Reader's Digest*
2. *TV Guide*
3. *Better Homes and Gardens*
4. *National Geographic*
5. *Good Housekeeping*
6. *Family Circle*
7. *Women's Day*
8. *Time*
9. *Ladies' Home Journal*
10. *My Generation*
11. *People Weekly*
12. *Rosie* (defunct)
13. *Westways*
14. *Home and Away*
15. *Sports Illustrated*
16. *Newsweek*
17. *Playboy*
18. *Prevention*
19. *Cosmopolitan*
20. *Guideposts*
21. *Via Magazine*
22. *American Legion Magazine*
23. *Maxim*
24. *Southern Living*
25. *Glamour*

(Source: The World Almanac and Book of Facts, 2003)

Leader of the Pack

Inquiring minds want to know—what *are* Americans reading in all these magazines? According to a comprehensive survey in the *World Almanac and Book of Facts*, the top 10 most popular topics for magazine articles are:

1. How-to articles (including self-help)
2. Interviews

3. Informational pieces

4. Inspirational pieces

5. Consumer-awareness articles

6. Entertainment

7. Opinion pieces

8. Humor articles

9. As-told-to (articles that retell harrowing experiences, such as members of the Donner Party eating each other)

10. Fillers (short, sometimes humorous fiction)

How can you get in on the writing? I'll teach you the nuts-and-bolts of writing magazine articles so you can craft your own lively and informative pieces. As Julie Andrews trilled in *The Sound of Music,* let's start at the very beginning, with the *lead.*

Take the Lead

The *lead* is the first sentence or paragraph of your article. It's the teaser. One or two paragraphs are all most readers are going to sample before they decide to stay with the article or do more exciting things like clean the lint from their navels. The lead fulfills a dual function:

1. It lets your reader know what the article will be about.

2. It entices your audience to read on.

Your lead is an audition. However, it has to do more than convince your reader that you can impart important facts or entertaining banter. Your lead must convince your readers that you're not taking their interest for granted, that you respect their investment of time, and that you're going to do everything in your power to repay their trust.

Leads follow three main formats: *startling statements, brief stories,* and *controversial statements.* In the following section are some samples of each kind. Match the method you select to the Big Three: topic, audience, and purpose. For example, don't use a startling statement about lowering the drinking age to start an article for Mothers Against Drunk Driving.

Words to the Wise

The **lead** is the opening sentence or paragraph in a magazine or newspaper article. It serves to introduce the topic and grab the reader's interest.

Sample Leads

Study the following three leads to see how each one accomplishes its purpose. As you read, decide how each method of introducing an article works with your personal writing style.

> **All the Write Stuff** _____
>
> Read the major feature magazines (or the magazines that you want to write for) and study their leads. Then adapt their techniques to your own writing style.

Startling statement:

The War Against Pornography

Of all the devices known to pornography—whips, chains, ropes, candles, razors, handcuffs, trusses, and objects too gross to describe here—of all these devices of debauchery, none, for the moment, is as important to the future of smut in America as a crisp, seven-page proposal now before the Los Angeles County Board of Supervisors.

Brief story:

The Mother of Kiddie Porn?

Tall, trim Catherine Wilson radiated wealth and style. She lived in a triplex home in a ritzy Los Angeles neighborhood and kept a small fleet of luxury cars. She took dutiful care of her children, personally driving them to their posh private schools every day. To all outward appearances, she was a pillar of the community—but, say L.A. police, a pillar erected on the muck and mire of child pornography. Working from a list of 5,000 names nationwide, Wilson allegedly built a $5,000,000-a-year mail-order business dealing in kiddie porn.

Controversial statement:

Pornography Through the Looking Glass

Television ushered in the new year by cracking what is breathlessly billed as "the last taboo": incest.

The 5 W's and H

Leads often answer the reporter's questions: *Who? What? When? Where? Why? How?* Some leads answer all the questions; other times, the lead addresses only the questions most important to the article. Read the following lead and then find the five W's:

An Offer We Couldn't Refuse

An important discovery I made recently about my uncle was that he introduced the mob to my family. This is important because my family came from Italy without any money and now we control most of Long Island. My Uncle Luigi gave us money, power, and control.

Who?_____

What?_____

When?_____

Where?_____

Why?_____

Sample Answers

Who?	The writer
What?	An important discovery about his uncle
When?	Recently
Where?	On Long Island
Why?	To gain power, money, and control

Next, we'll look closely at some specific types of magazine articles. You can match your writing style and interests with the requirements of each form. Then I'll show you some other writing methods you can use with many different types of articles.

Help Me, Rhonda: Writing Self-Help Articles

This publication cycle, self-help articles rule the pages. We're becoming a nation of wussies, and we need help from our magazine writers—you! Today's hottest of the hot topics include the following:

- Personal creativity
- Mood management
- Staying young
- Healing
- Mind/body integration

- Time management
- Relationship management
- Community building
- Being rooted
- Spirituality

It's not enough to jump on the bandwagon, however. You've got to see the wagon coming down the road and hop on it *before* it starts careening down publisher's row. Anticipate tomorrow's trends today if you want to write articles that sell.

Self-help articles follow a specific format:

- State the topic in a catchy way.
- Provide the information, the meat and potatoes.
- Conclude with general information/review the basics/offer a recommendation.

Depending on your topic, you may also want to include inspirational concepts, motivational tips, anecdotes, interviews, statistics, and recommendations. Here's the beginning of a how-to article on America's latest obsession: dieting.

Sin Food: A Fake Revival?

State the topic in a catchy way.

It was just a few years ago that food makers promised that fake fats would create a new world of guilt-free chocolate cake and french fries. They haven't delivered yet, but that hasn't stopped the industry from continuing its crusade. Here's an update from the front:

Provide the information, the meat and potatoes.

Salatrim: Nabisco claims it's more like real fat than the others. In other words, the reduced-calorie product recreates the texture of fat and has a better "mouth feel."

Olestra: Hundreds of millions of dollars later, Proctor & Gamble finally got the Feds to approve their fake fat, which the company is now using in fried snack foods such as potato chips. Good thing P & G hurried—Olestra's patents were almost running out.

Simplesse: Earlier this year, NutraSweet gave up its version of ice cream called "Simple Pleasures." Lousy mouth feel? Perhaps, but the fake stuff is still used in diet cheese and reduced-calorie mayonnaise.

Now, write the conclusion to this brief article. In a single paragraph, sum up with general information, review the basics, or offer a recommendation.

_____

_____

_____

_____

_____

_____

_____

Getting to Know You: Interviews and Profiles

An interview is nothing more than a conversation, hopefully with someone who is a lot richer, prettier, and sexier than you are. Otherwise, who would want to read your article?

Seriously, an interview with an everyday person can be just as interesting as an interview with a superstar. Like interviews, *profiles* are short biographies, normally addressing one facet of the person's life. A piece in *People* magazine, for example, might focus on a star's new film, while an interview in a local or regional magazine like *South Beach* could focus on a businessperson's latest venture. Whether your interview is funny or serious depends on your audience and writing style.

All the Write Stuff

Regardless of your topic and tone, always follow the cardinal rule of interviews and profiles: Get your facts correct. Check and double-check all data.

Here are 10 suggestions for conducting surefire interviews:

1. Always prepare your questions ahead of time. Write the questions out.

2. Prepare twice as many questions as you think you will need. You never know.

3. Bring a tape recorder, cassette tapes, and a spare set of batteries. Test all the equipment twice: once before you go to the interview and again when you set up.

4. Never tape-record a person without securing his or her prior approval, preferably in writing.

5. E-mail or call the person to set up the interview.

6. Follow up with a telephone call to make all the arrangements.

7. Call the day before the interview to confirm the time and place.

8. Dress like a professional.

9. Be polite and businesslike.

10. Send a follow-up thank-you letter.

From Famine to Gamin: Consumer Info

Consumer-information pieces follow the same format as how-to articles. Sometimes referred to as "service pieces," these articles provide information and make readers aware of important issues. The trick to these articles is hooking the reader right away. You have about five seconds before that page gets turned. In addition, you better provide a sound conclusion or your readers will be left feeling cheated and muttering in their soup. Check the articles in such magazines as *Reader's Digest, Consumer's Digest,* and *Ladies' Home Journal* for examples.

Basic Instinct: Methods of Organizing Information

Here are the basic ways that you can structure your articles:

♦ Problem/solution

♦ Cause/effect

♦ Comparison/contrast

♦ Spatial order

All the Write Stuff

Less pain, more gain: To get double duty out of your groundwork, write two (or more!) articles from one research session or interview. Then recycle the information from one article into another.

These patterns work with a wide variety of articles.

The structural problem you face in writing articles is how to include the basic information you have to supply. Otherwise, readers unfamiliar with the subject won't know what you're talking about. The following methods can help you solve this dilemma.

Problem/Solution

In these articles, writers state a problem and give one or more solutions. In most cases, the solutions will be arranged from most to least effective or least to most effective.

Here's the opening to a problem/solution article. As you read it, look for the problem and try to predict possible solutions.

A Taxing Situation

The deadline for filing federal income tax returns is less than two weeks away, triggering the familiar taxpayer laments about owing too much to the tax collector. The wealthiest taxpayers are as likely to complain as the less well-off, and sometimes more so, as the wealthy are more likely to owe the government money, while the poor are more likely to receive a refund. But everyone gripes about high taxes. And not without reason: Taxes *are* higher; each year the government takes more money out of our collective pockets. It's no surprise that the tax burden is distributed unfairly. How can the burden be redistributed to be more equitable?

The problem: How to make the tax burden more equitable.

The solution? That's your job. See what you can come up with.

_____

_____

_____

_____

_____

_____

_____

Cause/Effect

In these articles, you set up a situation and describe the results. In most cases, you will trace multiple causes and effects, even within a situation that seems relatively simple. To make your argument easier to follow, telegraph causes and effects with specific *transitions*. Here are the most common transitions used to show cause and effect:

- Because
- So
- So that
- Then
- Consequently
- Thus

- Since
- For
- For that reason
- Due to
- As a result
- Therefore

Below is an excerpt from an article developed by cause/effect. See how many causes and effects you can find. Check out some of the transition words, too.

That Lite Stuff

Diet foods aren't new, but the past few years have seen a striking upsurge in their popularity. Health-conscious Americans seem ready for foods that weigh less heavily on their consciences, and food manufacturers are eager to comply. Many products are marketed as "light" or "lite" versions of regular foods—that is, they contain less of such substances as fat, sugar, or alcohol (in the case of beer and wine) and they are usually lower in calories. The whole idea is so palatable that light foods and beverages are one of the fastest growing segments of the American food industry.

FDA Guidelines

Because consumers wonder whether those streamlined foods really do cut back on the calories, the Food and Drug Administration requires products claiming low or reduced calories to meet specific limits on calorie content. This helps consumers shopping with weight control in mind to choose products that represent genuine calorie reductions.

Under FDA guidelines, a food can be labeled "low calorie" only if a serving supplies no more than 40 calories and contains no more than 0.4 calories per gram (28.4 grams = 1 ounce). To be labeled "reduced calorie," a food must be at least one-third lower in calorie content than a similar food in which calories are not reduced, and it must not be nutritionally inferior to the unmodified food.

Food that is labeled low or reduced calorie must also bear nutrition labeling so consumers are not misled. Along with nutrients such as vitamins and minerals, the labels must also give the calories per serving and the serving size to which the figures relate, expressed in identifiable units of measurement such as a cup, slice, teaspoon, or fluid ounce.

Comparison/Contrast

When you write a comparison/contrast article, you show how two people, places, things, or ideas are the same (comparison) or different (contrast). With this type of article, you can present your material in two ways:

Method A	**Method B**
Introduction/Lead	Introduction/Lead
All of topic A	First aspect of topic A
All of topic B	First aspect of topic B
Conclusion	Second aspect of topic A
	Second aspect of topic B
	Conclusion

As with other types of organization, writers of comparison/contrast magazine articles often use transitions to alert readers to key parts of the argument. Following are the transitions you can use as you write these types of articles. First, some signal words that show comparison:

◆ Still

◆ In comparison

◆ Similarly

◆ Likewise

◆ Like

◆ In the same way

◆ At the same time

◆ In the same manner

Here are some signal words that show contrast:

◆ But

◆ Nevertheless

◆ However

◆ Yet

- Nonetheless

- Conversely

- Rather

- In contrast

- On the contrary

- On the other hand

Spatial Order

In this method, you arrange all the events in the article from a single reference point. Events can be arranged from top to bottom, bottom to top, inside to outside, outside to inside, point A to point B, and so on. You will probably use this method most often for descriptive articles, such as travelogues and descriptions of homes.

Below is part of an article whose details are arranged in spatial order. As you read the excerpt, try to see how the writer has arranged the details.

Nameless, Tennessee

Nameless, Tennessee, was a town of maybe ninety people if you pushed it, a dozen houses along the road, a couple of barns, same number of churches, a general merchandise store selling Fire Chief gasoline, and a community center with a lighted volleyball court. Behind the center was an open-roof, rusting metal privy with PAINT ME on the door; in the hollow of a nearby oak lay a full pint of Jack Daniel's Black Label.

Did you find that the writer followed the arrangement of stores along the main street?

The Least You Need to Know

- All things being equal, it's easier to publish a magazine article than a book.

- How-to articles (including self-help), interviews, and information articles are today's best-sellers.

- Effective openings, called *leads*, grab the readers' attention and reel them in fast.

- Use *transitions* to link related ideas and make it easier for readers to follow your logic.

For Better or Verse: Poetry

In This Chapter

- ◆ Define poetry
- ◆ Learn about the different poetic forms
- ◆ Pick the poetic techniques you need
- ◆ Write a poem

Poetry is one of the oldest arts, and until very recently, one of the most important ones. In olden days, poetry was as crucial as food, shelter, clothing, and super-premium ice cream (even though the latter hadn't been invented yet). Poetry was recited at important public occasions and learned by educated people as a part of their basic intellectual equipment.

A century ago, anyone aspiring to become a writer would, as a matter of course, practice writing poems, for they were considered the best way for a writer to learn order and discipline. To learn how to write an acceptable poem was to learn how to create art.

Today, poetry's place in the world has changed more radically than my hair color. In the past 75 to 100 years, poetry has declined from a noble art to become the bailiwick of small-time academics jostling each other for tenure. Poetry has lost its importance and much of its audience. Fortunately, large and small publishing houses still publish some poetry and a humble, hardy, and faithful band still read it.

In this chapter, I'll first teach you the basics of poetry. Then comes a detailed description of different poetic forms so you can decide which ones are right for your taste and talent. Throughout the chapter, I provide specific examples of famous poems that you can use as models. Finally, I'll have you write a little poem to get those creative juices flowing.

What Is Poetry and Why Should I Write It?

Poetry is like sex appeal: It's hard to define, but we know it when we see it. Edgar Allan Poe believed that poetry was "the rhythmical creation of beauty"; to Robert Frost, poetry was "a reaching out toward expression, an effort to find fulfillment." Percy Bysshe Shelley wrote, "Poetry is the record of the best and happiest moments of the best minds, the very image of life expressed in its eternal truth."

Try these definitions of poetry. See which suits your vision of your craft. Poetry is a type of literature …

- In which words are selected for their beauty, sound, and power to express feelings.

- That uses a kind of language that is more intense and expressive than everyday speech.

- That presents the speaker's emotions as they are aroused by beauty, experience, or attachment.

- That provides a fresh, unexpected way of looking at things.

- That gives pleasure, whether it appeals to the senses, emotion, or intellect.

Write Angles

The word *poem* comes from an ancient Greek word meaning "to make, compose." The implication is important: Poetry is made and the poet is the maker. The word *made* suggests materials; the word *maker* suggests effort.

To Emily Dickinson, poetry was …

My letter to the World
That never wrote to Me—
The simple News that Nature Told—
With tender Majesty
Her Message is committed
To Hands I cannot see
For love of Her—Sweet—countrymen—
Judge tenderly—of Me.

A Real Slugfest: Poetry vs. Prose

"Prose," claimed Samuel Taylor Coleridge, "consists of words in their best order. Poetry consists of the *best* words in the *best* order." The primary difference between poetry and prose is *concreteness*. A single word of poetry says far more than a single word of prose. That's because the language in poetry resonates worlds of other meaning. In a sense, the poet distills meaning in brief and vivid phrases. The poet's use of economy and suggestion evokes a response in the reader.

Taking the Road Less Traveled By: Becoming a Poet

It's not easy to write poetry (especially in today's world!), and most people aren't willing to do that much work for what seems like so little reward. But if you can write a single sonnet to equal one of Shakespeare's, you can forever call yourself a creative writer.

But regardless of what poems you eventually produce, writing poetry is crucial to your progress as a creative writer. Learning to work within strict forms, finding effective rhythms, selecting and using words properly, and constructing poems carefully will make you a better writer in any genre.

Poetic Terms: Walk the Walk and Talk the Talk

Since poetry comes in a wide range of forms, from haiku to rock lyrics, it's not a simple genre to define. Fortunately, we *can* put our finger on the elements that distinguish poetry from prose, so you can tell what you're writing and learn to write it with more precision.

Studying the following Big Three poetic terms and their definitions can help you learn to color in the lines on the blank canvas.

1. *Couplet:* two related lines of poetry, which often rhyme.

   True wit is Nature to advantage dressed,
   What oft was thought, but ne'er so well expressed.
   —Alexander Pope

2. *Refrain:* a line or a group of lines that are repeated at the end of a poem or song.

   Refrains serve to reinforce the main point and create musical effects. Folk singer Harry Chapin used a refrain at the end of each verse of his ballad "Cat's Cradle":

   Cat's in the cradle and the silver spoon
   Little boy blue and the man in the moon …
   —Harry Chapin

3. *Stanza:* a group of lines in a poem, like a paragraph in prose.

Each stanza presents one complete idea. Here's a stanza of poetry from Alexander Pope's *An Essay on Criticism:*

True ease in writing comes from art, not chance,
As those move easiest who have learned to dance.
'Tis not enough no harshness gives offense,
The sound must seem an echo of the sense.
—Alexander Pope

Poetic Tastes Change, So Do Your Own Thing

As conversation has given way to sound bites and facts to factoids, so the style of poetry has changed over the years. What was the crème de la crème of poetry in the past strikes some modern readers as sour milk.

Here's a stanza from an early-nineteenth-century poem called "A Tender Lay." The title alone is a hoot.

Be gentle to the new laid egg,
For eggs are brilliant things;
They cannot fly until they're hatched,
And have a pair of wings.

Some modern readers would consider this snippet as sappy as *Miracle on 34th Street* or *It's a Wonderful Life*. It's too mushy for jaded modern literary taste, like marshmallow fluff on white bread.

Now, here's a stanza from an Emily Dickinson poem. Even though Emily lived in the nineteenth century (1830–1886), she went her own way. How similar is this poem to your poetic style?

What shall I do when the Summer troubles—
What, when the Rose is ripe—
What when the Eggs fly off in Music
From the Maple Keep?

Dickinson's poems do not always rhyme, and her figurative language was too striking for the taste of her time. As a result, of her 1,775 poems, only seven were published during her lifetime, and all anonymously. It wasn't until 1955 that Dickinson's poems were accepted and even appreciated. Now Emily Dickinson is considered the Founding Mother of American Poetry, revered for her concrete imagery, forceful language, and unique style.

What does this mean for you, an aspiring poet? It means that you can study poems in magazines such as *The New Yorker, The Atlantic Monthly, Poetry, Quarterly West, Prairie Schooner,* and *Harpers* to see what today's poetry editors are buying in the big market magazines. Or, you can write what you wish. You're just as likely to find a publisher, and your poetry will be more honest.

Fortunately, poetry is a matter of individual taste. There is something to suit everyone. Don't let anyone box your muse into a poetic parcel. With poetry, individual voice, wrapped up in craftsmanship, is the whole point. Some people feel that modern poetry can be totally random if it's heartfelt, but in fact, even the most random-seeming language must be carefully crafted if it's to be good poetry.

All the Write Stuff

One of the most important resources for poets of all stripes is *Poets and Writers Magazine* (Poets and Writers, 72 Spring St., New York, NY 10012). This journal includes interviews with poets and writers, articles by editors, lists of grants and awards, and ads from publishers seeking poems for magazines, chapbooks (small book or pamphlet format), and anthologies.

Remembrance of Flings Past: Poetic Techniques

A good poet has as many tools and strict procedures as any handyman, even though in good poetry that structure may not be forced and obvious. Below is a list of the most useful poetic techniques. Mastering them will teach you why something poetic works on paper, or why it doesn't. You may use all of these techniques all the time, but it's more likely that you'll pick and choose depending on the subject, purpose, and audience in each poem.

Alliteration

Alliteration is the repetition of initial consonant sounds in several words in a sentence or line of poetry. Poets use alliteration to create musical effects, link related ideas, stress certain words, or mimic specific sounds. Here's an example from Dylan Thomas's "Fern Hill": "About the lilting house and happy as the grass was green." The phrase shows alliteration in the repetition of the *h* in *house* and *happy* and the *gr* in *grass* and *green*.

Blank Verse

Blank verse is unrhymed poetry, usually written in iambic pentameter (see "Meter" below for a discussion of iambic pentameter). Many English poets wrote in blank verse because it captures the natural rhythm of speech. Here's an example by William Shakespeare: "Time hath, my Lord, a wallet at his back,/Wherein he puts alms for oblivion."

Catalog

The *catalog technique* in poetry predates L.L. Bean and Victoria's Secret—Homer used it around 800 B.C.E., John Milton in the seventeenth century, and greedy children still use it around Christmas. It's nothing more than a list, but when used with brio, it's as overwhelming as Toys "R" Us on Christmas Eve.

Use Sonnet #43 from Elizabeth Barrett Browning's famous *Sonnets from the Portuguese* as a model of the catalog. The sonnet lists the ways she loves her husband.

> How do I love thee? Let me count the ways.
> I love thee to the depth and breadth and height
> My soul can reach, when feeling out of sight
> For the ends of Being and ideal Grace.
> I love thee to the level of everyday's
> Most quiet need, by sun and candlelight.
> I love thee freely, as men strive for Right;
> I love thee purely, as they turn from Praise.
> I love thee with the passion put to use
> In my old griefs, and with my childhood's faith.
> I love thee with a love I seemed to lose
> With my lost saints—I love thee with the breath,
> Smiles, tears, of all my life!—and, if God choose,
> I shall but love thee better after death.

Write Angles

Elizabeth Barrett Browning (1806–1861) was England's most famous female poet during her lifetime. She's most famous for *Sonnets from the Portuguese*, 44 sonnets that record her love for husband (and fellow poet) Robert Browning.

Figurative Language

Figurative language consists of words and expressions not meant to be taken literally. Figurative language uses words in fresh, new ways to appeal to the imagination. Figures of speech include *similes*, *metaphors*, *extended metaphors*, *hyperbole*, and *personification*. These are covered in the "Glossary of Writing Terms."

Images

An *image* is a word that appeals to one or more of our five senses: sight, hearing, taste, touch, or smell. Imagery can be found in all sorts of writing, but it's most common in poetry. The term *imagery* comes from the Imagism movement, which flourished during the early part of the twentieth century.

As sleek and stripped down as Sharon Stone, Imagism hawked radical and original images and hard truths. Shunning rhythm and rhyme, the Imagists depended on the power of the image itself to arrest attention and convey emotion. Here is a classic Imagist poem by Ezra Pound (1885–1972).

"In a Station of the Metro"

The apparition of these faces in the crowd;
Petals on a wet, black bough.

Meter

In life, a meter is an odd-shaped device that demands quarters on a regular basis. In writing, *meter* is a poem's rhythmical pattern.

Poetic meter is created by a pattern of stressed and unstressed syllables arranged in metrical *feet*. A poetic *foot* is a group of stressed and unstressed syllables in a line of poetry. A foot is composed of either two or three syllables, such that the nature of the foot is determined by the placement of the accent. There are six basic types of metrical feet in English. The first four are very common; the last two are as rare as a really bad hair day. The most common meter in English poetry is called *iambic pentameter*. It is a pattern of five feet, each having one unstressed syllable and one stressed one.

Poetic foot	Symbol	Definition
iamb	_ ´	1 unstressed, 1 stressed syllable
anapest	_ _ ´	2 unstressed, 1 stressed syllable
trochee	´ _	1 stressed, 1 unstressed syllable
dactyl	´ _ _	1 stressed, 2 unstressed syllables
spondee	´ ´	2 stressed syllables
pyrrhic	_ _	2 unstressed syllables

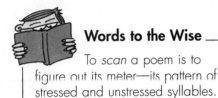

Here are some examples:

Iamb	I taste/a liq/uor nev/er brewed
Anapest	The Assyr/ian came down/like the wolf/on the fold
Trochee	Earth, re/ceive an/honored/guest
Dactyl	Out of the/cradle/endlessly/rocking

Onomatopoeia

Onomatopoeia is the use of words to imitate the sounds they describe. Here are three examples: *crack*, *hiss*, and *buzz*. Onomatopoeia is used to create musical effects and to reinforce meaning. Contemporary Irish poet Seamus Heaney uses onomatopoeia in his poem "Churning Day" to suggest the sounds of butter making:

> My mother took turn first, set up rhythms
> that slugged and thumped for hours. Arms ached.
> Hands blistered. Cheeks and clothes were splattered
> with flabbymilk.

Rock Around the Clock: Rhyme

Rhyme is the repetition of sounds at the end of words. Rhyming the last line of poems creates *end rhyme*; rhyming words in the middle of lines creates *internal rhyme*. Here is an example of internal rhyme: "Each narrow cell in which we dwell." *Cell* and *dwell* have internal rhyme because they share the same sound and one of the words is set in the middle of the line. The *rhyme scheme* in a poem is a regular pattern of words that end with the same sound.

Here's some strong end rhyme for you, courtesy of our old buddy William Blake:

> I was angry with my friend:
> I told my wrath, my wrath did end.
> I was angry with my foe:
> I told it not, my wrath did grow.

Friend rhymes with *end*; *foe* rhymes with *grow*.

Poets use rhyme to create a musical sound, meaning, and structure. Nowadays, except for Hallmark cards, rhyme is as out as John Denver, Crisco, and laugh lines. But there are those of us who like John Denver, Crisco, and laugh lines. To thine own self be true; there's nothing wrong with sticking by your style, even if it's out of style at the moment. Who knows what tomorrow will bring?

Groovin' to the Beat: Rhythm

Rhythm is the pattern of stressed and unstressed words that create a beat, as in music. Rhythm is created by poetic meter. When you write a poem, use the punctuation and capitalization in each line to help your reader decide where to pause and what words to stress to make the rhythm clear. Traditional poetry follows a regular rhythmical pattern; much of modern poetry does not.

Write Angles
Prose, as well as poetry, has rhythm. The artful arrangement of words creates a graceful, seemingly artless flow of ideas. Read your favorite novel out loud to see if you can sense the writer's rhythm.

Thirty-One Flavors and Fifty-Seven Varieties

Poetry takes all life as its realm. Its main concern is not with beauty, moral truth, or persuasion, but with experience. Beauty and truth are parts of experience, and so poetry often interprets them. But poetry as a whole is concerned with all types of experience, the good and the bad, the beautiful and the ugly, the strange and the common.

To embrace all these themes, poetry must take a variety of different forms. While some famous poets have become closely linked to specific forms (Shakespeare and the sonnet, Dylan Thomas and the villanelle, Robert Frost and the lyric), others experiment with many different forms. I suggest that you do the same. Try 'em all and see which ones suit your style, audience, and purpose.

Ballads

A *ballad* is a story told in song form. Ancient ballads such as "Sir Patrick Spens" were passed down by word of mouth from person to person; as a result, the words are simple and the ballad has a strong beat. Two of the most famous literary ballads are Coleridge's "Rime of the Ancient Mariner" and Keats's "La Belle Dame Sans Merci." They are both way too long to reprint here, but make great models for your own ballads.

Epics

These are long narratives in an elevated style, presenting highborn characters in a series of adventures that depict key events in the history of a nation. Homer's *Iliad* and *Odyssey* are epics. I know you have both of these memorized.

Free Verse

Free verse isn't poetry marked down for a quick sale. Rather, it's poetry without a regular pattern of rhyme and meter. This kind of verse uses a rhythm that reinforces the meaning and sounds of spoken language in lines of different length. Walt Whitman (1819–1892) gets the nod as the inventor of the form. (Noted word slinger Robert Frost, a good ol' boy from Vermont, said that writing free verse is like playing tennis with the net down.) Here's a sample of Whitman's free verse, the opening lines of "Out of the Cradle, Endlessly Rocking." Notice the strong rhythm, uneven lines, repetition, and alliteration:

> Out of the cradle, endlessly rocking,
> Out of the mocking-bird's throat, the musical shuttle,
> Out of the Ninth-month midnight,
> Over the sterile sands and the fields beyond where the child leaving his bed
> wandered alone, bareheaded, barefoot …

Haiku

Haiku is a Japanese poetic form that uses three lines for a total of 17 syllables. The first and third lines have five syllables each; the second line has seven syllables. Haiku creates a distinct emotion and suggests a spiritual insight, often through images from nature. Use the following two samples as models. They were written by the Japanese poet Moritake (1452–1540).

> The falling flower
> I saw drift back to the branch
> Was a butterfly.

> Fallen flowers rise
> back to the branch—I watch:
> oh … butterflies!

Hooked on Sonnets

A *sonnet* is a lyric poem of 14 lines written in iambic pentameter (a rhythm with five accents in each line). Originated by Italian poets during the thirteenth century, the form reached perfection a century later in the works of Petrarch and came to be known as the *Petrarchan* or *Italian* sonnet.

To scan the rhyme, assign a letter to each new sound. For example, if line #1 ends with *oe'r*, give it the letter *a*. If line #2 ends with *bed*, assign the letter *b*. If line #3 ends with *led*, assign *b*, because *bed* and *led* have the same sound. And so on.

The first eight lines, called the *octave*, rhyme *a-b-b-a*, *a-b-b-a*, and present the problem; the concluding six lines, called the *sestet*, rhyme *c-d-e*, *c-d-e*, and resolve the problem.

Here's a Petrarchan sonnet by Henry Wadsworth Longfellow you can use to learn the form. You might wish to scan the rhyme by assigning a letter to each end sound.

> **Nature**
>
> As a fond mother, when the day is o'er,
> Leads by the hand her little child to bed,
> Half willing, half reluctant to be led,
> And leave his broken playthings on the floor,
> Still gazing at them through the open door,
> Nor wholly reassured and comforted
> By promises of others in their stead,
> Which, though more splendid, may not please him more;
> So Nature deals with us, and takes away
> Our playthings one by one, and by the hand
> Leads us to rest so gently, that we go
> Scarce knowing if we wish to go or stay,
> Being too full of sleep to understand
> How far the unknown transcends the what we know.

See how "Nature" uses these features of the Petrarchan sonnet:

♦ Structure: The octave presents the problem—an unwillingness to let go of life. The sestet resolves the problem: Death is not to be feared because of the unimaginable glories of heaven.

♦ Length: There are 14 lines.

♦ Rhythm: The sonnet is iambic pentameter because it has five accents in each line and uses the unstressed/stressed pattern.

◆ Rhyme: Here is the rhyme scheme:

Word	Rhyme
o'er	a
bed	b
led	b
floor	a
door	a
comforted	b
stead	b
more	a
away	c
hand	d
go	e
stay	c
understand	d
know	e

Sixteenth-century English poets swiped the sonnet format but changed the rhyme to *a-b-a-b, c-d-c-d, e-f-e-f, g-g*. With the *Elizabethan* (or *Shakespearean*) sonnet, the poet describes the problem in the first 12 lines and resolves it in the final couplet. Shakespeare pounced on the form and succeeded in doing for the love sonnet what Godiva did for chocolate.

Here's an English sonnet by Edna St. Vincent Millay that will help you learn this poetic form:

Pity Me Not

Pity me not because the light of day
At close of day no longer walks the sky;
Pity me not for beauties passed away
From field and thicket as the year goes by;
Pity me not the waning of the moon,
Nor that the ebbing tide goes out to sea,
Nor that a man's desire is hushed so soon,
And you no longer look with love on me.
This I have known always: Love is no more
Than the wide blossom which the wind assails,
Than the great tide that treads the shifting shore,
Strewing fresh wreckage gathered in the gales;
Pity me that the heart is slow to learn
What the swift mind beholds at every turn.

Let's analyze the form so you can make it your own:

- Structure: The first 12 lines describe the situation—the poet is growing older and her lover no longer desires her. The final couplet resolves the problem—"At last, I understand what is happening in my life with my heart as well as with my mind."

- Length: There are 14 lines.

- Rhythm: The sonnet is iambic pentameter because it has five accents in each line and uses the unstressed/stressed pattern.

- Rhyme: Here is the rhyme scheme:

Word	Rhyme
day	a
sky	b
away	a
by	b
moon	c
sea	d
soon	c
me	d
more	e
assails	f
shore	e
gales	f
learn	g
turn	g

Limerick

A *limerick* is a type of humorous poetry. Limericks have five lines, a strong rhyme, and a set rhythm: *a-a-b-b-a*. The first, second, and fifth lines rhyme with each other, and the third and fourth rhyme with each other. The rhyming words are sometimes misspelled to create humor. Most limericks are bawdy; the clean ones usually don't involve buckets and girls from Nantucket. I had to look far and wide to find a limerick clean enough to reprint that didn't involve buckets and Nantucket:

> There was a young lady of Lynn
> Who was so uncommonly thin
> That when she essayed
> To drink lemonade
> She slipped through the straw and fell in.

Nearly all limericks are anonymous. If not written anonymously, they soon become so, because of repeated oral transmission and reprinting without credit.

Lyric Poetry

Poet Emily Dickinson, who made the *Phantom of the Opera* look like a party animal, was a champ at writing lyric poems. These are brief, musical poems that present a speaker's feelings. In the distant past, people sang lyrics as they played stringlike instruments called *lyres*. This is where we get the word *lyric*.

Narrative Poetry

Narrative poetry tells a story, either through a narrative storyline told objectively or through a dramatized situation. Examples of narrative storylines include Alfred Noye's "The Highwayman" and Robert Browning's "The Pied Piper of Hamelin." An example of a dramatized situation is Robert Frost's poem "The Death of the Hired Man."

A special form of the dramatized situation is the *dramatic monologue*, in which a character speaks, using the first-person point of view. We don't hear the other character's responses, but we can infer them from hints in the poem. It's like listening to one end of a phone conversation. Use Robert Browning's "My Last Duchess" as a model.

Give It a Shot

It's time to flex your poetic muscles and do some heavy word lifting. Use the following guidelines to write a poem about yourself. Then feel free to adapt the format to create other poems.

Line 1: Your first name

_____

Line 2: Four traits that describe you

_____

Line 3: Relative of

_____

Line 4: Lover of ... _____ (3 people or ideas)

Line 5: Who feels _____ (3 responses)

Line 6: Who needs _____ (3 responses)

Line 7: Who gives _____ (3 responses)

Line 8: Who fears _____ (3 responses)

Line 9: Who would like to see _____ (3 responses)

Line 10: Resident of _____ (city, etc.)

Line 11: Your last name _____

The Least You Need to Know

◆ Everyone defines poetry a different way; take it as "a type of literature in which words are selected for their beauty, sound, and power to express emotion."

◆ There is a wide variety of poetic forms and styles; feel free to express yourself— but learn the techniques and forms.

◆ Study poems as you would short stories and novels.

◆ As Archibald MacLeish said in his poem "Ars Poetica,"

A poem should not mean
But be.

Part 4

Drama, Scripts, and Screenplays

He's as nervous as a badly abused laboratory animal, first kept awake for too long, periodically electrocuted, then given large doses of dangerous drugs and placed in a maze with no exit. In short, he's a scriptwriter.

Okay, every job has *some* stress, but writing a script doesn't have to be as painful as root canal, an IRS audit, or an elementary school orchestra concert. In this part, I'll show you how to write dramatic literature—plays and scripts—without becoming a wreck. The process may not be as easy as programming your VCR or as peaceful as the pit of the Chicago Board of Trade, but we'll have a glorious time anyway.

Chapter 18

Finding the Shakespeare in *You:* Writing Drama

In This Chapter

- ◆ Learn dramatic terms
- ◆ Survey the different forms that drama can take
- ◆ Create structure, conflict, and dialogue in your plays
- ◆ Revise and edit your plays
- ◆ Package and present the play

Ever since Zog returned to the cave and put on a show about the size of the saber-toothed tiger that got away, people have delighted in theater. Although we don't have Zog's complete script, we do know from cave paintings and various artifacts such as primitive masks, wigs, and costumes, that men and women since prehistoric times have enjoyed the spectacle of theater.

This chapter opens with a survey of dramatic terms. Then comes a discussion of the different types of drama, so you'll be able to pick the dramatic form that suits your talent and creativity. I'll teach you how to structure dramatic plots, invent exciting conflicts, and create realistic dialogue. Next, you'll revise and edit your dramatic writing. Finally, it's time to package and present the play. Let's raise the curtain.

Aside from That, Mrs. Lincoln, How Did You Like the Play?

Drama is literature written to be performed in front of an audience. The elements of drama are similar to the other forms of fiction you've learned in *The Complete Idiot's Guide to Creative Writing*, such as novels and short stories, but in drama, actors play the parts of characters and tell the story through their interpretation of your words.

Words to the Wise

Drama is a piece of literature written to be performed for an audience. The actors tell the story through their actions.

Like novels and short stories, plays follow a defined format. For example, you've learned that short stories are a specific length and deal with one main character, conflict, and setting. Plays follow an equally specific set of conventions. These conventions bring up some drama-specific concepts and terms. Here are the top 10 playwriting terms that you need to know to write with assurance.

1. *Acts.* Plays consist of one or more *acts*, the main divisions in the action.

2. *Cast of Characters.* Most scripts begin with a list of all the characters in the play. Sometimes each character is described briefly, and these descriptions often show the relationships among characters. The characters are generally listed in the order in which they appear on stage.

   Here's part of the cast of characters from George Bernard Shaw's play *Major Barbara:*

   SIR ANDREW UNDERSHAFT

   LADY BRITOMART UNDERSHAFT, *his wife*

   BARBARA, *his elder daughter, a Major in the Salvation Army*

   SARAH, *his younger daughter*

   STEPHEN, *his son*

   ADOLPHUS CUSINS, *a professor of Greek, in love with Barbara*

   CHARLES LOMAX, *a young-man-about-town engaged to Barbara*

3. *Dialogue.* Plays are written almost entirely in *dialogue*, conversation between two or more actors.

In novels and short stories, dialogue is set off with quotation marks. This is rarely the case in a play. In plays, the characters' names are capitalized and the dialogue follows without any quotation marks. Start a new paragraph for each speaker's words. Here's an example:

STEPHEN: Not at all, mother.

LADY BRITOMART: Don't make excuses, Stephen.

4. *Playwright.* A playwright is a person who writes a play. From now on, that's you.

5. *Props.* Props are objects that the actors need to perform the play, such as books, knives, and bowls.

6. *Scenes.* Acts may be further divided into scenes.

7. *Scenery.* These are the decorations on stage that help show the play's setting.

8. *Script.* The script is the written form of a drama.

9. *Stage Directions.* Stage directions are instructions to the actors, producer, and director telling them how to perform the play and set the stage. Stage directions are included in the text of the play, written in parentheses or italics. They can describe how actors should speak, what they should wear, and what scenery should be used, for example.

   Here's a sample from Shaw's *Major Barbara.* The stage directions are easy to spot because they are in italics and parentheses.

   LADY BRITOMART: Bring me my cushion. (*He takes the cushion from the chair at the desk and arranges it for her as she sits down on the settee.*) Sit down. (*He sits down and fingers his tie nervously.*) Don't fiddle with your tie, Stephen: there is nothing the matter with it.

10. *Soliloquy.* A soliloquy is a speech one character speaks while alone on the stage. Sometimes there will be other characters present. If this is the case, they seem to become instantly deaf. In the soliloquy, the character often voices his or her deepest thoughts or concerns. Hamlet's "To be or not to be" soliloquy is an example.

Write Angles

The first dramas in England were the miracle plays and morality plays of the Middle Ages. Miracle plays told biblical stories; morality plays, such as *Everyman*, personified key virtues and vices.

All the World's a Stage

Playwriting has come a long way since Zog and his saber-toothed tiger. In the last century alone, "play" writing has come to include works not only for the stage but for the screen as well. Since writing for television and the movies is such a fast-growing field, I treat it separately in chapters 19 and 20. In this chapter, we're going to concentrate on the characteristics of stage plays.

Works for the stage fall into three categories:

1. *Full-length plays.* A full-length play is often a two-act play with one intermission or a 90-minute play with no intermission. Few three-act plays are produced any more because many producers feel that audiences have developed a shorter attention span. The script for an average full-length play is 85 to 90 pages long.

2. *One-act plays.* One-act plays usually feature five to seven characters and one or two locations. The script runs about 30–40 pages.

3. *Musicals.* Musicals use songs to advance the plot, develop the characters, and create the mood and tone. The length of their scripts depends on whether they are full-length or one-act plays.

The vanilla and chocolate of drama are *comedy* and *tragedy.* A traditional subdivision of comedy is *farce.* But in these wild and wacky days, we get hybrid dramatic forms of all kinds. Some work well, but others seem about as successful as chicken-fat ripple ice cream.

Below is a list of the different types of drama being written today. Use this list to decide which type or types suit your style, purpose, topic, and audience.

◆ *Absurdism.* Plays that show that the human condition is irrational and silly. In *Rhinoceros,* for example, a rhinoceros runs through the center of town. *Waiting for Godot* (by Samuel Beckett) is another example.

◆ *Black Comedies.* Bad things happen to the characters, but the events are so horrible that they're funny. *M*A*S*H,* for instance, shows the horrors of war through comedy.

◆ *Comedy.* A *comedy* is a humorous play that has a happy ending. *The Producers* comes to mind.

◆ *Docudramas.* Plays (and television shows) with a realistic, documentary tone are called docudramas. Steven Spielberg's award-winning story of the Holocaust, *Schindler's List,* is a docudrama.

- *Dramadies*. A happy/sad combo, the hog and heifer of theater. Neil Simon has penned a few of these.

- *Farce*. A *farce* is a humorous play that is based on a silly plot, ridiculous situations, and comic dialogue. The characters are usually one-dimensional stereotypical figures. They often find themselves in situations that start out normally but turn absurd. Often, humor is created through an identity switch and the other characters' reaction to it. Moliere's *The Doctor in Spite of Himself*, Chekhov's *The Bear*, and W. S. Gilbert's plays are farces.

- *Naturalism*. Characters are closely analyzed in a kind of artistic dissection. Humans are at the mercy of the forces of nature. Clifford Odets' *Awake and Sing* is a naturalistic drama.

- *Satires*. The vices of a person, society, or civilization are held up to ridicule. Check out Moliere's *The Misanthrope*.

- *Surrealism*. Plays that interpret the unconsciousness. Harold Pinter (*The Dumb Waiter*) and Edward Albee (*The Zoo Story*) are famous for writing surrealistic plays.

- *Tragedy*. The leading character has a fatal flaw or weakness that brings about his or her downfall. This results in a disastrous ending, usually death. The most common flaw is overwhelming pride. Arthur Miller's *Death of a Salesman* is likely the most outstanding contemporary American tragedy.

Days of Whine and Poses: Structuring Your Play

About 2,300 years ago, Aristotle pointed out in the first great piece of dramatic criticism, *The Poetics*, that the most important element of theater is the *plot*. Aristotle actually called it the *fable*, and some people call it the *story*. Whatever you call it, there can be little argument that what goes on and how it happens is the single most important consideration for the dramatist.

In the past, audiences strolled into the theater, sat down, and listened to one or more characters introduce the other characters, setting, and action. The character might have spoken into a telephone or addressed a minor character. The ancient Greeks used a chorus to accomplish the same thing. It was the classic beginning, middle, and end structure you learned in Chapter 8. Not in today's theater.

Today, an effective play starts with action. The action serves to define the main character, suck in the audience, and propel the play forward. No more leisurely exposition in these frantic days.

Remember the plot diagram you learned in Chapter 8. You use the same structure when you build a play, with a few variations:

♦ *Structuring a Full-Length Play.* If you're writing a full-length play, use the diagram twice. Build a climax at the end of Act One and provide a *hook*, a thread of unfinished action that will set off the action in Act Two. Then repeat the diagram and build to a full climax at the end of Act Two.

♦ *Structuring a One-Act Play.* With a one-act play, use a compressed version of the plot structure. There will be fewer conflicts and only one climax.

Why Can't a Woman Be More Like a Man? Conflict

Regardless of the structure you ultimately select for your action, a play without conflict is like freeze-dried kelp made of recycled Styrofoam: empty and tasteless. You'll recall that *conflict* in literature is a struggle or fight. Conflict makes a play interesting because readers want to find out the outcome.

As you learned in Chapter 9, there are two kinds of conflict. In an *external conflict*, characters struggle against a force outside themselves. In Tennessee Williams' steamy drama *A Streetcar Named Desire*, Blanche DuBois has an external conflict with her hot brother-in-law, Stanley Kowalski. In an *internal conflict*, characters battle a force within themselves, as Biff Loman does in Miller's *Death of a Salesman*. Plays, as with novels and short stories, often contain both external and internal conflicts. This is true in Arthur Miller's *The Crucible*, for example, as John Proctor battles with Abigail Williams and his own conscience.

PC or Not PC: Dialogue

Since plays use speech to develop action and character, dialogue is the linchpin of successful drama. Great dialogue can make your play; aimless prattle can break it. Dialogue is not just talk.

Here are some hints for creating realistic, effective dialogue in your plays:

♦ Think of each character's speech as a fingerprint: unique. Match the level of diction to the character's personality. Think how Archie Bunker's use of slang and non-PC language conveyed his character.

♦ To create effective, realistic dialogue, read what you've written into a tape recorder. Then play it back and see if each character emerges as an individual.

◆ Make sure there is an active motive behind what your characters say. Everything they say must be linked to a specific action or feeling.

◆ Use fragments. People rarely speak in complete sentences. Using too many complete sentences can make your characters sound stilted and artificial.

◆ Create a rhythm in each character's speech. Listen to everyday speech patterns to capture these beats.

Good Help Is Hard to Find: Revising and Editing

Revising and editing are vital steps in writing any creative literature. Use the following checklist to focus your work. Make photocopies and use a new sheet each time you go back over your play.

1. Structure

   ❏ Is the opening exciting?

   ❏ Is there adequate character development?

   ❏ Is there conflict and action?

   ❏ Is the plot clear and unified?

   ❏ Does the play fall within a recognizable category and follow the conventions of that form?

2. Characters

   ❏ Is each character clearly defined?

   ❏ Are the characters consistent?

   ❏ Are the main characters fully developed?

   ❏ Are the minor characters important enough in the plot to be included?

3. Conflict

   ❏ Is the conflict introduced in a believable manner?

   ❏ Is the conflict dramatic and exciting?

   ❏ Is the conflict resolved in a logical way?

   ❏ Is the play something that *you* would enjoy seeing?

4. Dialogue

❑ Is each character's speech recognizable and unique to that character?

❑ Is each character's motive clear and logical?

❑ Is dialogue used to advance the plot as well as reveal character?

❑ Have you created realistic dialogue through the use of fragments, diction, and slang?

❑ Does the dialogue follow the rhythms of everyday speech?

5. Script

❑ Is the script in the correct format?

❑ Does the script have a title?

❑ Is the work neatly typed?

❑ Are the pages numbered?

The Moment of Truth: Presenting the Script

You've got a rough draft and a really bad case of nerves. Now you're ready for a *cold reading*. That's when you gather a group of friends to read your play through. A reading is just that: You read the play, sitting around a table, without performing any actions or moves at all. Tape-record the cold reading and solicit responses. See what works—and what doesn't—for you and for others.

Wrong Turn

An *anachronism* is a chronological error that places a person, event, or object in an impossible historical context—like a character in a Shakespearean tragedy wearing a Timex. Check for anachronisms as you revise and edit.

After you make any necessary revisions to your script, it's time to pass it on to professionals to read. Then comes a *workshop performance*, in which actors perform the play. The input from a real audience helps you gather more information about how the play is working.

That's a Wrap: Packaging the Script

"It's all in the packaging," a friend of mine once said. He was right up to a point. The play's package has to conform to the conventions of the genre: no plot summaries spelled out in pepperoni on a pizza, please. Below are guidelines for presenting your script.

Name of the Game: Title Page

Place the following information on the title page:

1. The title of the play, centered in the middle of the page

2. Your name, under the title

3. Copyright statement in the lower left corner

4. Contact information in the lower right corner (including your telephone number). If you have an agent, his or her number goes there instead of yours.

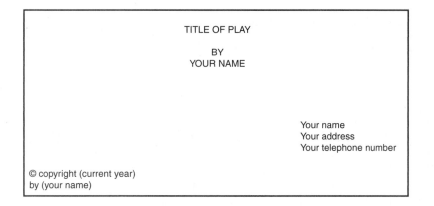

Cast List

The cast list appears on the second page. Here's what it contains:

1. A list of all the cast members and a brief description of each one

2. The cast size and gender breakdown

3. The setting (time and place of the action)

4. Length (three acts, one act)

5. Other information (date of the draft, production history of readings, any awards the play has received)

```
+-------------------------------------------------------------+
|                                                             |
|                       TITLE OF PLAY                         |
|                                                             |
|                                                             |
|  CAST:                                                      |
|                                                             |
|  NAME OF CHARACTER                    Brief description     |
|  NAME OF CHARACTER                    Brief description     |
|  NAME OF CHARACTER                    Brief description     |
|  NAME OF CHARACTER                    Brief description     |
|                                                             |
|                                                             |
|  Cast Size:  Four Men                                       |
|  Time: The play begins in 1992 and spans three months.      |
|  Place: Armpit, Idaho                                       |
|  Length: A play in two acts; one intermission               |
|                                                             |
|  Third draft revision:  7/20/97                             |
|                                                             |
|                                                             |
|  TITLE OF PLAY - History of readings and awards             |
|                                                             |
|                                                             |
|  1996 Winner, Hobart Award                                  |
|  Arena Stage Theatre Reading, April 1996                    |
|                                                             |
+-------------------------------------------------------------+
```

Pit Bulls and Alarm Systems: Protecting Your Work

Of course you'll have backup disks and spare hard copies of your play. But what about the risk of plagiarism? What's to stop someone in a cold reading or workshop from stealing your idea? The law, that's what.

The best way to protect your play from literary theft is to copyright it. To do so, write to the Library of Congress, Register of Copyrights, Washington, DC 20559. Ask them to send you copies of the copyright forms and the information you need to fill them out correctly. Mail back the forms, fee, and a copy of your play. Save the copyright certificate forever. Put it in a safe place, such as a bank vault or under your teenager's bed. No one would *ever* dare go there.

You can also contact the Dramatists Guild (234 W. 44th St., New York, NY 10036, 212-398-9366). It provides a newsletter that lists contests, awards, and the latest marketing and legal news. It also provides quarterly listings of theaters and contacts.

The Least You Need to Know

- ◆ *Drama* is literature written to be performed in front of an audience.
- ◆ *Comedy* and *tragedy* are the two main types of plays, but there are a slew of hybrid forms nowadays.
- ◆ Effective plays have zippy action, exciting conflict, and realistic dialogue.
- ◆ There's a specific way to package, present, and protect your play.

Chapter 19

California Dreamin'

In This Chapter

- ◆ Learn about the different film genres
- ◆ Toon into animated films
- ◆ Write soap operas
- ◆ Discover the biggest markets for scriptwriters
- ◆ Explore scriptwriting software

Gone with the Wind, Nightmare on Elm Street, Love Story, Dune, Die Hard, 101 Dalmatians, The English Patient, Evita, The Big Chill: Movies offer something for everyone. As a scriptwriter, you are in the enviable position of being able to craft a movie that people are really going to want to see. That's what this chapter is all about.

First, I'll take you on a survey of the different types of movies so you can learn the basics of each variety. Then you'll focus on writing animated films, a.k.a. "cartoons." Next, ever think about writing for daytime television—the soaps? I've included a section on this type of scripting as well. Then you'll explore the largest markets for scriptwriters and discover what you need to write these types of films. Finally, we'll survey computer software that can make it easier for you to generate and format your scripts.

Can't Tell the Players Without a Scorecard: Feature Films

Before you start to write your script, you have to figure out what kind of movie you're writing. The success of many scripts hinges on whether the structure is appropriate to the genre. You learned earlier that a *genre* is a major literary category. In literature, the major genres are *prose* (novels and short stories), *drama* (plays), and *poetry*. Here are the most common movie genres:

◆ Comedy (farce, parody, slapstick, screwball)

◆ Action/adventure

◆ Thriller

◆ Horror

◆ Romance

◆ Westerns

◆ Science fiction

◆ Drama

◆ Children's

◆ Mystery

◆ Historical

◆ Epics

Few screenplays fall neatly into one genre. Many are a mix of genres, a thriller with some romance and comedy, for example. Feel free to combine complementary genres, as long as you understand the boundaries of each one. Let's take a closer look at some of the most popular movie genres—comedy, action, thrillers, and horror—so you can pick the one that's right for you.

Laugh Riot

Here's the basic rule for writing comedy: "A comedy needs to be funny." I know, I know, that's so *obvious*, but if it's so obvious, why do we have so many embarrassingly unfunny flops?

A successful comedy is either funny or it's not funny. There's no middle ground. Being a little funny is like being a little pregnant: not possible. In addition, comedy is a very unforgiving genre. If you're working on a love story and the third act is a little weak, the script can be doctored up a bit here and there. But if a comedy isn't funny, it just isn't funny.

Before you write your script, study the hit comedies. Look at the classics—movies like *Bringing Up Baby, Desk Set, Adam's Rib, A Night at the Opera, Duck Soup*—as well as flicks by Mel Brooks, Albert Brooks, and Woody Allen. See what devices the writers use to create humor. Here are some techniques to watch for:

- Dialogue
- Sight gags
- Characterization
- Physical comedy
- Silly, absurd plot turns

Nonstop Action

The Matrix, X-Men, Die Hard, Lethal Weapon, T3, Predator, 48 Hours. When they make it, action movies make it big. Why? Well, it's clear that many theatergoers enjoy a well-done escapist piece, but an action movie needs more than mad car chases to be a blockbuster. Action movies hinge on these five qualities:

1. Admirable heroes
2. Villains worth fighting
3. Emotional depth
4. Universal themes (freedom, patriotism, justice, love, family, destruction of evil)
5. A fresh take, not a stale rehash

Thrills and Chills

Successful thrillers are driven by edge-of-your-seat suspense and a gripping plot that accelerates like a commuter about to miss the last bus. These movies sweep us into the emotional maelstrom of the characters and situation by creating genuine suspense and mounting tension. To work, the plots have to hang together logically; no holes large enough to drive a Buick through, please.

Here are some ways that you can make your thrillers really thrilling:

◆ To heighten the terror and suspense, create a terrifying villain.

◆ The villain must have a very strong motive. It is often revenge.

◆ Make the villain (as well as the hero) a three-dimensional, complex character.

◆ Have the hero completely deceived by the villain at first.

◆ Isolate your hero from his or her support system.

Again, watch the winners over and over to see how it's done. Anything by Alfred Hitchcock is ideal, especially *Psycho, Rear Window, Vertigo,* and *Notorious.* Modern nail-biters that make good models include *Basic Instinct, The Temp, Fatal Attraction,* and *Silence of the Lambs.*

The Horror! The Horror!

What do *Nightmare on Elm Street, The Hills Have Eyes, Shocker,* and *The People Under the Stairs* all have in common? They were all created by one of the modern masters of shock-a-roonies, Wes Craven. Here are some of Craven's suggestions for crafting a truly horrifying horror film:

1. Write sympathetic central characters.

2. Don't exploit your characters, especially women.

3. Create charismatic, powerful, frightening villains.

4. Craft a clear, compelling storyline.

5. Deal with the forbidden.

6. Tap dreams and daydreams.

7. Hit the areas where there are deep disturbances in our psyches.

Fine Tooning

Come on, you can tell *me* your secret little vice: You watch cartoons, don't you? Okay, so it's *South Park* and *The Simpsons* rather than *Teenage Mutant Ninja Turtles* and *Beavis and Butthead*—but they're still cartoons. Not to worry; you have plenty of company. Everyone likes cartoons, those delightful moving images known in the business as "animated films." This is one of the most exhilarating and wide-open types of script-writing.

Are you childlike but not childish? Do you like videos and comic books? Then you might have a flair for writing cartoons. Cartoon writers need to produce strong visual storytelling, pared-down dialogue, and fast pacing. Tooners must also be able to appeal to children without talking down to them or talking over their heads.

There are many different kinds of animation writing. You're probably most familiar with Saturday morning cartoons, beloved by late-sleeping parents and early-rising tots. But there are also animated feature films (*Who Framed Roger Rabbit?*, *Toy Story*), *anime* (as fans call Japanese animation), interactive games, computer animation, and animation-as-art films.

Words to the Wise

Anime is Japanese animation.

Fan Fare

Cartoons can be divided into two categories:

1. Soft: comedy, fairy-tale cartoons with a soft look, such as *Rainbow Brite*. These are generally targeted at girls and boys ages 3–8. Focus on fun stories that kids can relate to.

2. Hard: quasi-realistic action/adventure shows, such as *X-Men*. These are generally aimed at older boys, ages 5–12. The tone can be a little harder; the situations a little more sophisticated.

Both types of animated features follow the same script format.

Bam! Pow! Zowie!

Scripts for animated features are fraternal twins to scripts for live-action movies. Scripts for toons are different in three major ways:

1. There's more visual description.

2. There's less dialogue.

3. The description is much more specific.

As a result, half-hour cartoon scripts tend to run from 36 to 46 pages, as contrasted to 24-page half-hour live-action scripts. That's because directors of live-action scripts require only guidelines for movement and action. But cartoon artists need to know exactly what to draw and how it will fit in with the whole sequence. In effect, the writer of an animation script is like a director.

Animated films come together in different ways. In some instances, you write a script, it gets bought, the producer hires an animator, and the film is done. In other cases, the scriptwriter is also an animator. Some writers seek out an animator to create storyboards for them. The process depends on the writer's reputation and skills.

To learn how to get the visual aspect of animated features, you can study comic books. Since a comic book doesn't move, the panels function as a kind of shorthand. In effect, you "read between the pictures" to fill in what's missing. In an animated show, the writer has to provide this linking information.

Here's part of a comic book script. It was written by Bob Rozakis, author of more than 400 comic book stories. Use this sample as a model when you write scripts for animated features.

> Panel 1: Charlie Chipmunk is sitting in his tree house, looking down, curiously, at a pile of chestnuts on the ground below.
>
> CHARLIE (thought): Hmmm, those look delicious. I wonder who left me a present.
>
> Panel 2: Shooting over the shoulder of Farmer Bill, holding a net in his hands. He's laughing as he sees Charlie in the tree looking down at the nuts.
>
> BILL: Heh heh! That's it, my little chipmunk friend. You just come down and get those nuts—
>
> #2:—and THEN I've got you!!

Toon In

How can you break into this type of screenwriting? Getting your finger in this pie is easier than writing feature films or television scripts because the money is much less. In cartoons, the writer is paid once, unlike writers of live-action features. Because the writers' fees are lower, producers risk much less money when they hire a novice writer. There is also a lot less competition. Follow these steps to become a tooner:

1. Pick a cartoon show you like.

2. Focus on a syndicated show; they do more episodes and consequently need more writers.

3. Call or write Local 839 (4729 Lankershim Blvd., North Hollywood, CA 91602-1864, telephone 818-766-7191) and ask for a studio list. It's free and lists all the union companies.

4. There are nonunion companies as well. You can get these from the lists of animation producers in trade magazines, such as *Daily Variety* and *The Hollywood Reporter.*

5. As you write, use the model of the comic book panel here.

That's all, folks!

Daze of Our Lives

Will upright Bernie bed Bridget, that slut? Is Harriet homosexual, bisexual, or asexual? When will Brittany admit that she really loves the reformed alcoholic Colin (her first boss, second cousin, and third husband), and not that reprehensible rake William?

Call it melodrama, voyeurism, or real life. Whatever you call it, soap operas ("daytime TV" in the industry) are daily fare for millions of viewers. That makes the soaps a rich market for scriptwriters like you. Most people in the daytime TV industry agree that a new writer with talent and persistence will eventually get hired.

To write the soaps, start by reading the classics: Dickens, Thackeray, and Austen. The classics deal with timeless human themes like love, revenge, jealousy, and so on, and soaps play on the same heartstrings. Soaps are the same classic stories in modern clothing.

Here are three terms you have to know to write for the soaps:

♦ *Script:* the dialogue in the form of a 35- to 40-page shooting script.

♦ *Breakdown:* the story outline for a single show in narrative form. Figure 1–12 pages.

♦ *Sample:* a trial script or breakdown.

Soap Suds

Being a great writer doesn't guarantee success in the soaps, however. The following five qualities are essential:

1. The ability to write for already-existing characters

2. A complete knowledge of the show's plot and style

3. The capacity to tell a great story

4. The aptitude to interweave plot lines (since each hour show interweaves five to seven story lines)

5. The ability to create realistic dialogue

To get the dialogue right, turn the show on and close your eyes. You know the characters well enough to write their dialogue if you can distinguish them from their voices and speech patterns alone.

How can you acquire these skills?

1. Select and study a specific soap opera.

2. Know how many acts "your" show has.

3. Discover which plot is primary.

4. See what role humor plays in the show.

5. Study the camera angles. Since soaps are generally videotaped with three cameras, there are limited camera angles.

6. Pay close attention to scene openings.

7. Explore the ending *tag*, the punch.

8. Be able to write *fast*.

Words to the Wise

A **tag** is the dramatic closing scene in a soap opera, the cliffhanger.

Down and Dirty

In Chapter 20, you'll learn the basics of writing a script: structure, characters, plot, and dialogue. Here are some specific guidelines for writing a soap script:

Each episode contains 18–24 scenes. The opening segments, called *teasers*, serve to catch the audience's attention. Every 60-minute show has a teaser as well as six acts; each act includes two or three scenes each labeled A, B, C. Each drama is divided into three stories, ranked according to their importance. The first, or main story, is usually introduced in teaser C and continued in act 1, scene A. Cliffhangers are used to carry the audience through commercial breaks. They are also added at the ends of the teasers in acts 3 and 6.

The script must also follow a specific format. Write the following information on page 1:

◆ The title of the show

◆ The episode number

◆ Tape date and airdate

◆ Creator's name

- Producer's name
- Writer's name
- Complete cast list

Write the following information on page 2:

- A list of all scenes
- The sets in which they play

Typically, freelancers are hired to write dialogue. Most are assigned a 35- to 40-page script each week, which they write at home. Fees vary with experience.

Not-So-Silver Screen

IBM has solutions for a small planet ... and they show it on film. GTE makes good things come to light ... and they show it on film. Same with JC Penney, Kodak, Ford, GEICO, Little Caesar's Pizza, Farmers Insurance Group, and heaps of other large and small firms. Then there are corporate and industrial videos. Ever wonder who writes the scripts for industrial and commercial films? That "who" can be you!

Industrial and commercial scripts are a different kettle of film. Each calls for different skills. Most of what follows is about corporate and industrial films. Check with people in the field or in books on the topic for additional information.

Take all the multiplex movies ever produced, add all the television shows, and you're still nowhere near the miles and miles of corporate, industrial, and educational films and videos that have been produced. Scriptwriters with their sights set on Hollywood often overlook this juicy market. It's a great source of income while you learn the ropes for writing a blockbuster film. It can also be a great creative writing career itself.

These films fall into the following main categories:

- Education
- Business
- Motivational
- Sales
- Training
- Safety
- Product introductions

All the Write Stuff

The International Television and Video Association (ITVA), which has chapters throughout the United States, is a good way to get leads for writing business and training scripts.

More and more companies are relying on films and video. In some cases, they are even using news videos instead of or in addition to newsletters. Many larger production companies have writers and producers who work on staff, but smaller companies use freelancers. Advertising agencies are another source for this type of filmmaking. Ad agencies often produce training films and business-related shows.

See Chapter 20, "Tales from the Script," for step-by-step guidelines for writing your script.

Sleepless in Seattle

One of the chief advantages of making educational, training, and sales films is that you don't have to live or work in Hollywood or New York. Companies that make nonfeature films are scattered throughout the United States. As a result, it's much easier for you to network and make personal contacts no matter where you live. You don't have to be based in California or the Big Apple.

The rules are the same, however. If you want to break into this creative writing market, you have to market yourself.

Fast Track

Try the following ideas if you're interested in this type of creative writing:

♦ Study the format. You can find scripts in most libraries and bookstores. In addition, script software such as *Final Draft, Movie Magic Screenwriter 2000,* and *Scriptware* formats the script for you.

♦ Get experience. If you don't have a track record, hook up with a volunteer project, such as a charity. Write a great script. You can even get a friend to produce it. In addition, public access cable allows the community to use its production facilities for free for community-oriented projects.

♦ Use this script and video as a sample.

♦ Do a sample script on speculation for a company.

♦ Send letters.

♦ Make phone calls.

- Join professional organizations. The International Television Association and the International Association of Business Communicators focus on business and educational scriptwriting.

- Stay current. Be sure to keep up with the latest trends in your field.

A lot of big companies have their own corporate video departments with on-staff producers and directors. There are also small production companies (usually listed as video production facilities or producers) that are hired to do the whole thing but farm out the scripting. Management consulting firms like American Management Association often produce generic skills video courses for sale to corporations.

Get with the Program

It seems like there's computer software to aid us in everything we do, from getting a date to writing our wills. But perhaps no aspect of human endeavor is as inundated by software as writing.

Over the past few years, heaps of programs have magically appeared to serve a wide range of writing functions: from sparking creativity to formatting scripts to selling your finished work. Since scriptwriting is so hot, many Bill Gates wannabees have churned out a slew of scriptwriting software. These programs fall into two distinct groups: *story development* software and *formatting* software. And not to worry; there are programs for both Mac and PC users.

I know that you're too busy writing your script to crawl the mall, so here's a roundup of the latest and greatest scriptwriting software. But since programmers stay up all night eating donuts and turning out more and more stuff, you'll still have to visit some monster chain computer stores and read computer mags like *PC World* to stay up to speed. Or you could always befriend a computer geek of your very own. It worked for me.

Story Development Software

Sick of staring at a blank piece of paper or an equally blank screen? Then you might want to take a look at some of these programs. Since they focus on the creative side of scriptwriting rather than mechanical concerns such as formatting, they might be able to help you round up the usual suspects: plot, characters, structure.

- *Dramatica.* The biggest-selling "story development" software, Dramatica allows users to draw on examples such as Shakespeare's *Hamlet* by answering hundreds of questions. Based on your answers, the program offers feedback and constructive criticism. The program is unique among the ones I examined because it encourages scriptwriters to create their own format rather than filling-in-the-blanks with a preestablished template. The entire program is very versatile and interesting to use. (Around $269)

- *IdeaFisher.* Created 25 years ago to help spark ideas, IdeaFisher still has an early Windows interface but many users like its unique approach to creative associations. (Around $200)

- *Inspiration.* This program features idea graphing and outlining. Although originally aimed at students, the program has gained a following among professional scriptwriters as well. (Around $69)

- *StoryLine.* The self-help movement squared: StoryLine is a 22-step program to building a film. The breakdown of three hit films lets you see what works and what doesn't. (Around $300)

- *Collaborator.* Collaborator is like a small child, asking question after question. The questions become an outline built on the time-honored three-act dramatic structure. There's a detailed analysis of the weepy Christmas perennial, *It's a Wonderful Life*, that's nice for studying dramatic structure. (Around $300)

Formatting Software

There's a specific format to professional screenplays/scripts. If you send in a script that's not in the proper form, your work will scream "AMATEUR"—and then it's rejection-slip time. Your handy-dandy computer and some of the following software can take care of this aspect of writing with surprising ease.

- *Final Draft.* According to most accounts, this is the most widely used program, especially in television. This program formats scripts to industry standards, which lets you focus on writing without getting stalled on form. Press the return key and the cursor leaps to the next logical script element, such as dialogue or character. This program even inserts the words *More* and *Continued* at the top and bottom of pages for page breaks. There's a spell check, thesaurus, and "A and B" pages that convert submission scripts into production scripts. Tech support is also available. (Around $200)

♦ *Movie Magic Screenwriter.* Movie Magic Screenwriter is similar to Final Draft, but some users rate it higher. It is the second best-selling formatting program. This program even generates male and female voices to read through the script for you! (Around $249)

♦ *Scriptware.* Once the most popular scriptwriting software, it has fallen from favor because it is somewhat out-of-date (although update online patches are available). You can keep a running list of scenes with a feature called "Dialogue Box"; "Scene Shuffle" lets you rearrange scenes to get drama to the max. "Format Types Box" matches your writing to film-submit, film-shooting, TV standard, and TV sitcom format. (Around $300)

All the Write Stuff

If you don't have a computer, make two columns, "video" on the left and "audio" on the right. Single-space video descriptions in all caps; double-space dialogue and narration in upper- and lowercase.

♦ *ScriptWright.* This is a template add-on for Microsoft Word, featuring many word processing features. Prompt, free tech support is provided by e-mail. (Around $129)

♦ *Power Structure.* Designed to guide story and character development, this program is strong on structure. (Around $269)

The Least You Need to Know

♦ There are many different film genres: comedy, action, thrillers, horror, and so on.

♦ Consider writing animated films, a.k.a. cartoons.

♦ Scripting soap operas can provide steady work.

♦ There's a giant market for business and educational films. Jump right in!

♦ Scriptwriting software can make your task easier.

Chapter 20

Tales from the Script

In This Chapter

◆ Master the script trinity: story, structure, character

◆ Learn how to write a premise

◆ Find out how to create a treatment

◆ Decide if collaborative writing is right for you

"Best picture of the year!" "Two thumbs up!" "Hugely entertaining!" "A blazing triumph!" "A stunning achievement!" "Provocative and entertaining!" The movie is a smash and people are clamoring to see it. Lines stretch around the block; there's even talk of a major award. It's happened to a lot of script writers, even first-timers. It could happen to you.

In this chapter, you'll learn the basics of writing a movie or television script: story, structure, and character. I'll also teach you how to write a *premise*, and explain why you should. Then you'll explore story *treatments*. Finally, I discuss writing in teams so you can decide if collaboration is right for you.

Hot Stuff

If you choose to play the Hollywood game, realize that people who read your script are usually not looking to put their heads in a noose. They want to recommend a script that will make them look good. The burden of proof is on *you* to write that script.

So what are the movie moguls looking for in a winning television or movie script? Here's a checklist you can use:

Concept

❏ Is the concept striking and original—but not too original to be alien to audiences?

❏ Have similar ideas done well in the marketplace?

❏ Does the concept have mass appeal?

❏ Does it have blockbuster potential?

Story

❏ Does the story hook me right away?

❏ Might the story offend certain people? If so, who and why?

❏ Is there a strong emotional pull?

Plot and Structure

❏ Is there a clear beginning, middle, and end?

❏ Is there strong conflict that engages the audience?

❏ Are the scenes logically connected?

Character

❏ Is the main character identifiable?

❏ Can the main character carry the weight of the role?

❏ Are the characters revealed through action?

Dialogue

❏ Is the dialogue believable, intelligent, and compelling?

❏ Does each character have his or her own manner of speaking?

❏ Is the dialogue too profane or sexually explicit for the target audience?

Television and movie producers want a powerful story, sturdy plot, and strong characters. The dialogue must sparkle; the conflict must sizzle like a well-marbled steak on the barbecue. Let's look again at the Big Three: plot, structure, and character, this time as they apply to writing scripts and screenplays.

Story Hour

Story is the tale itself; plot is how the events are arranged. If your script doesn't ignite by the first few pages, it's nothing more than a heap of wet ashes. Most script readers truck home a bundle of scripts every night. If you don't hook these poor overworked, overpaid schnooks from the start, you've earned a one-way ticket to Palookaville. If someone likes what he's reading from the start, he'll keep on reading and be much more willing to overlook flaws down the line.

Unlike novels and short stories, the internal conflicts in a film script must be made visible. After all, a personal struggle may make a great novel, but nobody's going to sit for two hours and watch someone on screen sitting in a chair and grimacing. Further, the story pacing must be tailored to fit the time (half-hour, two hours, or whatever).

Words to the Wise

A **hook** (or **teaser**) is a striking incident or action at the opening of a plot that captures your audience's attention.

Hook your audience from the get-go. A *hook* (or *teaser*) is a striking incident or action at the opening of a movie that captures your audience's attention. It's most often a bit of dialogue or action, such as a murder, car crash, or sex.

You know a good story when you see one, hear one, or tell one. A good story has a strong central conflict that can sustain the action over the long haul. Remember that a *conflict* in literature is a struggle or fight. Conflict makes a story interesting because readers want to find out the outcome. Here are the essential conflicts:

- External conflicts (person vs. person, person vs. society)
- Internal conflict (person vs. himself or herself)

Film scripts often contain both kinds of conflicts. For a conflict to be effective, it must be important. The stakes have to be high enough to matter.

Set up the central conflict as early as possible. Ditch the gauzy atmosphere and go for the gusto. Once you've established what's going on, then you can throw in the smoke and mirrors because you've conveyed the core of the story. In movies, you can get rid of a lot of the description and set-up you use in novels and short stories. Since the visual setting in a movie creates immediate atmosphere, you can put leader text on screen to establish time and place quickly. You can also use music and sounds to convey emotions and a change of mood. None of this applies to other forms of fiction.

Build a Better Mousetrap: Plot and Structure

Structure is the arrangement of events in the plot. You've learned in previous chapters that *plot* is the arrangement of events in a work of literature. Plots have a beginning, middle, and end. You arrange the events of the plot to keep the reader's interest and convey the theme. Here's your basic structure:

♦ Act 1: Exposition

♦ Act 2: Rising action

♦ Act 3: Climax and resolution

While there's no hard-and-fast rule for script structure, most often the conflict is apparent in the first 10 minutes of the film. The rising action builds for most of the movie to create edge-of-your-seat suspense. You'll find the climax and resolution in the last 20 minutes. As you can see, the three acts listed above don't fall into three roughly equal parts.

Set up the conflict in the first act by establishing what the protagonist wants or what he or she is up against. Build the tension in the second act by creating an increasing sense of jeopardy, tension, or urgency. Solve the central conflict in the third act. Tie up all the loose ends in the resolution. Too much can't be left to the audience's imagination. Be sure there's a climax at the end of each act.

The script must move, build, and intensify to hold the audience's attention. There must be a logical connection between scenes. Avoid predictable plotting. The payoff has to be satisfying. Reward the audience for paying attention.

The construction of Sophocles' *Oedipus Rex* and George Bernard Shaw's *Mrs. Warren's Profession* have much in common with the construction of last night's episode of *Frasier* or the movie *Forrest Gump*.

Talking Heads: Character

No matter what kind of movie or screenplay you're writing—comedy, drama, musical, bang-bang shoot-'em-up—the characters bring it to life. Create characters who are textured enough that you and your viewers really want to get to know them:

- ◆ Introduce all your major characters and conflicts as early as you can, preferably in the first 25 pages.

- ◆ Introduce each character with a brief *sound bite*. Short, sweet, and evocative.

- ◆ Check your dialogue to make sure that every important character sounds unique and can be easily distinguished from every other character.

What the industry also wants is "castable" characters, star roles. Hollywood is a star-driven town, and stars can get movies made. Provide your characters with charisma and depth and the stars will want to play them. There aren't a lot of directors who can make that happen, but there are some stars with the clout. Take the time to create star roles. Make your leading heroes and villains unique, powerful, and dynamic.

Film is a visual medium. It's all about revealing characters through behavior. Characters have a way of developing lives of their own and sometimes the plot has to be shimmied to fit them. Writing is a process of discovery. Stay open to the idea of radical plot shifts.

A sure sign of a novice writer is when character is revealed through dialogue rather than through action. Although dialogue can reveal character, it is limiting. Viewers learn a lot more about characters by what they do.

Bite Me

A word or two about taste. We're all grown-ups here, and we know where the lines are drawn. If a script passes too far over the line, it's going to be bounced. In today's political climate, film executives are definitely concerned with the societal impact of a film and how it will be interpreted.

Here are some boundaries to watch:

- ◆ Excessive violence

- ◆ Sexual abuse

- ◆ Excessive profanity

- ◆ Racism

- ◆ Sexism

- ◆ Blasphemy

- ◆ Mistreatment of animals

*Killer Bimbos from Hell Eat *!%#@ Squirrels?* If you're targeting major studios, you're better off not writing a script that can be easily seen as offensive, degrading, tasteless, or vulgar.

Plot Lite: The Premise

You're sitting all alone, staring at the computer screen. There's a cup of stale java on your right; a half-eaten cookie on your left. Now what? Now you write the premise.

A *premise* is a basic idea for a script, what the story will be about. It's the seed for the story, and like a seed, it contains all the elements of the fully grown plant. A premise is *not* ...

- An idea.

- An area.

- A concept.

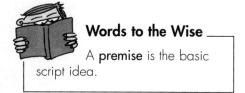

Words to the Wise

A **premise** is the basic script idea.

A premise *is* your entire story distilled to the fewest possible words, a summary. As such, it should be no more than two pages long, preferably shorter. It contains your characters, setting, central conflict. Take your time crafting your premise, because it can help you clarify your thinking about the entire story line.

An effective premise accomplishes three main goals. It ...

- Names and describes the main characters.

- Explains the primary conflict.

- Hints at the story's resolution.

An effective premise, like the plot that develops from it, makes sense. It engages your audience with its emotional tension, humor, or action. Follow these 10 steps as you write your premise:

1. Come up with an idea. Make it a snazzy, fresh one.

2. Expand or contract the idea to fit the length you need: a full-length motion picture, a one-hour television movie, a half-hour television show, and so on.

3. If you're writing an episode for a television series, start with the continuing characters. Fit your story around them.

4. If you're writing a movie, use any characters you wish.

5. Visualize the characters as the premise takes shape. If you can't get a mental image of your characters, neither will the people judging your premise.

6. Create a time and place for the action.

7. Come up with a problem the main character has to solve. The problem must engage the audience, usually through an emotional link.

8. Decide how the problem is solved.

9. Check the characters' motivations to see that everything makes sense.

10. Check your logic. Make sure every action has a logical reason behind it.

Double-check the rough draft of your premise before you make a final copy. Use this checklist:

❑ Does the premise have an interesting "hook" that grabs my attention from the very start?

❑ Do I want to find out more about this idea?

❑ Are the characters realistic and motivated?

❑ Is the central conflict clear and logical?

❑ Is the action intriguing?

❑ Is the ending emotionally satisfying?

❑ Is the overall premise interesting?

❑ Do all the events hang together?

If you answered "yes" to all eight questions, you're ready to move ahead. If not, it's time to retool. Go back over your premise and hone it until it's logical, interesting, and intriguing.

Words to the Wise

A **treatment** is a script outline.

Trick or Treatment

Would you build a nuclear reactor without a blueprint? Does anyone invade a banana republic without a battle plan? Scriptwriters plan and now, so will you.

Before they actually start to write the screenplay, most professional scriptwriters first map everything out in an outline, called a *treatment*. They go act by act, scene by scene, piece by piece. The treatment is so important, in fact, that many script contracts often include a treatment stage. The executive works closely with the writer to noodle the story, plot, and characters in preparation for the actual screenplay.

Following is a basic outline for your treatment. Expand it to suit your needs. Use your premise (about a paragraph long) to build your treatment. You should have about two pages.

Fill in this worksheet to create your story treatment.

ACT ONE

time and place

_____

Scene 1

_____

Scene 2

_____

Scene 3

_____

Scene 4

_____

Scene 5

_____

ACT TWO

time and place

_____

Scene 1

_____

Scene 2

_____

Scene 3

_____

Scene 4

_____

Scene 5

_____

ACT THREE

time and place

_____

Scene 1

_____

Scene 2

_____

Scene 3

_____

Scene 4

_____

Scene 5

_____

Now it's time to flesh out the treatment into a full-fledged script. Use what you learned in Part 2 to select a point of view. Then add dialogue, flashbacks, and characters as you've learned. With a script, you even get music, sound effects, and special effects!

Formatting the Script

Using the correct script format can overwhelm beginning screenwriters. But once you get it down, you'll do it without even thinking, like climbing that Stairmaster.

Here are some basics:

1. Use standard $8^{1}/_{2}$" × 11" white paper.

2. Start with FADE IN. Every script starts this way; it's like "The Curtain Rises" in a stage play.

3. Two spaces below FADE IN is the first image or *shot*. Each shot is written in capital letters. One or more shots make up a scene. The first shot tells if the scene is inside (INT) or outside (EXT); whether it's day (DAY) or night (NIGHT). You also give the location (APARTMENT—KITCHEN).

4. Two spaces below this is a description of the characters and scene, written in lowercase letters, margin to margin.

5. Capitalize characters' names the first time they are listed.

6. If you describe the characters, be brief. Here's an example: "LOU, a ruggedly handsome man in his early thirties."

7. Write basic shot descriptions. Specify a close shot, CLOSE ON, if you want something in sharp focus; use ANGLE ON if you want a different perspective.

8. Center dialogue on the page. It is written in lowercase letters, single-spaced.

9. Write the name of the character who is speaking in capital letters two spaces below the shot description.

10. Include directions to tell the actors what to do in a scene. If the descriptions are long, write them single-spaced in lowercase letters, margin to margin. If they are short, write them in brackets within a speech.

11. Write CUT TO: or DISSOLVE TO: at the end of a scene. Place the words on the right side of the page.

12. When a character's speech continues to the next page, write MORE on the line under the last sentence, indented to the same margins as the character's name. Then write the character's name and CONTINUED on the top of the next page.

For additional information on formatting your script, you may wish to use one of the scriptwriting formatting programs described in Chapter 19 or *The Complete Guide to Standard Script Formats, Part One, The Screenplay* by Cole and Haag (CMC Publishers).

Learn the Lingo

Here are some other terms you may wish to use in your script:

- ESTABLISHING SHOT: wide-angle shot
- TIGHT ON: close-up shot
- ANOTHER ANGLE: a new viewpoint
- CLOSER ANGLE: closer perspective
- CLOSE UP: tight shot
- CLOSE SHOT: tight shot
- POV: point of view
- REVERSE ANGLE: opposite of point of view; other person's view
- BACK TO: return to POV shot
- FAVOR (CHARACTER'S NAME): focus on that character
- CUT TO: end of a scene
- DISSOLVE: old scene fading out and new scene fading in
- FADE OUT: image fades to black
- INSERT: text inserted into a scene
- AD LIB: off-the-cuff comments
- DOLLY: move the camera to or from a subject
- PAN: camera moves from side to side
- VOICE OVER (V.O.): spoken narration
- OFFSCREEN (O.S.): character speaks offscreen
- BEGIN TITLES: when credits start
- END TITLES: main credits end

All the Write Stuff

Remember that all directions are written from the camera's point of view.

It's a Lock

Here's a sample page from a script. Use it as a model. And remember: It's easier than it looks at first blush. As a rough measure, figure that one page of script equals about 45 seconds of running time, give or take.

TITLE

FADE IN

1 INT. AIRPORT BAR—NIGHT 1

LOUISE and RITA, two attractive women in their late twenties, are sitting at the bar. LOU, a ruggedly handsome man in his early thirties, walks in and takes a seat at a table a few yards away. The room is illuminated only by a few lamps. There is a long bar and half a dozen small tables. Soothing elevator music plays softly in the background.

2 ANGLE ON LOUISE'S FACE 2

LOUISE

Louise, do you remember that man?

RITA (bemused expression)

I should think so, seeing as I was married to him, I think. Or maybe it was his brother.

LOUISE (astonished expression)

Married to him!

RITA (calmly)

It wasn't legal. I've been married to no end of men. No use going into it.

MORE

EXT. AIRPORT GATE—NIGHT

Circle the Wagons

By now, you should have hammered out a premise, treatment, and perhaps even a rough script. Keep writing. As you do, remember that less is more. Go light on camera angles and moves. Avoid lengthy descriptions. Let the visuals, music, and sound effects do your work. You're writing a screenplay, not a novel.

Complete this worksheet to make sure you're on track.

1. Describe the setting, the location.

_____

2. Describe the protagonist, the hero.

_____

3. Describe the antagonist, the villain.

_____

4. Summarize the plot in 25 words or less.

_____

5. What problem does the protagonist have to solve?

_____

6. What is the inciting moment, the event that sets off the plot?

_____

7. What is the climax, the high point of the action?

_____

8. How is the conflict resolved?

_____

9. How do the characters change as a result of their experience?

_____

A script is long—whether it's for a half-hour sitcom, a one-hour dramatic special, or an hour-and-a-half feature film. Figure at least 100 pages. You'll write, write, and write. You won't get anything else done, other than eat, breathe, and get older. What happens when you've bitten all your fingernails down to the quick and eaten all the super-premium ice-cream in three states? Here are 10 tips to keep you going.

1. Keep the action moving. That's why they call it *motion* pictures.

2. Avoid scenes where the characters sit around schmoozing.

3. Even though it seems that every action flick is a remake of *Lethal Weapon* and every comedy is another *48 Hours*, be original. Does the world really need another movie or TV show about buddy cops, drug busts, or damsels in distress?

4. Create a believable world for your characters. Even a sci-fi film has to have an internal logic to be believable.

5. Don't condescend to your audience.

6. Don't plagiarize.

7. Go out on a limb. Remember: You're the only one with the saw.

8. Everything on the screen must have a point and provide information; if not, remove it.

9. Stick with it.

10. Write the movie you want to see when *you* go to the movies.

The Least You Need to Know

◆ Winning scripts have a compelling story, a three-part structure, and intriguing characters.

◆ Write a *premise* and a *treatment* to plan your script.

◆ Use the right format to create professional-looking scripts.

◆ Don't give up. It will be worth it in the end.

Part 5

Living the Writer's Life

We write for many different reasons: pleasure, posterity, recognition. Whatever *your* reason for being a creative writer, you'll want to explore different types of creative writing classes, contests and grants, and self- and peer editing. This part of the book also covers self-publication and publishing on the Internet and how the publishing industry works.

Writers are often bedeviled by fear—fear of rejection, fear of offending, fear of running dry, even fear of success. To help you overcome these common obstacles, we'll explore some of these fears in detail and then demystify them. I'll also show you how to conquer writer's block and the thousand insecurities and doubts that go with it.

Chapter 21

Class Is in Session

In This Chapter

- Explore different types of creative writing classes: on-site, online, and community-based
- Learn about writer's retreats and conventions
- Consider setting up your own writers' group

According to literary legend, Nathaniel Hawthorne locked himself in his bedroom for 12 years (from 1825 to 1837) to learn how to become a writer. He barely communicated with the other members of his household, his mother and sister, and left his lair only for nighttime walks. Now, these 12 years did in fact result in an astonishing burst of creativity, but is it really necessary to become a hermit to learn to be a creative writer?

No, it's not.

You *can* lock yourself in your room for a dozen years and write in solitude as Hawthorne did, but *why*—when there are so many more interesting and pleasant ways to learn to write? Among the most successful ways are taking classes, attending writers' retreats, and setting up your own writers' groups. That's what this chapter is all about.

School Daze

Creative writing classes are offered through colleges and universities, both in classrooms and online. Such classes are also offered by writers, editors, and private companies not affiliated with a university or college. Virtually every community offers classes in fiction, nonfiction, and poetry writing through adult education classes, too. With the ever-increasing interest in creative writing today, these programs have become commonplace.

For example, in the past few years, more than 50 colleges have added a creative writing program to their undergraduate offerings, bringing the total to well over 300 degree-granting creative writing programs in public and private colleges across the United States. Usually, these programs are under the auspices of the English department and offer students the opportunity to earn a bachelor's degree with a major or minor in creative writing. These programs are wildly popular. For example:

- Oberlin College's creative writing program, begun in 1978, now has three times more applicants for positions in the courses than they have available space.

- Southern Vermont College, a tiny college with only 400 students, offered a creative writing major for the first time in 2001. They had 12 students the first year, 25 students the second year, and expect this exponential growth to continue.

- When Susquehanna College (Selinsgrove, PA) started its creative writing program five years ago, it had to beg for office space. Now, the program is the toast of the college, attracting huge grants and many students.

The results show that students enrolled in university creative writing programs are learning, producing, and winning. To whit:

- Students in the creative program at Carnegie Mellon University (Pittsburgh, PA) create their own chapbooks (small pamphlets of poems). The creative writing program, founded in 1968, is one of the oldest in America.

- The creative writing program at Columbia College in New York City emphasizes summer internships in writing-related fields, such as public relations.

- Each year the best undergraduate novel produced by a student in Wofford College's creative writing program is published in a limited edition of 2,000 copies. Since 1995, 40 students at this South Carolina college have written novels.

- The winner of the Sophie Kerr Prize at Maryland's Washington College for "greatest ability and promise for future fulfillment in the field of literary endeavor" gets far more than a handshake and a scroll: Last year's winner received a check for over $62,000.

Write Angles

Likely the most out-there creative writing program sponsored by a university is the writing department at Naropa University in Bolder, Colorado. Originally called "the Jack Kerouac School of Disembodied Poetics" by its founders Anne Waldman and Allen Ginsberg in 1974, the program is now referred to as the "Writing Department." Despite the name change, the program retains the vision of its founders, so that along with taking classes in creative writing and critical reading, you can expect classes in Sumi brushstroke and Aikido to help you "cultivate mindful awareness."

Traditional Creative Writing Classes: The Iowa Writers' Workshop Model

Likely the most famous creative writing program in America is the Writers' Workshop at the University of Iowa. Located in Iowa City, the Iowa Writers' Workshop was the first creative writing degree program at an American university (1936). In addition to being the best-known creative writing program, it is also the best ranked, according to the 1999 *US News and World Report* evaluation.

The Iowa Writers' Workshop has a two-pronged approach, as follows:

Program	**Workshop**
You can earn a Master's of Fine Arts in English	You can take seminars and classes from well-known and well-respected writers

Most creative writing programs have patterned themselves on the Iowa Writers' Workshop. As a result, this division into a degree-granting program (requiring a specific number of classes, manuscripts, and other qualifying factors) and seminars (on a pick-and-choose format) is common in many college and university programs. Iowa offers the following classes, many of which are offered at other colleges as well:

Writing Classes

- Creative Writing
- Fiction Writing
- Poetry Writing
- Fiction Workshop
- Poetry Workshop

- Graduate Poetry Workshop
- Graduate Fiction Workshop
- Basic Play Writing
- Broadcasting and Script Writing

Literature Classes

- Form of Poetry
- Form of Fiction
- Translation Workshop (famous literature in translation)

You'll notice that the classes can be divided neatly into two types: those that teach writing and those that teach the study of literature. The theory is the same as the one I have been using in this book and in my writing classes: You learn to write creatively by studying fine writing and by practicing writing.

A Different Paper Chase

While studying at Yale Law School, Matthew Pearl found the time to write *The Dante Club*, a historical thriller that was on *The New York Times* best-seller list for five weeks. Pearl signed his book contract in April 2000, a month before he graduated from Yale. Pearl isn't the only successful creative writer from Yale law school: law Professor Stephen Carter wrote the best-seller *Emperor of Ocean Park* and third-year law student Adam Haslett wrote *You Are Not a Stranger Here*, which made the short list for the Pulitzer Prize in Fiction. Other Yale law students who penned well-received books include Jedediah Purdy (*For Common Things*), Mark Costello (*Big If*), and Michael Johnston (*In the Deep Heart's Core*).

What conclusions can we draw?

- You don't have to take a formal creative writing class to become a more imaginative writer. Many different college classes, especially those that emphasize logic, clear thinking, and writing skills, will help you become a better writer. Consider taking a wide variety of college classes to learn different skills and subjects that you can apply to your creative writing.

- An emphasis on writing—even if it's not creative writing—helps people become better writers. Write as much as you can, as often as you can.

- Being a member of a community of writers and thinkers encourages creative writing.

- You can keep your individuality in a group of people who encourage you to be true to yourself.

- Despite the much-trumpeted warnings against stress, many people produce extremely well under pressure. Stress can help you be more prolific.

- If they can do it, you can do it.

Are Traditional University Creative Writing Programs for You?

There's no doubt that a reputable and well-run college or university creative writing class can teach you a great deal about the craft of writing. Although we can argue (as many do) that neither creativity nor persistence can be taught, talent *can* be developed.

Further, many of these programs can provide valuable contacts in the publishing world, if you wish to publish. In addition, colleges are centers of intellectual stimulation. You'll be in the vortex of energy and brains. Colleges take ideas and language seriously, so you are more likely to get the encouragement you need to succeed as a creative writer.

However, here are some questions to consider before you sign on the dotted line:

- Is the program reputable? Just because a program is offered by a college or university doesn't mean that it's any good. First make sure that the program is accredited by a recognized accreditation agency. Then talk to people who have been in the program; sit in some classes to judge the quality of the education for yourself.

- Does the program meet your needs? Some colleges allow you to take classes without enrolling in a degree program. Others, in contrast, insist that you enroll and matriculate (earn a degree). Decide whether you want to be able to pick and choose classes at will or wish to pursue a degree. Then see which program fits your needs.

- Will taking the class help you write more? The discipline of a classroom and community of learners helps some people focus more closely on their writing. It's the same psychology behind Weight Watchers™, Alcoholics Anonymous, and other collective programs. For others, however, class becomes a substitute for actual writing. They *talk* about writing so much that they don't get around to actually *doing* much of it.

All the Write Stuff _____

According to reliable estimates, 30 million people surf the Net. Capitalizing on this huge market, many writers have established online support groups. Romance authors are the newest (and currently the largest) group of writers, publishers, and booksellers using the Internet to promote themselves and the genre. Scores of published and unpublished romance writers have home pages with photos, bios, book covers, and whole chapters for readers to sample.

Online Creative Writing Classes

Evening to-do list:

- Check e-mail.

- Look up weather forecast for Friday's trip to LA.

- Post your creative writing assignment on the class bulletin board and "chat" in the online Writer's Café.

Thanks to the boom in online classes, Internet users can add "taking an online creative writing class" to the list of things that can be accomplished while sitting behind a computer. Traditional colleges, online colleges, and companies are adapting online culture and responding to people's increasingly busy lives by offering a variety of creative writing classes online.

Online classes are phenomenally popular. The University of Phoenix, for example, has 72,000 students enrolled nationwide in its 33 online degree programs. In addition to formal degree programs, most universities offer stand-alone online classes.

What Can I Expect from an OnLine Creative Writing Class?

Most online creative writing classes have four components:

- Formal instruction

- Group feedback

- Instructor feedback

- A virtual classroom

For example, the instructor will post a weekly lesson online, usually accompanied by an assignment. This lesson corresponds to the lecture in a traditional classroom. The instructor will probably also assign readings in a textbook and other homework assignments.

After you complete the writing assignment, you post it to a message board, where you receive feedback from one person, several people, or the entire class. The instructor is likely to require that you provide evaluations and comments on a specific number of peer writing assignments. The instructor also offers his or her comments on each paper, and these comments may or may not be shared with the entire class.

Finally, a virtual classroom will be provided where you can dialogue with other class members in real time or *asynchronously*.

Words to the Wise

Asynchronous communication is the term for e-mails and other electronic communications that are posted and read at different times. For example, if Brad Pitt or JLo sends you an e-mail at 10 on Tuesday, you might open and read it a few hours later. In contrast, we have real-time communication, in which people converse at the same time with one another. IM's (instant messages) take place in real-time communication.

As with traditional creative writing classrooms, some online instructors make attendance mandatory; i.e., you must sign on and participate in dialogues and offer feedback a certain number of times. You might even have to sign on at specified times. Other online classes, in contrast, do not make attendance compulsory.

Are Online Creative Writing Programs for You?

There's no doubt that online creative writing classes offer many advantages. In addition to the obvious—you have access to instruction even if you can't leave your home or choose not to—online education allows you to stay anonymous. This is important to people not comfortable receiving feedback on their creative writing in person.

Nearly all creative writing classes (both traditional and online) involve class critiques of your writing. Even the most gentle comments can draw blood. Consider the following issues as you decide whether online creative writing classes are for you.

◆ Do you have the computer equipment and access to it? You must have the hardware you need at home, and be able to use it when you need it. *Never* use your office computer for your creative writing—even at night or on weekends.

Recent court rulings have upheld the right of companies to access your office computer files, both work-related and personal. Even if you erase your files from your hard drive, the geeks can retrieve them easily. No one wants anyone at work reading the latest draft of their memoir or horror story—especially if they are one and the same ....

◆ Are you reasonably computer literate? Online classes are very user-friendly but many people are still frightened of technology. If you're not yet up to speed on your computer skills and you want to take some online creative writing classes, consider first taking a computer class in adult education, the library, or your local community college.

◆ Does online education suit your learning style? Some writers crave the stimulation of a classroom, the edgy interaction and stimulating exchange of live bodies. Others prefer the safety of sitting alone in front of their terminals. Some writers need a formal class at a formal time to get them working; others are self-directed enough to sign on at random times and complete their work. Know the way you learn before you sign on.

Adult Education Creative Writing Classes

How many of these classes look familiar?

◆ The Poetry/Writer's group meets the third Friday of every month in the North Kingstown Free Library, 12:00. Bring a bagged lunch and your latest writing. No charge.

◆ The Creative Writing Circle meets the fourth Thursday of every month at 7:30 P.M. at the VFW Hall on Main Street. Class is free.

◆ The Recreation and Parks Association sponsors Wednesday morning creative writing classes at the Neighborhood Guild. The 10:00 90-minute sessions include assignments and critiques by an instructor. The fee is $2 per class.

Communities offer creative writing classes for free or a nominal cost through the library, community center, public schools, recreation and parks associations, and so on. These classes can be a great way to hone your creativity.

Don't shake your head and mutter: "The instructors are probably the same people teaching macramé and underwater fire prevention." Not so fast. One of the creative writing programs in my decidedly suburban neighborhood is taught by a celebrated novelist; another by a poet on the short list for the prestigious Pushcart Prize. Both are superb teachers as well as accomplished writers.

Writing is a lonely business and writers often welcome the opportunity to get out and share their craft. When it comes to adult education and other community classes, professional writers are in it for the fun, not the money or networking. And since many of these classes meet a few times (such as four, six, or eight sessions), it's easy to attract top-notch people to teach.

Scriptourism: Writer's Retreats

Consider these options:

- A seven-day creative writing retreat in Belize run by *Zeotrope: All-Story*, the magazine financed by movie director Francis Ford Coppola.

- An eight-day writing retreat in Yelapa, a small Mexican fishing village 45 minutes from Puerto Vallarta by boat. The program also features intensive work with yoga instructors.

- A five-day creative writing seminar in Chappell Hill, Texas (or Costa Rica, New Mexico, San Francisco, and probably Pluto).

Search on Google for the term "writers' retreats" and you'll get more than 50,000 hits, showing that there's no lack of get-away-from-it-all creative writing events. Today, the muse has moved from attics to Arizona, from Manhattan to margaritas. Some writers' retreats are decidedly Spartan affairs in local motels, while others are lavish resort-style vacationing with writing workshops. The top-of-the-line literary retreats can include massages, wine tastings, evenings in the sweat lodge, kayaking down the rapids, and sojourns in ancient Aztec ruins. The subtext isn't difficult to decode: with the right pampering, everyone can access their muse.

The writing retreat business has been dubbed *Scriptourism* because participants require nothing more than a pen, paper, a desire to write—and a fat wallet. The price tag for such luxury is as steep as you'd expect: The programs typically cost $750–$3,500 a week.

Words to the Wise

Scriptourism is the newly coined term for creative writing retreats.

However, prestigious writers' retreats will pay the way for experienced or very promising new writers: Among the most esteemed are Yaddo, MacDowell, and Breadloaf. These retreats are different from the "scriptourism" ones because of their strictly literary focus.

The following chart details the pros and cons of these programs.

Advantages	Disadvantages
You're out of the house so you can focus on creative writing.	You're out of the house so you can focus on fun—and the other writers.
You can learn useful creative writing techniques from experienced teachers.	The teachers may be neither experienced nor good.
You can get useful feedback.	The programs are pricey.
You might make some valuable contacts in publishing.	You might meet a lot of people seeking to make valuable contacts in publishing.
Creative writing is hard work. Why not make it fun?	Sorry: Creative writing is damned hard work. There's no way to make it fun.

Creative Writing Conventions, Seminars, Workshops

There's a staggeringly wide variety of writing conventions, seminars, and workshops to spur creativity and provide you with exposure to professionals who can help you sharpen and refine your writing skills. A quick web search yielded nearly 15,000 this year alone ... and that's not counting the ones not posted on the web.

All the Write Stuff

You can find a listing of writers' retreats and conventions in magazines like *Poets and Writers* as well as on the web. A handy list can be found at http://writing. shawguides.com. Search by time (month, years); location (state, country); specialty (memoir, children's fiction, mystery, romance, etc.); or any combination of terms.

Attending writer's conferences can be a good way to validate yourself as a writer and compare notes with fellow writers who are at different stages of their experience. You'll also have the opportunity to learn from informative presentations by experts in the publishing industry, such as agents and editors.

Start Your Own Writers' Group

Writing is a solitary activity. Writing classes, conferences, and retreats can give you a break as well as teach you valuable skills, but a close-knit group of fellow writers can provide the support you need to grow as a creative writer.

Traditionally, writers' groups are made up of people who read their material aloud. Then the rest of the group offers feedback. Some groups are based on genre (nonfiction, fiction, romance novels, memoir, etc.) while others include writers with varied interests.

The following suggestions can help you get started with a writers' group:

♦ Decide if you want a balance of skills, from novice to experienced writers.

♦ Experiment with different methods of running the group until you find the method that works best for members. For example, you may wish to have each writer provide printed copies of what is being read or have someone besides the author read the piece.

♦ Make sure that people who join your writers' group are interested in writing. Writers' groups, like writers' conventions, are notorious for nookie.

♦ Meet on a regular basis and keep to the schedule. This helps make writing a priority and builds cohesiveness. You can meet weekly for an hour and a half, every other week for two hours, and so on. Try to meet at least once a month.

♦ Don't let a few members monopolize everyone else's time. Individual readings should be no longer than 15 minutes to keep everyone's interest and make sure that everybody gets a chance to participate. Everyone doesn't have to read every time, but make sure that all participants feel they are being treated fairly.

If you decide to join an established writing group, shop carefully, based on your needs. For example, if you're just starting out, you might want a group that is supportive, offering criticism only as you ask for it. If you're looking for in-depth suggestions for improvement and have a thick skin, look for a group that is willing to tear into your work.

Critique Checklist

Use the following questions as a springboard to critiques:

1. What specifically did I like about this piece?

2. What technique was especially successful? Why?

3. What was the main conflict?

4. How did the writer create suspense?

5. Does the dialogue sound realistic?

6. Is the point of view consistent?

7. Were the characters like real people? Explain why or why not.

8. Was anything confusing? If so, how could the piece be clarified?

Play Nice

Let's face it: People have agendas. They might be jealous of someone with more talent or someone who just works harder. Or they may *think* they're being nice, but they're using a sarcastic tone and causing pain. And even if everyone is kind, sharing your creative writing can be like opening a vein. You can avoid some of these landmines by using a moderator. Assign one person to this role or rotate the leadership.

Always begin and end a critique with a comment about something you enjoyed in the piece, something that was successful. Then guide the group to focus on technique rather than content, unless the content is so objectionable that it's grossing everyone out. Above all else, be tactful.

Danger, Will Robinson!

Maura Stanton grew up in the Midwest, one of eight children. No slam to those who inhabit the middle of the country, but Stanton dreamed of escaping her colorless life. She put herself through college as a computer programmer. As a senior, she took a creative writing class and found her escape. That semester, Stanton wrote over 100 poems, sometimes penning as many as three a night. Maura Stanton went on to win the very prestigious Yale Younger Poets Prize and has published four collections of poetry. Creative writing class worked for her.

However, keep in mind that just about anyone can hang out a shingle and set up a creative writing program, hold a seminar, or organize a retreat, which makes careful shopping a must. Otherwise, you could do yourself more harm than good. Consider the following issues:

- ◆ Decide what you need. Do you need a year in college or will a one-shot class or weekend seminar give you the impetus to write more creatively?

- ◆ Get a recommendation and visit the class. Shop carefully before you sink a lot of time and money into any class.

- ◆ Check credentials. How long has the program been established? Is it accredited? Be sure the people who are promised to teach really do teach.

◆ Beware of extravagant promises. Many famous writers have attended well-respected programs. Whether these glittering literati became famous *because of* the level of instruction or *as a result of* the contacts they made is open to debate.

The Least You Need to Know

◆ You can sharpen your skills, write more, and network by taking creative writing classes in colleges, online, and in adult education.

◆ Ditto on writers' retreats, groups, and conventions.

◆ Make sure that all formal programs are reputable, accredited, and meet your needs.

◆ Don't let writing workshops become a substitute for writing.

22

We're in the Money: Contests and Grants

In This Chapter

◆ Explore different kinds of writing awards

◆ Learn how to apply for contests and grants

◆ Find the writing contests that are right for you

Ever think that it takes as long to sell your writing as it does to create it? If so, you're not experiencing one of those controlled-substance flash-backs. Sometimes it *can* take much, much longer to sell a memoir, novel, or script than it ever took to write the manuscript in the first place.

What can you do if you just want to write without having to worry about selling your work, but you need enough money to keep the wolf from the door? Consider entering writing contests, applying for writing grants—and winning. That's what this chapter is all about.

You, Too, Could Be a Winner!

Are you a saint or a sinner? *Story*, now defunct but once the most widely circulated literary magazine in America, and *Encyclopedia Britannica* sponsored the *Story* Seven Deadly Sins Competition a few years ago. The judges were looking for devilishly good stories based on any of the Seven Deadly sins: anger, avarice, lechery, envy, sloth, gluttony, and pride. Only original unpublished entries of 5,000 words or less were considered; there was a $10 entry fee. The winning manuscripts were published in *Story* for the regular fees. The winners got a nice piece of change *and* a leg up in the business.

Is poetry your passion? Every year, the winner of the Empress Publications Poetry Contest receives $250 and publication in an anthology. Applicants submit original, unpublished poems of up to 25 lines in any form or style. This contest offers great freedom of expression, money, and publication.

Do you want to use your personal experiences—a memoir—to help others and make the world a better place? *The Baton Rouge Advocate* invites breast cancer survivors to share their stories in a letter-writing contest on "The Beauty of Early Detection … Pass It On." Survivors are asked to write letters of 300 words or less sharing their stories of how early detection saved their lives. One letter will be selected from each of Louisiana's seven congressional districts and finalists will be featured on a statewide poster to be unveiled in a ceremony at the Governor's Mansion commemorating National Breast Cancer Awareness Month. The contest is sponsored by the American Cancer Society, the women's caucus, Louisiana Health Care Review, and the Louisiana Cancer Control Partnership.

More on memoirs: The Writers' Workshop in Asheville, N.C., invites entries to the "Hard Times" writing contest. Writers are asked to write about a difficult experience in their lives, how they overcame it, and how it changed them. Winning stories will be chosen for originality and creative writing style; first prize is $500, second prize, $350; third prize, $250; and 10 honorable mentions will be awarded. Stories should be unpublished and should not exceed 5,000 words double-spaced, 12-point font. You can enter up to eight times. Enclose a self-addressed, self-sealing stamped envelope and a reading fee of $18 per entry.

As this handful of examples illustrates, there are awards for all writers, in all subjects, at all levels of expertise and experience. Let's see how you can go about getting your slice of the pie.

On Your Mark …

Nearly every day, new writing contests and awards are announced online and in various writer's magazines. I'm not going to fool you; competition for contest money is keen. To give yourself the winning edge, make sure that you read the contest requirements carefully. If they are not posted online or included in the journal article, send a stamped self-addressed envelope to the contest requesting the rules *before* entering to get the information you need. When you get the facts, check and double-check the following details on the brochures, literature, cover letters, and actual applications:

- Contest contact names

- Addresses

- Deadlines

- Entry fees (if any)

- Rules and requirements for submissions

Wrong Turn

Get the very latest writing contest information that you can. Some groups lose their funding; some publications fold. Don't waste your time unless you know the contest information is timely and accurate.

Read the guidelines carefully to make sure you don't enter a contest for which you are not qualified. Here are some matters of eligibility to consider:

1. *Writer's age.* Many contests are open only to writers who are specific ages (under 21, over 50, and so on).

2. *Previous publications.* Sometimes you must be a published author; other times, unpublished. Sometimes it doesn't matter whether you've published before or not.

3. *Geographic location.* Where you live can sometimes affect your eligibility.

4. *Type of writing.* Most contests are centered on specific genres and subgenres, such as memoirs or one-act plays.

5. *Length of work.* Your submission must often conform to specific word and line counts.

As someone who has judged both poetry and prose writing contests for many years, I can tell you that we take our guidelines seriously. Entrants whose submissions do not conform to the guidelines are not considered at all. This means that we don't even read their submissions.

Winning a contest or award is about more than fast cash, however. Snatching the right brass ring on the award merry-go-round has launched many a successful writing career. Winning an award makes your writing more interesting to publishers. The more prestigious the award, the greater the interest, too.

Get Set ...

To give yourself the winning edge, do some careful research before you decide to apply for a specific writing contest or award. Here are some suggestions:

◆ Get a list of previous winners. This list will often be posted online at the same site as the contest announcement or be reprinted in the magazine or previous year's book.

◆ Analyze their work. See if you can figure out what qualities in each winning entry appealed to the judges.

◆ Attend the staged reading of an award-winning entrant. Analyze the writing to see why it won.

◆ If you're applying for an award sponsored by a magazine, read several issues of the magazine to familiarize yourself with its style.

◆ When you submit your entry, send only your best work.

◆ Make sure your writing is letter perfect. I strongly suggest that you keyboard your work; handwritten entries look amateurish.

Sometimes, you will have to be nominated for an award. If this is the case, select prominent, well-respected, and well-connected people to toss your hat into the ring. Be sure to allow them sufficient time to write the letter of nomination. As a courtesy, you may wish to send the person making the nomination a copy of any relevant awards, grants, or other honors you've already snagged. Also include a list of your publications. Keep copies of this information so you can use it again to enter other writing contests.

Go!

Most large public libraries carry lists of funding sources for writers. Increasingly, sources of funding are listed on the Internet, posted on Websites and online bulletin boards. Below are some resources to check. Every effort was made to keep the following list up-to-date, but contests and organizations change often so be sure to double-check any listing before you apply.

◆ *Foundations and Grants to Individuals* (Foundation Center, 79 5th Ave., New York, NY 10003)

◆ *Grants and Awards Available to American Writers* (PEN American Center, 568 Broadway, New York, NY 10012)

- *Poets and Writers* (72 Spring St., New York, NY 10012)

- *Associated Writing Programs Newsletter* (Old Dominion University, Norfolk, VA 23529)

- *Annual Register of Grant Support* (National Register Publishing Company, 30049 Glenview Rd., Wilmette, IL 60091)

You May Already Be a Winner! Grants

Another way to support your writing is to get funding from foundations and agencies. There is *grant* money available even in tough economic times, so seek and ye shall find. Here are the most open-handed sources:

- Private sources. These include individuals, foundations, and companies. Small as well as large companies endow grants, so don't overlook any possible source of funding.

- Service organizations. A *service organization* is a group of people who help others. Notable service organizations include Rotary International, Lions, Kiwannis, Junior League, and the Women's Club.

- Government agencies. The federal government sponsors programs to support writers and other artists. Further, every state has an office for the support of the arts. You might have heard about your state poet laureate, for example, or your state Council for the Arts.

Most of the largest foundations in the United States are headquartered in New York City, but every state and large city has foundations that give grants to projects they consider worthy. Write, e-mail, or call your local art agency. Let your fingers do the walking through your telephone book to find the arts/cultural commission in your region.

Foundations, like banks, invest in worthy projects (that's *you*) and expect a return. Like banks, the first "loan" (grant) is the hardest one to get. I received my first grant in 1986, an Empire State Challenger Fellowship. It was renewed the following year. Others followed.

Words to the Wise

A **grant** is a subsidy furnished by an agency to finance a project. There may or may not be strings attached (such as residency requirements, number of publications, age, and so on). There are usually fewer strings attached to an outright award.

Don't Take It for Granted

"Ah, a *foundation* would never give me any money," you lament. "I'm just not famous enough as a writer yet." Don't be so sure. What could you do as a writer that would interest a local foundation? Here are some ideas:

◆ Give readings of your work at schools, hospitals, retirement homes, or prisons

◆ Develop a writing program at any one of the above institutions

◆ Write a history of your region

◆ Write a history of the foundation

◆ Write a biography about a famous person in the area or in the foundation

Laundry List

Following is a list of some general grants for writers. I compiled this list by surveying states to give you an overview of the types of organizations you can expect to find. Of course, you'll do a thorough search of your own to find the organization whose mission most closely matches your writing style and personal needs. Then apply, already! (And be sure to include your name, address, and telephone number on all applications. You'd be astonished at how many applications come in incomplete and so can't be processed!)

◆ Annual Associateship
Rocky Mountain Women's Institute
7150 Montview Blvd.
Denver, CO 80220
303-871-6923

Words to the Wise

A **foundation** is an institution created by a donation or legacy. With their endowment, the foundation can carry out the founders' or directors' wishes.

Recipients are provided with a work space, small stipend, support, and services for one year.

◆ Annual Grant Award Program
Witter Bynner Foundation for Poetry, Inc.
Suite 118, 105 E. Marcy St.
Santa Fe, NM 87501
505-988-3251

Grants for individual poets.

◆ Artist Trust Fellowship
#415, 1402 Third Ave
Seattle, WA 98101
206-467-8734

Grants in playwriting, screenwriting, fiction, and poetry.

◆ Artists Fellowships
Illinois Arts Council
Suite 10-500, 100 W. Randolph St.
Chicago, IL 60601-3298
312-814-6750
800-237-6999

Fellowships in fixed amounts of $5,000 and $10,000 to Illinois writers of poetry or prose.

◆ George Bennett Fellowship
Phillips Exeter Academy
Exeter, NH 03833-1104

Annual award of stipend, room, and board to "provide time and freedom from material considerations to a person seriously contemplating or pursuing a career as a writer."

◆ Commonwealth of Pennsylvania Council on the Arts Literature Fellowships
216 Finance Bldg.
Harrisburg, PA 17120
717-787-6883

Fellowships for Pennsylvania writers of fiction and poetry.

◆ Fellowships to Assist Research and Artistic Creation
John Simon Guggenheim Memorial Foundation
90 Park Ave., New York, NY 10016
212-687-4470

Extremely competitive fellowship to assist writers to engage in any field of knowledge and creation.

◆ GAP (Grants for Artist Projects) Fellowship
Artist Trust, Suite 415, 1402 3rd Ave.
Seattle, WA 98101
206-467-8734

The GAP is awarded to about 15 artists and writers every year; it is "no-strings-attached" funding. $5,000 maximum award.

◆ D. H. Lawrence Fellowship
University of New Mexico
English Department, Humanities 217
Albuquerque, NM 87131-1106
505-277-6347

Fellowships for published or unpublished writers of fiction, poetry, or drama.

◆ New York State Writer in Residence Program
New York State Council on the Arts, 915 Broadway
New York, NY 10010
212-387-7020

Awards $8,000 for a six-month residency.

Hey, You Never Know: General Awards

Below is an overview of some general writing awards so you can see what's out there. If you decide to apply for any of these funding sources, be sure to get the latest information. You can do so by writing a letter of inquiry or calling the award committee to request the guidelines.

Notice that many of these awards are targeted for specific geographic areas. There are a zillion more writing awards; this is just a very small sampling of what's available so you can do some browsing. Use this list as a springboard to do your own research to find the best match for your talents and interests.

◆ The Christopher Award
The Christophers
12 E. 48th Street
New York, NY 10017
212-759-4050

Award for outstanding books published during the year that "affirm the highest values of the human spirit."

◆ Editors' Book Award
Pushcart Press
Box 380
Wainscott, NY 11975
516-324-9300

Award for unpublished books; must be nominated by an editor in a publishing house.

◆ Louisiana Literary Award
Louisiana Library Association
P.O. Box 3058
Baton Rouge, LA 70821
504-342-4928

Award for published material related to Louisiana.

◆ Minnesota Voices Project Competition
New Rivers Press, #910
420 N. 5th St.
Minneapolis, MN 55401
612-339-7114

Award for new and emerging writers of poetry, prose, essays, and memoirs from Wisconsin, Minnesota, Iowa, and the Dakotas.

◆ Ohioana Book Awards
Ohioana Library Association
65 S. Front St., Room 1105
Columbus, OH 43215
614-466-3831

Awards for books published within the past year by an Ohioian or about Ohio and Ohioans.

◆ The Carl Sandburg Literary Arts Awards
The Friends of the Chicago Public Library
400 S. State St., 9S-7
Chicago, IL 60605
312-747-4907

Award for Chicago writers of fiction, nonfiction, poetry, and children's literature.

◆ Towson State University Prize for
Literature
College of Liberal Arts
Towson State University
Towson, MD 21204-7097
410-830-2128

Award for a book written by a Maryland author no older than 40.

Wrong Turn

Check to see if the contest has an entry fee. Some fees can be very steep, to defray the cost of the contest. Many contests are held as fund-raisers, too.

Folding Money for Fiction

Can't decide what to do with the trust fund that Grandma Buffy set up for you? Up to your ears in lottery winnings? Need a way to funnel off some stock profits? To get rid of all that extra cash, you can always do what many other well-heeled folks have done: Establish literary awards. Some of the awards listed below were started by publishers looking to find good writing, but many were established to honor famous writers and beloved family members, even pets.

Take advantage of someone's generosity and apply for a bunch of these awards today. When you become rich and famous from your writing, you can set up your own awards and give some other struggling writers a leg up on the ladder of success.

◆ AIM Magazine Short Story Contest
P.O. Box 20554
Chicago, IL 60620-0554
312-874-6184

Award for unpublished stories of no more than 4,000 words that "promote brotherhood among people and cultures."

◆ Nelson Algren Short Story Awards
Chicago Tribune
435 N. Michigan Ave.
Chicago, IL 60611

Award for unpublished short stories between 2,500 and 10,000 words by American writers.

◆ Birch Lane Press American Fiction Contest
Birch Lane Press English Department
Springfield College
Springfield, MA 01109
413-596-6645

Award for unpublished fiction by established and emerging writers (entry fee; many cash awards).

◆ Robert L. Fish Memorial Award
Mystery Writers of America, Inc.
17 E. 47th St., 6th Floor
New York, NY 10017
212-888-8171

Award for the best first mystery or suspense short story.

- Ernest Hemingway Foundation Award
  PEN American Center
  568 Broadway
  New York, NY 10012

  Award for the first published novel or short story collection by an American author.

- O. Henry Festival Short Story Contest
  O. Henry Festival, Inc.
  P.O. Box 29484
  Greensboro, NC 27429

  Award for unpublished short fiction (entry fee).

- Aga Khan Prize for Fiction
  The Paris Review
  541 E. 72nd St., Box 5
  New York, NY 10021

  Award for unpublished fiction of less than 10,000 words.

- Minnesota Ink Fiction Contest
  Minnesota Ink, Inc.
  27 Empire Dr.
  St. Paul, MN 55103
  612-225-1306

  Award for previously unpublished fiction.

- The *Writer's Digest* Self-Published Book Awards
  Writer's Digest National Self-Publishing Awards
  1507 Dana Ave.
  Cincinnati, Ohio 45207

  Award for self-published books in all categories.

Folding Money for Nonfiction

The Gordon W. Dillon/Richard C. Peterson Memorial Essay Prize awards bucks for essays on orchid culture, orchids in nature, and orchids in use. The Barbara Savage "Miles from Nowhere" Memorial Award forks over a $3,000 prize every year for unpublished books on hiking, mountain climbing, paddle sports, skiing, snowshoeing, bicycling—any adventure travel that doesn't involve public transportation. You can win awards for good writing on behavioral science, European history, biography, and early Spanish history, too. And that's just skimming the surface of the pot.

And you mean to say you haven't won a writing award yet? Let's remedy that situation right now. Read on to see if any of the following nonfiction writing contests suit your talents and interests. If not, there's a slew more that you can find on the web.

- ◆ George Freedley Memorial Award
  Theater Library Association
  New York Public Library at Lincoln Center
  111 Amsterdam Ave.
  New York, NY 10023
  212-787-3852

  Award for books relating to theater.

- ◆ Joan Kelly Memorial Prize in Women's History
  American Historical Association
  400 A Street, SE
  Washington, DC 20003

  Award for writing on women's history and/or feminist theory ($1,000).

- ◆ Literary Nonfiction Writers' Project Grants
  NC Arts Council

  Department of Cultural Resources
  Raleigh, NC 27601-2807
  919-733-2111

  Annual award to "recognize the literary value of nonfiction and encourage the artistic growth of the state's writers of nonfiction."

- ◆ Loft Creative Nonfiction Residency Program
  The Loft
  Pratt Community Center
  66 Malcolm Ave., SE
  Minneapolis, MN 55414-3551

  Award for six creative nonfiction writers and a month-long seminar with a resident writer.

- ◆ McLemore Prize
  Mississippi Historical Society
  P.O. Box 571
  Jackson, MS 39205
  601-359-6850

  Award for a book or biography on some aspect of Mississippi history.

◆ The Mayflower Society Cup Competition
North Carolina Literary and Historical Association
109 E. Jones St.
Raleigh, NC 27601-2807
919733-7305

Award for previously published nonfiction by a North Carolina resident.

◆ National Jewish Book Award—Autobiography/Memoir
Sandra Brand and Arik Weintraub Award
15 E. 26th St.
New York, NY 10010
212-532-4949

Award for an autobiography or memoir of the life of a Jewish person.

◆ National Writers Club Articles and Essay Contest
The National Writers Club
Suite 620, 1450 S. Havana
Aurora, CO 80012
303-751-7844

Award to "encourage writers in this creative form and to recognize those who excel in nonfiction writing" (entry fee).

◆ National Writers Club Nonfiction Book Proposals Contest
The National Writers Club
Suite 620, 1450 S. Havana
Aurora, CO 80012
303-751-7844

Award to "help develop creative skills, to recognize and award outstanding ability, and to increase the opportunity for the marketing and subsequent publication of nonfiction book manuscripts" (entry fee).

◆ PEN/Spielvogel-Diamonstein Award
PEN American Center
568 Broadway
New York, NY 10012
212-334-1660

Award for the best previously unpublished collection of essays on any subject by an American writer.

Shake the Money Tree

Here's what I've learned about writing contests and awards as a judge and long-standing member of various contest committees:

1. The more literary contests that you enter and the more grants that you apply for, the more you learn about the process.

2. The more you learn, the better your next application will be.

3. Entering contests and applying for grants teaches you a lot about your art, too.

4. People who don't win one year may very well win the next cycle.

5. You can't win it if you're not in it.

The Least You Need to Know

- ◆ There's a lot of contest and grant money out there for writers.
- ◆ Enter contests to win writing awards.
- ◆ Apply for grants to get a slice of the pie.
- ◆ Many prizes include publication as well as money.

23

The Importance of Editing

In This Chapter

◆ Define editing and understand why it's so important

◆ Learn how to edit your own writing

◆ Explore the advantages of peer editing

◆ Work with a professional editor

You need criticism—and not the "hurts so bad" variety, either. All writers need educated, specific feedback that will help them improve their work, making it stronger and better. That's why the editing process is so important.

In this chapter, we'll discuss the editing process and its various steps. Then I'll help you learn how to edit your own writing. Next, I'll cover working with a peer editor and a professional editor. By the end of this chapter, you'll be ready to experiment with different editing methods to find the ones that work best for you.

What Is Editing?

Editing is part of the creative process of writing. When you come to this step, you evaluate your writing to see what needs to be deleted, added, and moved to make your message and style more effective. Editing isn't one-stop shopping, however: Expect to rethink your writing several times before you're satisfied with it. As you make each round of improvements, you again assess your writing to see if it suits your audience and purpose.

Words to the Wise

Editing is evaluating your writing to find ways to make it better. The process involves deleting, adding, replacing, and moving words, sentences, and passages in the text.

Editing, like exercise and vegetables, is good and good for you. It doesn't mean that you didn't do a fine job on your rough draft or that you're not a good creative writer. In fact, just the opposite is the case. The finest creative writers tend to do the most editing.

Editing Your Own Writing

Producer Russel Crouse asked the award-winning playwright Eugene O'Neill if he would cut some passages in *Ah, Wilderness* to make the play shorter. O'Neill was adamant about not cutting a single word from any of his plays, but he finally agreed to trim a bit. The next day O'Neill called Crouse and told him, "You'll be happy to learn I cut fifteen minutes."

"How?" Crouse ecstatically replied. "Where did you do it? I'll be right over to get the changes."

"Oh, there aren't any changes in the text," O'Neill explained, "but you know we've played this in four acts. I've decided to cut out the third intermission."

Editing your own work is an important part of the writing process, but no one said it was easy! (And if you've ever sat through a Eugene O'Neill play, you know that shorter might very well be better ....) Looking at your work with a critical eye can help you catch awkward phrases and outright errors. Change a word here, slice a few words there and you've suddenly transformed lifeless prose into sizzling reading. Here's how to get started.

As you begin to edit your writing, think about your audience and purpose for writing. Remember that your *audience* is the people who will read your writing. To meet their needs, ask yourself, "What does my audience know about my topic?" Recall that your purpose is your reason for writing. To focus on the purpose, ask yourself, "What am I trying to accomplish in my writing?"

Next, revise the form and content of your work. Form is the shape of the writing. For example, the form of your writing may be a story or a poem. Adjust your draft until it meets the requirements for that specific type of writing. Plays, for instance, tell the story through dialogue, so your final version of a play will likely be virtually all conversation.

Content is what you're saying. When you revise for content, you make sure that each part of your draft is clear and logical.

Once you understand how editing works, you'll find the process relatively painless and even interesting. It's my favorite part of writing because it's like a puzzle, as I try to see how each piece fits best.

Getting Started

Use the following five suggestions to begin editing your own drafts.

1. Write what you want to write. Don't obsess about errors; instead, concentrate on getting your creativity down on paper.

2. Let your writing sit and "cool off." Leave it alone for at least a day.

3. Edit your paper several times. Each time, look for something different. The first time, for instance, eliminate obvious grammatical errors and flaws in logic. The second time, get into deep cuts. Look for ways to make your writing really achieve your goal. If you're going for publication, for instance, focus on including *only* what your target publisher will buy. Ax a word, phrase, sentence, or chapter if it's off your topic and would turn off your audience.

> **All the Write Stuff**
>
> Be sure to save each edit under a different file name, such as chapter1.doc, chapter1a.doc, chapter1b.doc, chapter1c.doc, and so on. This allows you to not only ease the pain of do-it-yourself surgery but also to save "deleted" material to use for another writing or perhaps return to the original document in another form or place.

4. Try reading your words aloud to see how they flow. Reading your words aloud helps you pick up bumpy patches and smooth them out.

5. Leave your ego in a drawer.

To make your task a little easier, I've created one possible hierarchy of editing tasks. Adapt it to suit your specific topic and your editing style.

1. Writing skills. Correct errors in grammar, usage, spelling, and punctuation.

2. Sentence construction. Check for active and passive voice, fragments, and run-ons.

3. Word choice. Choose vivid and appropriate words.

4. Plot. Make sure your plot has conflict and suspense.

5. Character development. Do the characters act like believable people? Do readers care about them?

6. Pacing and rhythm. Does the story build in a logical way? Does the writing have rhythm? (Prose as well as poetry has a beat or flow. If the rhythm is jarring, the prose sounds awkward.)

7. Theme. If you're writing fiction, check that readers come away with some meaning. Otherwise, they're apt to feel cheated.

8. Cleverness. If something strikes you as precious and ever-so-clever, it likely should get the heave-ho because it distracts from the story itself and draws attention to the writer's egotism.

Write Angles

Verbs show voice, the form of the verb that shows whether the subject performs the action or receives the action. English has two voices: active and passive.

- A verb is *active* if the subject performs the action: "The pilot made a mistake."
- A verb is *passive* when the action is performed upon the subject: "A mistake was made by the pilot."

In general, use the active voice instead of the passive voice because it is less wordy.

A good job of editing usually takes nearly as long as the initial creative writing—and it may take longer! Now, let's look at some specific ways to edit your work.

Edit by Deleting

Editing involves deleting material that's off the topic or repeats what you've already said. As you revise, look for ways to tighten your sentences by removing extraneous material that clogs your writing. The following chart provides some examples.

Look For ...	Revision
Repetition	*Cut the unnecessary material*
Bring it to **final** closure.	Bring it to closure.
Filler	*Cut the fluff*
The point that I am trying to make is that you should never miss a good chance to shut up.	Never miss a good chance to shut up.
Unnecessary modifiers	*Select the best modifier*
The big, huge, massive cloud completely covered over the sun.	The massive cloud covered the sun.
Passive voice	*Active voice*
Falling asleep is done by the average person in seven minutes.	The average person falls asleep in seven minutes.

There will be times when you simply won't be able to see how one of your golden sentences can be improved, much less shortened. The problem is even more acute when you're working with a word limit and so *must* cut something out. If you didn't think all those words were really necessary, you wouldn't have included them in the first place, right? In the back of your mind, you're thinking, "Once someone reads my article/memoir/chapter, they'll see that it has to be this long." You know the truth, but it's too grim: If you're submitting a piece for a contest or publication and it doesn't meet the guidelines, they won't read it at all.

Edit by Elaborating

Effective creative writing uses relevant support to bring your topic to life and engage your readers. This "support" can be details, facts, definitions, examples, statistics, and quotations. Adding them to a draft is called *elaboration*.

As you read your draft, see where you need to add more detail to make your writing come alive. Use the following chart to help you focus your exploration.

Look For ...	Revision
Unclear topic	Audience analysis
	Never assume that your audience has your level of knowledge about a topic—especially if you've done research or work in the field.
Lack of sensory details	Add details on five senses
	Focus on things you can see, smell, touch, taste, and hear.

Edit Punctuation

Often, you'll have to change, add, or delete punctuation to make your meaning clear. That's because punctuation creates meaning just as words do.

Try it yourself on the following letter by adding the punctuation you think is necessary. (You'll have to add capitalization, too, to show the start of a new sentence.)

Dear John

I want a man who knows what love is all about you are generous kind thoughtful people who are not like you admit to being useless and inferior you have ruined me for other men I yearn for you I have no feelings whatsoever when we're apart I can forever be happy will you let me be yours

Mary

Here are two variations. See how the change in punctuation drastically alters the meaning in each case.

Version #1:

Dear John,

I want a man who knows what love is all about. You are generous, kind, thoughtful. People who are not like you admit to being useless and inferior. You have ruined me for other men. I yearn for you. I have no feelings whatsoever when we're apart. I can forever be happy—will you let me be yours?

Mary

Version #2:

Dear John,

I want a man who knows what love is. All about you are generous, kind, thoughtful people, who are not like you. Admit to being useless and inferior. You have ruined me. For other men, I yearn. For you, I have no feelings whatsoever. When we're apart, I can forever be happy. Will you let me be?

Yours,

Mary

So don't neglect the little guys—commas, periods, semicolons, and colons—as you focus on editing the words, phrases, and sentences in your writing.

Edit by Rewording

Other times, you'll have to select new words to get your meaning across. When you revise by rewording, you replace words and revise sentences to make your writing accurate and fresh. Here's how to do it:

◆ Look for words that you use too often.

◆ Replace repeated nouns with pronouns.

◆ Substitute other repeated words with synonyms.

◆ Ditch empty, overused adjectives such as *excellent* and *nice*.

◆ Sharpen your words by finding the precise word you want, not a close relative.

Edit for Unity

When you edit for unity, also look for sentences that are off the topic. If your ideas don't cling together like teenagers in love, you can add *transitions*. A transition can be a word (such as *also*) or a phrase (such as *for example*) that shows how ideas are related. Each transitional word and phrase indicates a slightly different shade of meaning, so choose your transitions as carefully as you choose your peaches.

The following chart shows the most common transitions and their meanings. I've lumped related transitions together, but you should tease out their gentle shades of meaning. For example, *and* joins two equal things, but *also* indicates that something has been added to the mix.

Transitions	Meaning
and, also, besides, finally, further, furthermore, in addition, moreover, next, too, then	addition
as a result, because, consequently, for that reason, therefore, since, so, thus	cause and effect
for example, for instance, namely, specifically	example
different from, in comparison, in contrast, in the same way, like, likewise, on the one hand, same as, similarly, unlike	comparison
certainly, granted, naturally, of course, to be sure	concession
however, in contrast, on the contrary, on the other hand, nevertheless, nonetheless, still, yet	contrast

continues

continued

Transitions	Meaning
better, best, finally, first, last, least important, more important, most of all, second	importance
above, across, adjacent, at the side, below, beside, here, in the distance, in the back, in the front, near, nearby, next to, there, where	location
accordingly, as a result, consequently, due to this, so, therefore	result
As a result, finally, hence, in brief, in conclusion, in short, in summary, on the whole	summary
after, at length, before, currently, during, eventually, finally, first, immediately, in the future, later, meanwhile, next, now, second, secondly, soon, subsequently, then, third	time order

Wrong Turn

Combining sentences isn't always the way to go. Sometimes, you'll want to keep your sentences short and crisp to get a staccato rhythm going, as this Rodney Dangerfield joke shows: "Once when I was lost, I saw a policeman and asked him to help me find my parents. I said, 'Do you think we'll ever find them?' He said, 'I don't know, kid. There are so many places they can hide.'"

Peer Editing

Thinking of asking a friend or lover to read your drafts to help you edit them? It's a great idea from your standpoint, but your reader may not be as enthusiastic. British Prime Minister and writer Benjamin Disraeli (1804–1881) had a standard reply unmatched for diplomatic ambiguity for people who sent him unsolicited manuscripts to read: "Many thanks; I shall lose no time in reading it."

Good peer editors know how to put you on track without demolishing your self-esteem. They are able to encourage your creativity and writing aspirations while being brutally honest. They are tactful and honest, never malicious. Often, a good editor will include at least one true, positive point about a manuscript, even if the rest is a total mess. They'll find that glimmer of potential in your work that keeps you going when the going has gotten tough.

So you've got this manuscript. You've squandered the best years of your life on it, lavishing your energy with abandon. Your best friends say it's the greatest thing since sliced bread; your spouse is bowled over by the beauty of your prose—even your mother-in-law is impressed with your exquisite turns of phrase. Now what?

Don't trust your nearest and dearest to have the final word, but do ask them for a read-through. The more eyes on your writing, the better. After all, you're free to accept or reject any and all suggestions.

Peer Editing in Writing Workshops

Writer's groups aren't all about punch and cookies, sex and scandal. They are also about members critiquing each other's manuscripts to improve the quality of everyone's work. In an effective writing workshop, the other writers comment on each other's work and make suggestions for revision. Fellow writers can let you know which of your characters are as slimy as Leisure Suit Larry and which parts of your story are as riveting as Rosie. You can then sift through this advice and make your own decisions about which to keep and which to reject.

Another advantage of writing workshops is consensus. An individual editor, no matter how skilled, might be having a bad day, week, or life. He or she might have strong personal feelings for (or against!) you that can influence how the criticism emerges. With a group critique, however, you're canceling out individual preferences.

Further, critiquing other writers' work is also a good way to build critical faculties in yourself that you can apply to your own writing.

Peer Editing on the Internet

An increasing number of writers are posting their work on the World Wide Web and soliciting suggestions for revisions. Like any other method, posting your work for editing on the Web has its good and bad points.

Advantages:

- ◆ It's free.
- ◆ It's easy and doesn't involve any travel.
- ◆ It gives you many different opinions.

Disadvantages:

◆ Anonymity is dangerous. You have no guarantee that the people reading and editing your work are who they say they are. Your online reader could be a skilled editor trolling the Web for the next hot writer du jour—or a 12-year-old with too much time and technotraining.

◆ Someone may download your work and publish it as their own.

◆ Listening to unskilled editors can damage your writing as well as your self-confidence.

Professional Editing

So you've signed a contract and you've been assigned an editor. Now it's time to get to work. In this situation, good teamwork is essential for success. Follow the following 10 guidelines to get the most from the writer-editor relationship.

1. Remember that everyone has his or her own taste. How else can we explain the sale of Donnie and Marie Osmond albums? Consider your editor's personal taste when you decide to accept or reject criticism.

2. Be careful of editors who impose their own ideas of what a story should be on your work. There's a subclass of editors who love to write your stories for you— it's easier than writing their own. But even well-meaning people will guide you to write the story *they* want to write. Sift comments carefully.

3. Try to get editors to focus on what is on the page—what works and doesn't work for them. Most important, encourage your editor to articulate the reasons why something is a hit or miss. Ask him or her to identify these areas:

   ◆ Weak spots

   ◆ Places where there's potential for development

   ◆ Passages that seem to be missing something

   ◆ Errors in logic

4. Remember that every genre generates its own standards of criticism. The criticisms for novels, short stories, poems, screenplays, and essays are all different. For example, the points an editor critiques in a novel (theme, characters, conflict, plot, setting) are different from those an editor critiques in a poem (rhythm, rhyme, tone, and so on).

5. Take all suggestions, but resist the urge to have the editor do the rewriting for you. Do it on your own.

6. Be wary of editors who psychoanalyze the process of writing. These editors tend to say things like, "I think you stopped writing here because you're scared. I *know* there's more, if only you'd delve a little deeper." These editors can be well-meaning, but it's still psychobabble. Also, it can undermine your confidence. Guide the editor to stick to the text.

7. Look for recurring issues in your writing in the editor's comments. This can help you identify larger style issues you should work on in your writing in general.

8. Try to translate unhelpful criticism into direct questions that you can use. If your editor says something is murky, press for more specific information.

9. You can help prevent miscommunication by rephrasing what your editor said to make sure you understood it. This also gives the editor a chance to correct any misunderstandings that may have occurred.

10. If you can't figure out how to incorporate the feedback into your story, don't get into a lather. Think about it. Let it sit awhile unmolested. If the feedback does indeed contain something important, it will become clear eventually. The important thing is to keep on writing.

Your Momma, Too!

When an editor comments on your work, try to listen quietly and respectfully. Resist the urge to leap back with defenses. I suggest you let the editor's comments sit at least a week before you respond. This will give you the time to process and absorb what has been said about your work. After all, your writing is an extension of yourself, so even the gentlest suggestion might provoke some resentment. Criticism that seemed ludicrous on Monday often makes a lot more sense by Friday.

Be Professional

Here are some more ways to make your work sessions with your editors both smooth and productive.

◆ *Check for inferences.* Identify your editor's nonverbal as well as verbal clues. This can help you identify the real (as opposed to the stated) problem with your writing, if there is one. If you're conferencing on the phone (most often the case), listen for changes in tone and phrasing.

◆ *Keep an open mind.* Don't be quick to leap to conclusions. After all, you've got plenty of time to make unwarranted assumptions.

◆ *Check for feelings.* Identify the emotions your editor is stating outright or implying through body language. Gauge the emotional temperature of the conversation to keep it within normal ranges.

◆ *Determine how important each criticism is to your editor.* Some comments are minor. Others, however, will matter a great deal more to your editor. This can help you decide where to put the most thought and effort.

◆ *Avoid counterattacking.* When we're attacked (or perceive that we're being attacked), our natural reaction is to defend ourselves—perhaps by counterattacking. The counterattack may prompt the editor to strike back, and the conflict will escalate. Feelings get hurt and issues become muddy and difficult to resolve. No matter how much a specific comment may sting, remember that you're a pro. Sit tight and think.

The Least You Need to Know

◆ Always start by editing your work yourself.

◆ Next, you may wish to have your writing peer edited by a friend, relative, or fellow writer.

◆ You may work with a professional editor as well.

◆ Listen carefully to what your editor says, even though you're not obligated to take all of his or her suggestions.

Chapter 24

Creative Ways to Publish Creative Writing

In This Chapter

- ◆ Explore self-publishing
- ◆ Learn about on-demand publishing
- ◆ Discover the pros and cons of publishing on the web
- ◆ Investigate ways to support yourself as a writer

About a decade ago, a successful doctor in Washington, D.C., decided to write a book about the radical shift in medicine from a vocation to an industry. He very much wanted to publish his book to alert people about the disturbing commercialization of medicine.

Since he was a creative writer, the doctor decided to couch his concerns in fiction. He took creative writing classes at a major university to hone his skills; he set aside his evenings and weekends to write. After a great deal of work, he produced a murder mystery on his theme of medicine as an increasingly cold business.

The doctor sought out scores of publishers and agents, but got nary a nibble. A handful of editors actually skimmed his manuscript and offered some constructive criticism, but most of the people he approached wouldn't even crack the spine of his manuscript. Rather than giving up, the doctor ultimately decided to self-publish his book at the leading print-on-demand publisher, iUniverse.

More and more creative writers are going this route for a number of reasons. In this chapter, we'll explore self-publishing, publishing-on-demand, and publishing on the web. Once considered highly untraditional, these publication methods are gaining in popularity. By the end of the chapter, you'll have the tools to decide if these routes to publication suit your needs and personality.

Do-It-Yourself: Self-Publishing

A few years ago, a group of writers in San Francisco calling themselves the "Wild Writing Women" wanted to publish their stories about voodoo, bus accidents, and lost panties. Their pieces were a bit too brazen for the usual outlets, and so they couldn't find a mainstream publisher willing to take a chance on them.

After months of trying to interest conventional publishers, the women decided to self-publish their book. The result was *Wild Women Writing: Stories of World Travel*. A hit, the book sold out its initial print run and was picked up by the traditional publisher Globe Pequot.

Simply put, *self-publishing* is contracting with a packager or printing company to be your production department. You own all rights to the book and only pay for those services you need to get your book printed.

Why self-publish? Here's the straight scoop: Lacking celebrity status or a proven publication track record, your chances of landing a book contract with a major publishing house are slim. That's why do-it-yourselfers comprise the fastest-growing segment of the publishing industry.

Created with lots of free help and printed in small runs, self-published books by individuals and writing groups can sell well and have some staying power. Usually peddled by the author and friends, these books are the Girl Scout cookies of the literary world: tasty sellers to a loyal following. A surprising number of runaway hits started as self-published books, including …

- ◆ *The Erroneous Zones* by Wayne W. Dyer
- ◆ *The Celestine Prophecy* by James Redfield

- *What Color is Your Parachute? A Practical Manual for Job Hunters and Career Changers* by Richard Nelson Bolles

- *Chicken Soup for the Soul* by Jack Canfield (which has hatched a series).

Words to the Wise

Self-publishing is contracting with a packager or printing company to print your work.

The Advantages and Disadvantages of Self-Publishing

The following chart shows some of the main advantages and disadvantages of self-publishing.

Advantages	Disadvantages
You control the entire publishing process.	You don't have the help and advice of a professional editing team.
You get all the profits.	You have to put up all the money for publishing and eat any losses.
You don't have to deal with rejection.	You have to distribute the book yourself.
You can make valuable contacts in many fields.	You lose time you could be spending writing.
You can establish your platform to launch conventional publishing or a career as a writer, if you are so inclined.	You are setting up a business and must do all the bookkeeping.

Getting bound books is just the beginning, because do-it-yourselfers face the challenge of promoting and marketing their texts. Further, when you publish your own book, you have to keep track of sales and taxes for your Uncle Sam. In effect, you're running a business. There are other drawbacks as well:

- Mainstream book buyers and booksellers tend to be skeptical of self-published books. As a result, these books usually do not to sell well.

- Distribution is difficult.

- Publicity is near impossible. Few self-published books get reviewed in magazines and newspapers.

- As a result, few people have found publishing success this way.

Should You Self-Publish?

Laurie Notaro was an Arizona advice columnist in 1994 when she started sending her manuscript for *The Idiot Girls' Action Adventure Club* to mainstream publishers. As the rejection letters filled her mailbox to bursting, Notaro decided to self-publish. For less than $100, she got a box of bound books. The book was just the beginning, how-ever; Notaro then began a publicity campaign to sell it. She knew that she had to set up a *platform*, a fan base, so she first posted a chapter of the book on her web page and alerted all her newspaper column read-ers about her book.

All the Write Stuff

Agents and publishers look for writers who have estab-lished a platform, a fan base. This platform ensures at least a core group of potential book buyers.

Next, she bought some Internet ads. Wisely, Notaro said, "I wasn't really expecting to make money on the book; my goal was to make it available to that one person out there who would do something with it."

Notaro's determination paid off when an ad posted at Amazon.com caught the eye of an agent with a New York literary agency. The agent visited Notaro's website, read an excerpt of the book posted there, and took her on as a client. The agent soon sold the book to Random House.

There's no doubt that it takes a colossal amount of effort, determination, and savvy to get a self-published book picked up by an agent and sold to a mainstream publishing house.

Consider self-publishing if you feel you …

1. Can afford the investment of time and money.

2. Are willing to promote your book on your own. This means vigorous attempts to sell your book: linking to appropriate websites, sending out marketing mate-rials, paying for Internet and print ads, pushing your book at public appearances, arranging network opportunities, and so on.

3. Want to maintain complete control of your book.

4. Want to start and run a business.

5. Have a thick skin and don't get overly discouraged by rejection.

6. Can support yourself by other means as you toil to create a writing career.

On-Demand Publishing

On-demand books are printed in small runs by printers. The process can easily be done online. Basically, you follow these steps:

1. Find a publisher you like

2. Sign a contract

3. Enter your credit card number

4. E-mail your manuscript

A few weeks later, you get the manuscript—warts and all. Some on-demand publishers will do some editing work and offer moral support. Of course, these services cost more, but they are well worth it. I strongly suggest that if you do decide to go the on-demand route, use a company that will offer substantial critiques of your manuscript and detailed suggestions for improvement. *Everyone* needs to be edited—even me!

So far, on-demand publishing is the same as self-publishing. Here's the big difference: When you self-publish, you pay for and receive a set number of books, say 100. That's it: You won't have any more dealings with the publisher, unless you sign another contract to have another load of books printed.

Words to the Wise

On-demand books are printed in small runs as the sales orders come in.

On-demand companies, in contrast, establish an ongoing relationship with you. They keep printing books as you need them, on a demand basis. For example, say you publish your book on-demand with iUniverse, one of the major print on-demand houses. If you can sell 30 copies to a bookstore, you call iUniverse and they crank out 30 copies. If you can sell one copy, they print one copy.

Big companies often publish huge print runs: for example, Hillary Rodham Clinton's book had an initial press run of one million copies. Should those copies fail to sell, Simon & Schuster, the publisher, has to take back the returned books. For small publishers, it's clearly less expensive to print on demand so they can take a chance on an unknown author. Thus, even conventional publishers are going the on-demand route to save money.

With some on-demand publishers such as Publish America, the author pays for the initial work. The cost can range from a few hundred dollars to $1,000. With other on-demand publishers, the author does not pay anything up front. Instead, the company gets a share of all sales and the author receives a royalty of the cover price, usually around 8 percent. The royalty rate rises if more than a specific number of books are sold.

Poetry rarely sells—whether published by the author, on-demand, or conventionally. The following on-demand books sell best:

- Self-help books

- Cookbooks

- Sports books

- Nonfiction essays

Electronic Printing

You can also publish your book on the web and not create any print copies at all. With so many opportunities to market digital content through websites, CD-ROMs, and other online services, many writers are no longer asking, "Should I publish electronically?" but rather, "How do I publish electronically"? The trend isn't limited to newcomers, either; best-selling author Stephen King published a novel online in installments, having readers send a voluntary donation of $1 for each chapter.

You can simply post your writing on your web page, which I discuss in detail in the next session. Or, you can hire a company to do the work for you, much as you would with a self-publisher or on-demand publisher.

Some online publishers edit in the traditional way, correcting errors and rough spots in a manuscript. However, the most prominent online publisher, Xlibris, believes that readers act as a quality filter for the author. In other words, if the book isn't any good, it won't sell. Thus, the writer's manuscript goes straight to the consumer with almost no editing by the publisher. Of course, if you post your manuscript directly on your personal web page, you can edit as much or as little as you want.

Post It

If you want to publish your book on the web yourself, follow these steps:

1. Convert your word processing file to a web document that uses HTML (Hypertext Markup Language). You can do this with newer versions of Word or WordPerfect or specially designed programs such as Adobe PageMill and Microsoft FrontPage. These programs are very easy to use.

2. Upload the file to the place where your website is hosted. If you want to charge a fee, password-protect your site.

The following chart summarizes the pros and cons of electronic publishing.

Advantages	Disadvantages
It's easy.	Your book won't be carefully edited.
There's the potential for a massive readership.	You probably won't earn anything.
It's free.	It's not protected by copyright.
You don't have to leave your chair.	Only people online can read it.
There's no publisher to deal with.	There's no publisher to deal with.

E-Books

What about publishing your manuscript as an e-book? Everybody's talking about e-books, but so far, the same people who surf the web with brio are staying away from e-books ... far away.

But some e-book proponents believe that e-books are similar to paperbacks, issued just after World War II. At first, paperbacks were regarded as shoddy, cheap substitutes for "real" books, hardbound copies. By 1950, however, paperback books were completely accepted. These e-book cheerleaders predict that e-books will soon be as mainstream as paperbacks. Nonetheless, most publishers do not predict the easy acceptance of e-books and the demise of print books. They view e-books as enhancements, just as videos have helped the film industry rather than replaced movies in theaters.

There's no doubt that e-books offer opportunities for new writers because it is an easy way to get your book published. Why? Because very few e-book publishers offer an *advance*, money paid up front against your royalties. Those that do usually pay $100–$500; traditional publishers usually fork over $5,000–$10,000 advances on the low end of the scale.

On the other hand, e-book royalties are potentially much sweeter, ranging from 24 percent to 85 percent of retail sales; traditional publishers rarely pay more than 15 percent. E-book publishers can afford to pay so much more in royalties because they have virtually no production costs: no paper, no printing.

So how does e-book publishing work? Some publishers charge small fees for converting digital files into e-books. For instance, 1stbooks

Words to the Wise

An **advance** is money you receive when you sign a contract with a traditional publisher. In theory, this is the money you live on while you are writing the book. The advance has to be paid back through royalties (the money a book earns through sales) before you receive another dime.

charges a $159 set-up fee and a $300 deposit to take a manuscript in Word or WordPerfect and convert it into a PDF file that can be read with free Adobe Acrobat Reader software. It takes two to three months for the e-book to be available for downloading. Authors receive 100 percent of the purchase price until they recoup their deposit and then 30 percent of the cover price. 1stbooks currently carries more than 2,000 titles; they sell for 20–50 percent less than paperback books. Most authors don't sell very many copies, however.

Supporting Your Writing Habit

Fortunately, writing is a career that lends itself to part-time devotion. Unlike roofing, it's portable; unlike brain surgery, it doesn't require expensive equipment.

But what if you want more than writing at night until you sell a zillion copies of your self-published novel? What if you want to find work that not only uses your writing skills but also sharpens them?

Many careers offer the opportunity for you to use and develop your writing skills. Here are a few:

Career	Writing Skills
Publishing	Get the inside track by reading and editing manuscripts
English, history teaching	Read and grade papers to hone writing skills
Technical writer	Grasp formatting and clarity
Reporter	Learn to write clearly, directly, and succinctly
Law	Emphasize logical thinking

The Least You Need to Know

♦ Self-publishing through on-demand printing or on the web has advantages and disadvantages.

♦ If you self-publish, you have total control over your book but you must edit and distribute the book on your own.

♦ Self-publish only if you can afford the investment of time and money.

♦ Electronic publishing is easy and free, but you're not likely to see any profits.

♦ Careers in writing help you learn your craft as you support yourself.

Writer's Block (or, Just Shoot Me Now)

In This Chapter

◆ Explore the most common fears that writers share

◆ Learn some quick fixes to overcoming writer's block

◆ Resort to stern measures

◆ You *can* conquer writer's block

We live in a stressful world. There's more pressure than ever before: tension on the job, convoluted family situations, less clean water and air, startling new technology. Are you trying to be a writer on top of all of this? If so, you're probably attempting to carve out the time to write in addition to carrying a full-time job. Of course you feel "blocked" at times. And that's just when you have enough energy to realize how exhausted you are.

In this chapter, you will learn what writers fear—and why. You'll soon discover that you're not alone in your concerns. In fact, you've got plenty of company. Then I'll teach you a variety of different ways to overcome *writer's block*. Best of all, each method is surefire and completely painless!

The Five Deadly Fears

Milton and the medieval crowd had the Seven Deadly Sins; writers have their own demons. Do you know what bedevils you but you can't quite put it into words? You can use the following list to put a name to your own particular writing demon so you can whip it into submission.

Words to the Wise

Writer's block is a temporary inability to get words on paper. Like grief, it has a life cycle: denial, despair, acceptance, and finally recovery.

Fear 1: Fear of Failure

This is the one that kicks you in the face. You are afraid that you will toil away for years ... and no one will care. Your best shot will fall short of the mark. Your friends, family, neighbors, and co-workers will think you are an idiot for wasting your time. Worst of all, you'll think you've made a horrible mistake by deciding to become a writer.

Fear 2: Fear of Rejection

When you write, you expose yourself. Every time you write, you are revealing your innermost thoughts on paper. You might as well pull your pants down in public and moon the universe. As a result, it's not difficult to feel that if your work is rejected, you are being rejected as well. And rejection stings like the dickens.

Fear 3: Fear of Success

To succeed in something new means that you are breaking with the past. Writing success is virgin territory for you, completely uncharted. If you gain success as a writer, your friends and family might envy you—especially if they have been trying to break into print themselves. You may fear that your friends secretly wish that your success will conveniently vanish as quickly as it came. That way, you won't upset the status quo and be a threat to anyone. Besides, you think, if you succeed once, it was probably just a fluke.

Fear 4: Fear of Offending

What happens if you have too much to say on paper? Suppose a character in your novel makes rude remarks about another character—who just happens to resemble one of your relatives? You have nothing against this person, but your character does.

Imagine Auntie Josephina wagging her finger at you during the next family gathering as she says, "You have shamed the family with your nasty writing. We can never hold our heads up in the community again."

Ever consider writing about sex? Can you imagine what your mother or father will say if you write about your first sexual experience and the book gets published and sells a zillion copies? Ouch.

Fear 5: Fear of Running Dry

What if you have nothing to say—or you think that what you say has been said a million times before? What happens if your writing doesn't offer startling new insights? "No one will want to read my stuff," you think, "because I have nothing new to contribute to the world's storehouse of knowledge." With this fear, you are actually sabotaging the idea of being a writer before you give yourself a chance.

One Step at a Time

Let's look at some of these fears in detail and see if we can demystify them.

Fear #1: *Fear of failure.* You can't win it if you aren't in it. You have the choice between risking the discovery that you were not cut out to be a writer versus spending the rest of your life wondering if you could have done it—if you'd only had the nerve.

Besides, you don't have to shout your intentions from the rooftops. In Part 1, I advised you to tell people that you want to be a writer. If that suits your style, fine. If not, keep your writing to yourself. For what it's worth, the more you want to become a writer, the more likely you are to succeed.

Fear #2: *Fear of rejection.* No matter how the news is delivered—phone, fax, or FedEx—rejection hurts. What's nice about being rejected as a writer, however, is that it's rarely personal. Unless you've dallied with the editor's significant other during the last Christmas party, the rejection is always for your work, not for *you*.

Editors may reject a book because:

◆ They can't take on another project at this time.

◆ They already have a book just like it on their list (this has happened to me twice!).

◆ The publishing company doesn't have enough money in the budget right now to take a chance on a book by a beginning writer.

◆ Books of the type you're proposing aren't selling particularly well right now.

♦ You haven't targeted the right publishing company for your book. This is a very common mistake among novice writers.

♦ The company is undergoing some internal upheavals and you're caught in the cross fire.

♦ Your book needs a little more polish before it's ready for publication.

Keep in mind that there are different levels of rejection. Anything but a preprinted letter of rejection is encouragement to submit again. With each rejection, your novel, story, poem, or script is a step closer to acceptance.

Fear #3: *Fear of success.* It's natural to feel a letdown after any momentous event: graduation, marriage, the birth of a child, winning the lottery, a promotion, and the sale of a book. But after the hoopla dies down, your life is still basically the same: Your corns still ache, your middle is still spreading, and your aging pooch still needs to be let out every 10 minutes.

There's also the worry that people will treat you differently once you hit the big time. And some will. I have lost one friend who could not accept my success. She had been a professional writer before she started her family and found it difficult to keep up the pace after. She chose other work and is a success at it, but she still resents my success as a writer. That's life. In the grand cosmic balance, I made many wonderful new friends among the writers and editors I have met and worked with. They encourage and support me in countless ways.

Fear #4: *Fear of offending.* Writing about alcoholic parents when you have alcoholic parents makes it tricky to face Pater and Mater at the next cocktail hour once the book is published. Yes, you might offend someone when personal revelations hit print. Eventually, they'll get over it. And if they don't, that's something *they* have to deal with. You can't tailor your art to suit individuals. This isn't carte blanche to wound everyone in a 20-mile radius. It *is* the okay to say what you have to say in print with honesty.

Themes that challenge society's morals or standards might offend entire groups of people, not just family and friends. Some of the world's greatest writing has sparked enormous public controversy. Many books, plays, and essays were so incendiary that they were even banned for a time, including these classics: Lawrence's *Lady Chatterley's Lover;* Twain's *The Adventures of Huckleberry Finn,* Salinger's *The Catcher in the Rye,* Nabokov's *Lolita,* Burrough's *Naked Lunch,* and Joyce's *Ulysses.* And don't forget the furor over virtually every play that George Bernard Shaw wrote!

This doesn't mean that you're going to deliberately set out to offend everyone to ensure your literary immortality. But if you're honest and your work has vision, you might find that your work changes the world. Upton Sinclair's novel *The Jungle* resulted in the passage of the Pure Food and Drug Act; Steinbeck's novel *The Grapes of Wrath* focused attention on the plight of migrant farmers. When seen in this light, what do you care if Aunt Ethel says your book is piggy and has stirred up a peck o' trouble?

Fear #5: *Fear of running dry.* Your life is composed of unique experiences and you see them as no one else can. If you have the desire to write, it's because you have something special and different to say. You can't run dry; there's too much in there. Someone might write it better, but no one will write it exactly the same.

Another great thing about writing is its diversity. If you really can't get started on your second novel, not to worry. Switch gears: Try a poem or essay instead. The different types of writing are similar enough to tap the same creativity but different enough to spark new ideas.

Quick and Dirty

Most of the time, blocked writers just need a little jump start to get back to work. Nothing drastic, just a gentle nudge with an electric cattle prod in the right direction. And that's what I have for you here. Following are 16 gentle nudges you can use when the creativity well seems to be running a little low. I suggest that you try 'em all and then pick the nudges that work best for you.

1. Brainstorm, freewrite, web, or use any other prewriting method to jump-start your creative engine. These techniques were covered in Part 1.

2. Redefine the audience. If you're writing for adults, try the same idea as a kids' book instead. And you never know; you might end up creating a better book: *The Little Prince, Alice in Wonderland,* and C. S. Lewis' *Narnia* series can all be read and enjoyed by children and adults.

3. Tell your ideas to a friend. It's often easier to speak to a real audience than to imagine an artificial one.

4. Reexamine your purpose for writing. For example, if you're writing to persuade, try writing to entertain instead. Upton Sinclair's *The Jungle* and Harriet Beecher Stowe's *Uncle Tom's Cabin* both persuade by entertaining. And each accomplished its purpose brilliantly.

All the Write Stuff

Too shy to share your writing ideas with a friend? Try "talking" to a tape recorder.

5. If a parameter such as line length or word count is holding you back, abandon it, at least for this draft. You can always go back and reshape your writing to fit a specific format.

6. Write the part that's easiest to write. You can fill in the rest later. There's no rule that says you have to start at the very beginning. Start in the middle, start with the conclusion—wherever you want.

7. Briefly do something else that doesn't require thinking, such as laundry, gardening, or washing the dog. (He probably needed it anyway.)

8. Try using a different method of transcription. If you're keyboarding, for example, try writing longhand. If you're writing longhand, try a tape recorder.

9. Draw a picture or a diagram to show what you mean. Use the visual to help you spark ideas and order your thoughts.

10. Change the point of view. Laura Ingalls Wilder wrote the initial draft of the first novel in her *Little House* series from the first-person point of view. Her daughter, a brilliant editor, suggested a switch to the third-person point of view. This gave Wilder the distance she needed to craft her life story into fiction.

11. Develop little rituals or routines that get you in the mood to write. In the winter, I make a cup of hot tea; in the summer, it's iced tea. This goes on the bookshelf to the right of the computer. Then I sharpen two pencils and I'm ready to go. This ritual tells my brain that it had better get ready to write, like it or not.

12. Visualize yourself writing. I've lifted this idea from professional athletes, who use visualization all the time. Here's the drill. Close your eyes and sit comfortably. Imagine yourself rereading what you wrote the day before, holding your fingers over the keyboard, and plunging right in. Imagine yourself feeling confident and successful. Stick with it, because it can take a few tries to get into the groove.

13. Write your material as a letter. This technique gives you a chance to relax and shoot the breeze on paper without the pressure of "producing." It can also help you develop your unique voice. When you're done, revise the letter into the first draft of your work.

14. Change your personae. Don't write as yourself; write as an entirely different person. If you're a stunning (and modest) female college professor/writer like myself, try writing as a male ice-skating champion, a world-weary diplomat, or a cross-dressing dominatrix. Once you take on a role, you'll feel less inhibited about writing.

15. Picture a scene, sound, taste, or smell. For example, to write a scene in a bakery, imagine the rich yeasty smell wafting through the air, the golden loaves of hot crusty bread emerging from the oven, the satisfying crunch of a buttery warm croissant. Start by describing the sensory feedback and then segue to the plot, characters, setting, or conflict. This method works especially well with poetry or descriptive passages.

16. Never end a day at the real "end" in the writing. The next day, it's off to the races as you're anxious to finish what you started the previous day. You won't be stuck trying to figure out how to get started, because you'll be busy finishing!

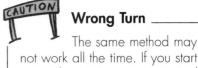

Wrong Turn

The same method may not work all the time. If you start to run dry again, vary your attack by trying different methods.

Help! My Brain Is Filled Up!

Sometimes you're just too tired to work. That's not writer's block—that's exhaustion. Learn to tell the difference between burn-out and block. I suggest that you start by giving yourself a good rest. Get enough sleep for a change; eat nourishing food. Let someone else deal with the daily stress for a while. Treat yourself to a massage and some vigorous physical activity. If you still can't write after a few days on my R & R regime, you may really be blocked. If that's the case, we have to take sterner measures.

Stern Measure #1: Punch a Time Clock

Are you stuck? Go back over what you've written. Noodle with it. Play a little here, adjust a little there. This is time well spent; after all, much of creative writing is rethinking and revising.

If this doesn't work, you can establish a strict schedule. This will help you get back into the groove. Try these three steps:

- ◆ Write for 15 minutes a day—no more.
- ◆ As you write, don't think or analyze.
- ◆ Write as fast as you can.

Write Angles

Many writers get blocked when they have to move from planning to actual writing. Once writers get started writing, it's usually smooth sailing.

If this goes well, add a few minutes to the schedule at the end of the week. A week later, try to write for half an hour without a break. Keep lengthening the amount of time until you're back into the writing routine.

Stern Measure #2: Work Overtime

Getting desperate? The following unblocking technique is like the total day of beauty regime I subject myself to every six months … a last-ditch effort. When things start looking so bad that I just have to do it all—hair, nails, skin, clothes—I bite the bullet and go for it. Same for writer's block. Chomp down.

Set aside a full day—and I mean a full day—to write. Plant your butt in the chair *and stay there*. Don't answer the phone, don't putter in the yard. Let the mail go unread and the dishes unwashed. Stock up on junk food to reward yourself for your determination.

The first hour is the hardest, but stick with it. Follow these three steps:

- Write anything.

- Don't doodle—write sentences.

- Stick with it.

Stern Measure #3: Home Alone

Some people can write any place, any time. Some people can also eat White Castle burgers and stay sweet-tempered at the motor vehicle bureau. Most of us are not that fortunate; we need real food and people who don't make us crazy. If you fall into this vast majority of sensible folks, this stern measure may be right for you.

Keep a log to discover when and where you write best. On the top of everything you write, note these details:

- Where you wrote the piece

- When you wrote it

- Weather conditions at the time you wrote (sunny, rainy, and so on)

- Who, if anyone, was present when you wrote

- What music, if any, was playing

- Any background noise

- Any special circumstances

Photocopy the following worksheet and clip a copy to everything you write for the next month. Fill it in at the end of each writing event.

Place:

Time:

Weather conditions:

People present:

Music:

Noise level:

Special circumstances:

You might find writing is easiest on the kitchen table at 4 A.M., or on the den floor at midnight. Maybe you have to write on a sunny porch after lunch or in a corner of the living room after everyone has gone to sleep.

Once you figure out when and where you write best, make that place your office. I'm a firm believer in having a room of one's own, a place where a writer can go and be creative unmolested. Maybe it's only a corner of a room, but make it your own, private and respected.

Setting aside your own "office" helps your brain know that it's writing time. The crib had a similar effect on my children when they were small. I put them in their cribs only when it was naptime or bedtime, never any other time. As a result, they were accustomed to falling asleep right away when they hit that mattress. Once you find your best writing situation, your brain will get programmed to kick in when you go there.

> **Write Angles**
>
> Best-selling writer Judith Krantz has a sign on her door that says: DO NOT COME IN. DO NOT KNOCK. DO NOT SAY HELLO. DO NOT SAY I'M LEAVING. DO NOT SAY ANYTHING UNLESS THE HOUSE IS ON FIRE.

Stern Measure #4: Get to the Root of the Problem

Occasionally, deep-seated psychological problems can block your ability to write. You may have developed a real fear of writing for some reason you can't fathom. Even though you can't put your finger on the problem, it is very real and it blocks your ability to write.

Take a few minutes to jot down your thoughts about writing. If the thoughts are negative, try to substitute positive ideas. For example, if you're thinking, "I just can't do this," try writing, "I can write. I can write very well." Here are some other positive thoughts you can use to replace the negative ones you may be thinking:

All the Write Stuff

Don't be shy about soliciting positive feedback from friends, relatives, and editors. Reread all the good comments you've gotten on your writing.

◆ "If I keep working, I can produce something that's good."

◆ "My other writing was great. This shows I can do it ... and well."

◆ "I got A's in creative writing in high school."

◆ "I love to write. It gives me great pleasure to put words down on paper."

◆ "Writing is worth the effort it takes."

Stern Measure #5: Define the Problem

Sometimes, you may not be suffering from writer's block at all—you may just have a case of regular old garden-variety procrastination. "Me?" you bluster indignantly. Yes, buckaroo, you may be a procrastinator. If that's the case, some of the techniques for shattering the block won't work for you. Take this simple quiz to diagnose your writing problem.

Circle the situations that apply to you.

You're a Classic Procrastinator If ...	You May Have Writer's Block If ...
You're still figuring out if bell-bottoms, love beads, and a Nehru jacket are the right look for you.	A blank sheet of paper makes you even more nauseated than the thought of wearing bell-bottoms, love beads, and a Nehru jacket.
You're just about ready to buy one of those newfangled TV sets—you know, the ones that show programs in color.	You're so frustrated that you're ready to pull out your liver through your lungs, chew ground glass, or watch reruns of *Gilligan's Island*.
You sent for your Woodstock tickets in 1969 and just noticed they haven't arrived yet.	You would spend a week in Woodstock—even in the winter—rather than spend another day trying to write.
You try to pay your bills the very same decade they're due.	You find bills reassuring because they show that *someone* can get some writing done.
You can't decide if you should vote for Nixon or Kennedy this year.	Vote? Make a mark on paper?

What can you do if you're really suffering from procrastination rather than writer's block? Setting your work aside for a while won't help; in fact, it's likely to make the situation worse. Try these ideas instead:

◆ Identify the problem that keeps you from writing. Deal with the problem, and then go back to writing.

◆ Set a regular time to write. Make it the same time every day.

◆ Force yourself to write for the specific amount of time you've set aside, even if you don't think you're producing anything usable. Write for the total time; no fudging!

◆ Keep your goals realistic. Decide to write a paragraph or a page at a time, not an entire chapter.

Write On!

Remember that writing is a deliberate act. Don't wait for the muse to come for a cup of tea and a donut. Call that baby in right now. You don't have to stare at a blank page day after day and suffer the torments of the damned. Writing should be pleasurable, not torture. Use the methods I described in this chapter.

If you've gotten this far, you've already gotten lots of good writing down on paper. Keep it up; I know you can do it.

The Least You Need to Know

◆ Even experienced writers sometimes have difficulty getting started.

◆ If you're a procrastinator, give yourself a kick in the pants.

◆ There are many easy and effective ways to overcome writer's block.

◆ Don't give up!

Chapter 26

Learn How Publishing Works ... So You Can Get Published!

In This Chapter

- ◆ Learn how your words become a book
- ◆ Discover which books editors buy ... and why
- ◆ See if you need a literary agent and learn how to find one
- ◆ Understand how publication rights and book contracts work

Not all creative writers want to get published. Some people write for the sheer pleasure of it. But there's nothing wrong with wanting to publish to get a little fame, fortune, and flattery. In this chapter, I'll show you how to get it!

Book It

Each publishing company has its own process for turning your raw manuscript into a bound book, but the general procedure is similar. Here's how it works.

Stage #1: Review

First, your book lands on an editor's desk. If an acquisitions editor signed your book, he or she will often be the one to traffic the manuscript. If your book was not acquired by a specific editor, it will be assigned to a general editor or a freelance editor, who gives it a quick look to see whether there is an obvious problem that needs immediate attention.

Acquisitions editors (also called *commissioning editors*) are the elite of the editorial department in terms of status and salary because they find and buy successful books. It is their taste, judgment, and negotiating skills that determine the success of their publishing house.

In some publishing companies, acquisitions editors may line-edit the manuscript they acquire. In other publishing companies, in contrast, acquisitions editors may never "edit" in the traditional sense because they never change a word of the text. Rather, the detailed line-by-line editing is done by subordinates.

Words to the Wise

Acquisitions editors find and buy manuscripts to turn into books. Freelance editors, people hired for specific jobs, can work on any stage of the editing process, from line editing to production work.

There's another possibility as well: Your manuscript may be turned over to a freelance editor for actual editing. These editors are hired on a book-by-book basis and usually work at home.

If you're publishing a scholarly book, the manuscript will next be sent to be peer-reviewed, which usually takes a few weeks. Depending upon the reviewer's recommendation, the manuscript could be accepted or rejected or, most likely, will be returned to you for some rewriting.

Stage #2: Production

During the production process, your manuscript is edited for content and then copy-edited. Then you'll be contacted by a production editor with questions identified by the editors in the first pass-through. These questions could refer to many different aspects of your manuscript, such as …

◆ Inaccuracies, inconsistencies, and unclear writing.

◆ Problems with author's voice, plotting, or resolution.

◆ Outright mistakes and typos.

Sometimes your book will need a second pass to resolve additional issues. If you make excessive changes not indicated by the copyeditor—*author's alterations*—you will be charged for them. You might be sent a bill or have the money deducted from your royalties.

Traditionally, changes were made on a print copy of the manuscript in red pencil and marked with flags (Post-Its™). Increasingly, however, the entire process is done electronically. Each editor is assigned a different color in the computer document of your manuscript, such as blue for the content editor, green for the copyeditor, and red for the acquisitions editor. You get your own color and respond to each editor's comments on the screen. Then you send the file back to the publisher. The number of editors and the exact editing process varies from publisher to publisher.

Some publishing companies then send *proofs*, printed copies of the corrected manuscript, for your examination and correction.

Stage #3: Marketing

Even before the book appears in bound copy, the editor and publicity department set up a buzz in the media and publishing community about your book. If the book is very high profile, the publicity may include a book tour, print and radio ads, television appearances, and favorable placement in bookstores. Other books, in contrast, receive much less publicity or none at all. As the author, you may be asked to assist in publicity efforts by filling out a questionnaire concerning your own publicity contacts in the media.

The very first mention of your book at the acquisitions meeting might affect its destiny. That's because your book is ranked according to its promise. Some companies rank books by letters, as follows:

- A: Top of the list, full-court treatment
- B: Minor effort and money expended on publicity
- C: You're on your own, baby

On a high-profile book, you might be consulted about the jacket design, jacket copy, and back-cover endorsements. You might be asked to help the publisher find someone to write a favorable foreword, too. If your book is very high profile, the publisher will hold a launch party to send your baby out into the world. This is unusual treatment, reserved for the superstars, so don't expect a brass band parade for your first (or even subsequent) book, unless you're coming to the table with a gilt-edged ready-made reputation.

Which Books Do Editors Buy ... and Why?

How many unsolicited novel manuscripts do you think are submitted to conventional publishers every year? About 10,000? Maybe 20,000? As high as 25,000? Guess again.

Every year, *more than 30,000 manuscripts* find their way to publishers' desks, sent over the transom, stuffed under the mat, and whizzed through the U.S. Mail. Only about 2,000 brand-new novels are published every year. Don't figure the odds; it's too grim. Besides, most of those novels were solicited by the publishers. Only a handful came from first-time novelists.

Don't throw your computer out the window yet, because things aren't as bleak as they seem. Publishers *do* buy the memoirs, novels, and nonfiction books by first-time authors. They *are* actively looking for fresh, new writing. It *is* difficult to get your writing published by a major publishing house, but it's not the impossible dream.

All the Write Stuff

Shameless Plug: If you're rusty on skills, get a copy of my book, *The Complete Idiot's Guide to Grammar and Usage*. It's a fast and fun way to brush up on your writing skills.

To publish with a publishing company, you need the three T's: talent, tenacity, and a tough skin. I *know* you have talent. Stick with me and you'll acquire tenacity and a tough skin.

Editors buy good books but no matter how good a book may be, no one will buy a book unless they need it. The words "need it" translate to "can sell it." Here are my top ten tips for selling your book:

10. Write a lot. You're not going to get good without practice. Try to write every day so you get into the habit.

9. Know your craft. Read a lot; take classes if you need the support. After you learn the basics, clean up any problems with skills such as spelling, grammar, punctuation, and usage.

8. Know your market. Publishing is far less difficult if you know what a publisher wants and you give it to them. You can do this by reading a lot of books in the genre you want to write. For example, if you want to write romance novels, read a lot of romance novels and analyze what elements are common to each different publisher.

7. Get the guidelines. Many publishers provide free guidelines for publication. You can often download these from the publisher's website or obtain them by mail. Then follow the guidelines to the letter.

6. Establish a track record by starting small. Submit your work to smaller publishers, less well-known magazines and newspapers, small journals.

5. Make contacts. Attend conferences and conventions. Meet editors and other writers. Find out how they broke into publication.

4. Seek advice—and follow it. Ask people whom you trust to read what you've written and listen to their feedback. Study rejection letters from editors and agents, too. (Not to worry; every writer gets rejection letters!)

3. Be creative. Can't get a break? Make your own luck by publishing on the web or self-publishing. Then promote your book heavily. When your book takes off, you'll have a platform to present to a big publishing house, if you wish.

2. Be professional. Don't badger people, whine, or act like a prima dona and thus feel entitled to special treatment. No one wants to work with a spoiled brat. When you send in a proposal or a letter, make sure that it's letter perfect.

And my number-one suggestion for getting published:

1. Don't give up.

Secret Agent Man: Literary Agents

According to legend, a popular writer requested in his will that upon his death, his body be cremated and 10 percent of his ashes thrown in his agent's face.

As this anecdote illustrates, agents tend to spark somewhat ambivalent feelings among their clients. Maybe that's because the author/agent relationship is likely the most significant relationship in publishing.

What Does a Literary Agent Do—and Not Do—for a Writer?

Let's start with a definition: A *literary agent* is an author's representative. Here are some of a literary agent's functions.

A literary agent ...

- Is your *exclusive* marketing representative.
- Finds the right market for your writing.
- Shops your books, plays, and screenplays around.
- Gets your book to the right editors.
- Sets up meetings with publishers.
- Negotiates contracts.

- Recommends you for other writing work.

- Collects all advances and royalties due to you.

- Shelters you from conflicts with editors and publishers.

- Tracks your publishing accounts.

- May or may not provide tax information to the IRS.

- Takes a percentage of your income.

You've learned what an agent *will* do for you. Now it's time to see what an agent *won't* do for you:

An agent won't ...

- Act as your editor.

- Proofread your work.

- Loan you money.

- Act as a therapist.

- Be your travel agent.

- Be your lawyer (unless this is part of the deal).

- Do public relations work (again, unless this is part of the deal).

- Function as a secretary.

- Be available 24 hours a day, seven days a week.

- Be your best friend.

Do You Need an Agent?

Consider these scenarios:

- You've finished half of your memoir. Do you need an agent now?

- An editor liked the synopsis and sample chapters from your first novel. Should you start agent shopping now?

- Happy day! A publisher wants to buy your memoir. Is it time to hire an agent to work the deal?

Say you're a beginning writer, plodding away on your first book. If you've created a strong synopsis for your novel and have several impressive chapters written, odds are you don't need an agent to sell the book. Therefore, at this point in your writing career, it may be premature of you to be thinking about hiring an agent to *sell* your work. Note the emphasis on the word "sell."

If this scenario fits your current situation, I suggest that you first try to publish some excerpts from your novel in literary or mass-market magazines. Once you succeed in this, you'll have the beginnings of a literary track record. This will make it easier for you to publish more fiction and nonfiction, especially longer pieces. It will also encourage an agent to want to represent you, if you decide that's what you want.

Even if you sell your first book on your own, you may wish to have an agent close the deal. That's because a good agent can often help you get better terms than you can get on your own. This paves the way for more lucrative contracts in the future, too.

Your first writing contract is important, perhaps the most important one you'll ever get. Mistakes at this point can cost you a great deal of time, money, and frustration. Losing time and money are bad enough, but having to endure frustration is simply not acceptable.

Only you can decide if and when you need an agent to represent you. As you read earlier in this chapter, lacking celebrity status or a proven track record, your chances of landing a book contract with a major publishing house are slim; ditto on finding a good literary agent.

Use the following worksheet now to decide if you should go out shopping for an agent today.

Check each statement that applies to you.

- ❏ I don't have a completed manuscript yet.
- ❏ I'm not sure I want to market my book now.
- ❏ If I do decide to sell my book, I'm tough enough to negotiate with the big kids.
- ❏ I'm comfortable in business meetings.
- ❏ I promise to read the contract all the way through.
- ❏ I understand legal terms, or know how to get their definitions.
- ❏ I'm not easy to intimidate.
- ❏ I have a thick skin.
- ❏ I'm willing to market my book somewhere else if I can't get the deal I want.
- ❏ I have the time, energy, economic savvy, and courage to deal with contract negotiations.

If you answered "yes" to most of these questions, you're likely best off lighting out for the territory ahead of the rest—alone. This may change later in your writing career, so keep reading.

Finding an Agent

So you decided that you need an agent. How do you find one? First of all, you can consult *The Literary Market Place*, a writer's reference book. It lists several hundred literary agencies and agents.

Here are some other sources to try:

♦ The Society of Authors' Representatives (P.O. Box 650, New York, NY 10113). This group offers a list of agents.

♦ *Guide to Literary Agents & Art/Photo Reps* (Writer's Digest Books). This is an annual directory that provides specific information about agencies. The Association of Authors' Representatives is not a regulating group. There are many reputable agents who are not members of AAR.

♦ *Publishers Weekly.* See which agents make the big deals, which ones represent the types of works you write, which ones are looking for clients, and so on.

♦ Genre-specific magazines. Agents often advertise in genre-specific magazines. Check the magazines for the genre you write: for example, *Romantic Times* for romance, *Locus* for science fiction.

I've always been a strong fan of the personal road to finding an agent—recommendations from fellow authors. This is another good reason to join (or create) a writer's group. Fellow writers can help you get in touch with suitable agents. If you don't know anyone who has used an agent, you might chat up writing instructors, booksellers, librarians, and publishers' sales reps. See which agents they know and how they feel about them. You may very well need that personal reference to get a foot in the door.

All the Write Stuff

According to *Literary Market Place*, about 40 percent of book agents will not read manuscripts by unpublished authors. Another 15 percent will not even answer query letters from them.

Literary agents often attend writers' conferences, conventions, seminars, and workshops to find new clients and to represent their existing stable of work-horses. As a result, these events can be great places to shop for an agent. If you decide to go this route, here are six guidelines to follow:

1. Be professional. Dress and act appropriately.

2. Try to arrange a private meeting with the agent.

3. Explain the project you're trying to sell.

4. Don't offer a manuscript; it's tacky.

5. If you decide to use the agent, send a letter reminding the agent where you met and how.

6. If you don't want to use the agent, follow up with a thank-you letter.

Caveat Emptor

All missions entail a certain risk, and it's true of agent shopping. Here are a few guidelines that can prevent a stay at Heartbreak Hotel.

First, beware of agents who push long-term contracts. Also avoid contracts that can't be broken by either party at any time. This is not to say you should discard agents like JLo discards husbands. On the contrary; when you find a good agent, stick around. But shun agents who claim that you'll bolt once they've given you the best years of their lives. If the agent is good, of course you'll stay.

Second, there are some so-called "agents" who charge a fee for reading your manuscript and then pay students to do the work. They make their money on these fees, not from placing the manuscripts. Think twice before paying an "agent" a reading fee. If you really feel that you need a professional opinion, hire a person or firm that does nothing else. Or, you may wish to join (or create) a writing group.

Finally, always get a written agreement with your agent. There are some writers who have enjoyed fine relationships with their agents with only a handshake to seal the deal. There are other writers, however, who have gotten badly burned on such deals. Agents can sell their businesses, go bankrupt, decide to raise commissions—and where does that leave you? If you have a good contract, that leaves you just fine.

Here are some other considerations:

♦ Will your agent respect the confidentiality of your dealings?

♦ Will your agent treat you as a professional?

♦ Will your agent remember that he or she works for you, and not the other way around?

♦ Will your agent work for you, not the publisher?

◆ Is your agent a professional in all areas of his or her dealings?

◆ What fees does the agent charge?

On average, agents charge between 10 to 15 percent of your writing income for domestic sales; 25 percent commission for foreign sales. Your agent should not charge you for normal business expenses, such as domestic telephone calls or bookkeeping. But it's very common for an agent to charge for special expenses, such as daytime overseas calls, photocopying, and book purchases.

It is virtually impossible to sell fiction without an agent, but remember that as much as agents work for their writers, they have to stay on the editor's good side so they can sell more books. This does give them some conflicting loyalties.

Legal Beagles: Rights, Contracts, and Payment

One size may fit all with T-shirts and spandex pants, but not when it comes to selling your writing. Contracts and agreements vary considerably from publisher to publisher. Some editors work only by a handshake agreement, while others have contracts as thick as the phone book. In this section, you will learn the basics of the business of contracts.

Know Your Rights!

Any time an editor buys a piece or asks permission to publish something, even without offering payment, the editor is asking you for *rights*. In so doing, the editor or publisher is obtaining the right to publish your work. When the rights are not specified, most writers assume that the publisher is buying one-time rights, but that's not always the case. Let me take you on a survey of the different kinds of rights you can sell so you know the score.

Words to the Wise

Rights give the publisher legal permission to publish your work.

◆ *First Serial Rights.* Under first serial rights, you grant a newspaper or magazine the right to publish your writing for the first time in any periodical. First serial rights can be applied to any type of writing: shorter writings such as essays, poems, and short stories as well as excerpts from novels, biographies, and screenplays. Under this agreement, all rights to further publication belong to you, the writer.

◆ *One-Time Rights.* This is different from first serial rights in that the buyer has no guarantee that he or she will be the first to publish the work. See "simultaneous rights."

◆ *Second Serial (Reprint) Rights.* Under these rights, a newspaper or magazine has the chance to print an article, essay, story, poem, or an excerpt from a longer work after it has already appeared in another periodical.

◆ *All Rights.* A writer who sells something to a magazine or newspaper under these rights cannot use the same material in its present form in any other publication. If you think you may want to reuse the article, story, poem (etc.) later on, ask the editor to buy first rights instead of all rights. Sometimes, an editor will reassign rights back to a writer after a given period of time, such as one year.

◆ *Simultaneous Rights.* If magazines don't have the same readers, you can often sell the same article to two or more places at the same time. For example, a cooking magazine might be willing to buy simultaneous rights to a story, even though they know a travel magazine might be using the story as well.

◆ *Foreign Serial Rights.* If you sold first U.S. serial rights, you are free to resell the same piece abroad. To do so, research magazines and newspapers that buy writing that has already been published in U.S. or North American magazines and newspapers.

◆ *Syndication Rights.* Like serial rights, syndication rights give magazines and newspapers the right to publish your writing. The difference is that your work will appear in many newspapers and/or magazines at the same time. The syndication takes a commission on the sale. The rest of the money is split between you and your publisher.

◆ *Dramatic, Television, and Motion Picture Rights.* These can be crucial rights if it seems even remotely likely that your work will get published in another medium. Therefore, I strongly suggest that you study any contracts carefully for these rights.

◆ *Subsidiary Rights.* These include serial rights, dramatic rights, rights relative to revised editions, translation rights, and so on. They are discussed in detail later in this chapter.

◆ *Electronic Rights.* Electronic rights concern any means of electronic transmission, such as the World Wide Web. This also includes electronic versions of your writing, such as compact discs (CDs). Since even the computer mavens can't predict the spread of the Net, I suggest that you carefully watch how you assign these rights.

Always talk to your editor and read your contract carefully to see what rights you are keeping and which rights you are signing away. Here are three special situations to scrutinize:

◆ If editors or publishers change, the rights may shift as well.

◆ Sometimes endorsing your check signs away rights.

◆ Beware of verbal rights agreements. Get it in writing.

Now, let's compare and contrast the two most common types of writing contracts: a work-for-hire agreement and a royalty structure.

Take the Money and Run: Work-Made-for-Hire Agreement

With a *work-made-for-hire* agreement, you're a hired hand. As such, you get a flat fee, a one-shot payment. Under this type of contract, you have no claim to what you write; everything belongs to the publisher. The minute you sign the work-made-for-hire agreement, you are signing away all future rights to the work.

A work-made-for-hire writing arrangement might be right for you if you …

◆ Want a set, guaranteed amount of money.

◆ Like short-term jobs with no strings attached.

◆ Are looking for a way to support yourself while you write harder-to-sell works such as poems, novels, and screenplays.

◆ Do not want credit for your work—it's rare that your name appears on a work-for-hire job.

Royal Flush: Royalty Contracts

Royalties are a percentage of the retail price of your book. You receive that percentage as a fee for writing. With certain types of writing, such as novels and biographies, you get royalties instead of a flat fee. Far more important, you also retain ownership of your writing.

An *advance against royalties* is a loan from the publisher to you. The advance is later deducted from how much your book earns in royalties after publication. Except in very rare circumstances, an advance is not repayable. Even if only one copy of the book is sold, the advance is yours to keep. Advances generally range from $100 up. They are generally paid in increments.

Words to the Wise

With a **work-made-for-hire** contract, you sign away all rights; with a **royalty** contract, you keep ownership of your writing. Royalties are a percentage of the retail price received on sales of your book.

The Least You Need to Know

♦ Manuscripts become books by being reviewed, edited, printed, and marketed.

♦ Editors buy books they can sell, so if you want to publish through a conventional publishing house, learn what they sell.

♦ Assess your professional situation carefully to decide if you need a literary agent. It takes a lot of effort to get a good agent, so don't be discouraged.

♦ Understand contracts and your rights to your work.

Glossary of Writing Terms

act   One of the main divisions in a play. Acts may be further divided into *scenes*.

active voice   In the *active voice*, the subject performs the action named by the verb.

adaptation   A script based on another work, such as a book or article.

agent   A person who tries to sell a writer's work, place the writer in the right job, and guide the writer's career.

alliteration   The repetition of initial consonant sounds in several words in a sentence or line of poetry. Use alliteration to create musical effects, link related ideas, stress certain words, or mimic specific sounds.

allusion   A reference to a well-known place, event, person, work of art, or other work of literature.

anecdote   A brief story that gets the reader's interest and sheds light on a main idea and theme.

antagonist   The force or person in conflict with the main character in a work of literature. An antagonist can be another character, a force of nature, society, or something within the character.

article   A short work of nonfiction.

author's purpose   The author's goal in writing a selection. Common purposes include to entertain, instruct, persuade, or describe. A selection may have more than one author's purpose, but often one purpose is the most important.

autobiography   A person's story of his or her own life. An autobiography is nonfiction and describes key events from the person's life.

ballad   A story told in song form. Ballads often tell stories about adventure and love.

biography   A true story about a person's life written by another person.

blank verse   Unrhymed poetry, usually written in iambic pentameter. Many poets write in blank verse because it captures the natural rhythm of speech.

catalog technique   A poetic list.

character   A person or an animal in a story. *Main characters* have important roles in a literary work; *minor characters* have smaller roles.

characterization   The act of telling readers about characters. Sometimes, writers tell about characters directly. Other times, writers let readers reach their own decisions by showing the comments, thoughts, and actions of the other characters.

chronological order   Arranging the events of a story in order in time from first to last.

climax   The highest point in the action. During the climax, the conflict is resolved and the end of the story becomes clear. The climax is also called the *turning point*.

collaboration   Cooperation with two or more people in the writing of a script or other work.

conclusion   The end of an article, play, poem, or book.

conflict   A struggle or fight. Conflict makes a story interesting because readers want to discover the outcome. There are two kinds of conflict:

- ◆ In an *external conflict*, characters struggle against a force outside themselves.

- ◆ In an *internal conflict*, characters battle a force within themselves.

Stories often contain both external and internal conflicts.

connotation   A word's emotional overtones. "Home," for example, suggests warmth and acceptance; "house" carries no such overtones. Compare the connotations of "svelte" and "emaciated" and "thrifty" and "miserly."

couplet   Two related lines of poetry, which often rhyme.

creative writing   A kind of writing that uses language in imaginative and bold ways.

denotation   A word's exact meaning.

denouement   The resolution of a story. At the denouement, all the loose ends of the story are woven together.

description   A kind of writing that creates a word picture of what something or someone is like.

dialect   The way people speak in a certain region or area. In a dialect, certain words are spelled and pronounced differently. Use dialects to define characters and setting more fully.

dialogue   Conversation in fiction or drama. It is the exact words a character says. In a story or novel, quotation marks are used to indicate dialogue.

diary   A writer's record of his or her experiences, ideas, and feelings.

diction   Word choice.

drama   A piece of literature written to be performed in front of an audience. The actors tell the story through their actions and words.

dramatic monologue   A type of poem in which a character speaks, using the first-person point of view.

dramatic poetry   A play written in poem form.

epic   A long narrative in an elevated style, presenting high-born characters in a series of adventures that depict key events in the history of a nation.

essay   A brief writing on a particular subject or idea.

exposition   A type of writing that explains, shows, or tells about a subject. The word can also be used to mean the opening parts of a play or story. During the exposition, the characters, action, and setting are introduced.

extended metaphor   An *extended metaphor* compares two things at length and in several different ways.

fable   A short, easy-to-read story that teaches a lesson about people. Fables often feature animals that talk and act like people.

fantasy   A kind of writing that describes events that could not take place in real life. Fantasy has unrealistic characters, settings, and events.

farce   A humorous play that is based on a silly plot, ridiculous situations, and comic dialogue. The characters are usually one-dimensional stereotypical figures. They often find themselves in situations that start out normally but soon turn absurd.

fiction   Writing that tells about made-up events and characters. Novels and short stories are examples of fiction.

figures of speech   *Figures of speech* (or *figurative language*) use words in fresh, new ways to appeal to the imagination. Figures of speech include *similes, metaphors, extended metaphors, hyperbole,* and *personification.*

flashback   A scene that breaks into the story to show an earlier part of the action. Flashbacks help fill in missing information, explain the characters' actions, and advance the plot.

foot   A poetic *foot* is a pattern of stressed and unstressed syllables arranged in metrical *feet.* A foot is composed of either two or three syllables, such that the nature of the foot is determined by the placement of the accent. There are six basic types of metrical feet in English. The first four are very common; the last two are rare.

foreshadowing   Provides clues that hint at what will happen later on in the story. Writers use foreshadowing to create suspense and link related details.

frame story   A shorter story within a larger one. Often, the longer story introduces and closes the frame story.

free verse   Poetry without a regular pattern of rhyme and meter. Walt Whitman's poetry is an example of free verse.

genre   A major literary category. The three genres are prose, drama, and poetry.

haiku   A Japanese poetic form that uses only three lines and a total of 17 syllables.

hero/heroine   Literary characters who we admire for their noble traits, such as bravery, selflessness, or cleverness. In the past, the term "hero" was used to refer to a male character, the term "heroine" for a female character. Today, "hero" is used for either male or female characters.

humor   Parts of a story that are amusing. Humor can be created through sarcasm, word play, irony, and exaggeration.

hyperbole   Exaggeration used for a literary effect such as emphasis, drama, or humor.

image   A word that appeals to one or more of our five senses: sight, hearing, taste, touch, or smell.

imagery   Imagery is the use of images (*see* image) and figurative language that helps readers visualize a person, place, thing, or situation.

inciting moment   The beginning of a conflict.

irony   Occurs when something happens that is different from what was expected.

◆ In *verbal irony*, there is a contrast between what is stated and what that statement suggests.

◆ In *dramatic irony*, there is a contrast between what a character believes and what the audience knows to be true.

◆ In *irony of situation*, an event reverses what the readers or characters expected.

limerick   A type of humorous poetry. Limericks have five lines, a strong rhyme, and a set rhythm. The first, second, and fifth lines rhyme with each other and the third and fourth rhyme with each other—*aabba*.

lyric poems   Brief, musical poems that express a speaker's feelings.

main character   The most important figure in a novel, short story, poem, or play.

memoir   A first-person writing about an event.

metaphor   A figure of speech that compares two unlike things. The more familiar thing helps describe the less familiar one. Metaphors do not use the words "like" or "as" to make the comparison. "My heart is a singing bird" is a metaphor.

meter   A poem's rhythmical pattern, created by a pattern of stressed and unstressed syllables. The most common meter in English poetry is called *iambic pentameter*. It is a pattern of five *feet*, each having one unstressed syllable followed by a stressed one.

minor character   A less important figure in a literary work, who serves as a contrast to the main character or to advance the plot.

mood   The strong feeling we get from a literary work. The mood (or *atmosphere*) is created by characterization, description, images, and dialogue. Some possible moods include terror, horror, tension, calmness, and suspense.

myth   A story from ancient days that explains certain aspects of life and nature.

narration   Writing that tells a story. Narrations that tell about real events include biographies and autobiographies. Narrations that deal with fictional events include short stories, myths, narrative poems, and novels.

narrative poems   Poems that tell a story, either through a narrative storyline told objectively or through a dramatized situation.

narrator   The person who tells a story. The narrator may also be a character in the work.

nonfiction   A type of writing that deals with real people and events. Essays, biographies, autobiographies, and articles are all examples of nonfiction.

novel   A long work of fiction. The elements of a novel—plot, characterization, setting, and theme—are developed in detail. Novels usually have one main plot and several less important subplots.

onomatopoeia   The use of words that imitate the sounds they describe—for example, words like "snap" and "crackle."

passive voice   In *passive voice*, the subject receives the action.

personification   Giving human traits to nonhuman things. For example: "The book begged to be read."

persuasion   A type of writing that tries to move an audience to thought or action.

plot   The arrangement of events in a work of literature. Plots have a beginning, middle, and end. The writer arranges the events of the plot to keep the reader's interest and convey the theme. In many stories and novels, the events of the plot can be divided as follows:

- *Exposition*: Introduces the characters, setting, and conflict
- *Rising Action*: Builds the conflict and develops the characters
- *Climax:* Shows the highest point of the action
- *Resolution:* Resolves the story and ties up all the loose ends

poetry   A type of literature in which words are selected for their beauty, sound, and power to express feelings. Traditionally, poems had a specific rhythm and rhyme, but such modern poetry as *free verse* does not have regular beat, rhyme, or line length. Most poems are written in lines, which are arranged together in groups called *stanzas.*

point of view   The position from which a story is told. Here are the three different points of view writers use most often:

- *First-person point of view:* The narrator is one of the characters in the story. The narrator explains the events through his or her own eyes, using the pronouns *I* and *me.*
- *Third-person omniscient point of view:* The narrator is not a character in the story. Instead, the narrator looks through the eyes of all the characters. As a result, the narrator is "all-knowing" (omniscient). The narrator uses the pronouns *he, she,* and *they.*
- *Third-person limited point of view:* The narrator tells the story through the eyes of only one character, using the pronouns *he, she,* and *they.*

prose   All written work that is not poetry, drama, or song. Examples of prose include articles, autobiographies, biographies, novels, essays, and editorials.

protagonist   The most important character in a work of literature. The protagonist is at the center of the conflict and the focus of our attention. *See* main character.

purpose   *See* author's purpose.

realistic fiction   Contains imaginary situations and characters that are very similar to people in real life.

refrain   A line or a group of lines that are repeated at the end of a poem or song. Refrains serve to reinforce the main point and create musical effects.

repetition   Using the same sound, word, phrase, line, or grammatical structure over and over for emphasis.

resolution   The *resolution* of a plot occurs near the end of a story, when all the remaining strands of the story are woven together.

rhyme   The repeated use of identical or nearly identical sounds. Poets use rhyme to create a musical sound, meaning, and structure.

   ◆ *End rhyme* occurs when words at the ends of lines of poetry have the same sound. Lines that end with the words *bat*, *cat*, *sat*, or *rat* would have end rhyme.

   ◆ *Internal rhyme* occurs when words within a sentence share the same sound. For example: "Each narrow cell in which we dwell." *Cell* and *dwell* have internal rhyme because they share the same sound and one of the words is set in the middle of the line.

rhyme scheme   A regular pattern of words in a poem that end with the same sound.

rhythm   The pattern of stressed and unstressed words that create a beat, as in music.

rituals   Little habits that provide structure to writers.

scene   A part of a play. Each scene in a play takes place during a set time and in one place.

science fiction   *Science fiction* (or *sci-fi*) is fantasy writing that tells about make-believe events that include science or technology.

sensory language   Words that appeal to the five senses: sight, hearing, taste, touch, or smell. Sensory language is used to create images and imagery.

setting   The time and place where the events of a story take place.

short story   A form of narrative prose fiction that is shorter than a novel; it focuses on a single character and a single event. Most short stories can be read in one sitting and convey a single overall impression.

simile   A figure of speech that compares two unlike things. Similes use the words "like" or "as" to make a comparison. "A dream put off dries up like a raisin in the sun" is an example of a simile.

sonnet   A lyric poem of 14 lines written in iambic pentameter.

speaker   The personality the writer assumes when telling a story. For example, the writer can tell the story as a young girl, an old man, or a figure from history.

stage directions   Instructions to the actors, producer, and director telling how to perform a play. Stage directions are included in the text of a play, written in parenthesis or italics. They describe how actors should speak, what they should wear, and what scenery should be used, among other things.

stanza   A group of lines in a poem, like a paragraph in prose. Each stanza presents one complete idea.

style   An author's distinctive way of writing. Style is made up of elements such as word choice, sentence length and structure, figures of speech, and tone. A writer may change his or her style for different kinds of writing and to suit different audiences. In poetry, for example, a writer might use more imagery than he or she would use in prose.

surprise ending   A conclusion that differs from what the reader expected. In most stories, the ending follows logically from the arrangement of events in the plot. In a surprise ending, however, final events take an unexpected twist.

suspense   The feeling of tension or anticipation a writer creates in a work. Writers create suspense by including unexpected plot twists. This keeps readers interested in the story and makes them want to read on to find out what will happen.

symbol   A person, place, or object that represents an abstract idea. For example, a dove may symbolize peace or a rose may symbolize love.

theme   A literary work's main idea, a general statement about life. The theme can be stated outright in the work, or readers will have to infer it from details about plot, characters, and setting.

tone   The writer's attitude toward his or her subject matter. For example, the tone can be angry, bitter, sad, or frightening.

transitions   Words and phrases that give writing coherence.

turning point   *See* climax.

verse   A stanza in a poem.

voice   The author's personality as expressed through his or her writing.

writing   A way of communicating a message to a reader for a purpose.

Index